T0291248

'This is not simply a book about Agile methodology. It is about how Organizational Development and Learning professionals can orient themselves and their practice to create experiences and development programmes for people that quickly and transparently drive business value. In *Agile L&D* is a way to deepen organizational consulting by centring people, focusing on incremental value, creating feedback loops and mastering the ability to respond to changing landscapes – essential skills for practitioners in contemporary contexts.'
Wayne Mullen, Partner and Chief People Officer, Sentiem

'Natal is able to crystallize, in expert and yet relatable language, the rationale for Agile L&D – laying out the urgent case for us to adapt and, indeed, why Agile is quite possibly the most viable response we have to the changing nature of work and skills – but also providing the guide to how we can do it. This book is truly something to get excited about.'
David James, Chief Learning Officer, 360Learning

'The most actionable Agile book I've read. If you're working in an L&D or People role, and don't read this you're missing a trick. Agile HR changed my entire philosophy on how to do "people" work. Agile L&D now brings me a practical toolkit, case studies galore and a whole host of inspiration that applies not only to learning but to every part of people experience. If you're in an L&D role and you don't own a copy of this book, you're missing out on the chance to gain some very special superpowers. It just makes sense!

Why didn't this book exist when I began my L&D career? The good news is, it exists now and should be a core text for anyone in the field of L&D and OD.'
Aisling Winter, Head of Culture, IAG Loyalty

'If you're an L&D leader looking to better engage and influence your C suite and deliver clear organizational impact, then this book is a must read. Using Natal's learnings and insight you'll soon be experimenting, prototyping and pivoting on your way to a new L&D mindset that really delivers for your people.'
Jodie Pritchard, Director of Learning & Development, Barnardo's

'What's great about the book is that it strikes the right balance between equipping you with practical tools and leading the way in real-time value creation in L&D and HR.'
Arne-Christian van der Tang, Chief HR Officer, TomTom

'In the ever-evolving landscape of HR, Natal stands out as a visionary leader, and her new book on Agile Learning and Development is a testament to her expertise.

Natal's unique perspective on Agile methodologies has transformed the way we approach product development within HR. The book seamlessly combines theoretical insights with practical applications, providing a road-map for L&D professionals to harness the power of agility. Her ability to translate agile concepts into actionable steps is unparalleled, making the book an invaluable resource for anyone striving to stay ahead in the fast-paced world of Learning and Development.
Charlotte Young, Director of Organizational Development, Cambridge University Press and Assessment

'This book is a real game changer, especially now as we navigate the rapid transformation in the world of work. I absolutely love the five super practical principles Natal lays out. They're like a secret weapon for anyone in L&D looking to shake things up. Consider this book your new sidekick for navigating the exciting changes in work. Grab your markers and sticky notes; you're in for a hands-on experience.'
Laura Keith, CEO Hive Learning

'This highly accessible book is for anyone who needs to evolve a traditional operational model for L&D and people teams into a multi-functional approach, powered with capabilities like human-centred design, experimentation and data analytics. It does an impressive job of bringing to life what can often be hazy concepts and translating them into practical tools and frameworks for any L&D or people team. Essential reading for our time.'
Belinda Gannaway, Co-author *Employee Experience by Design: How to create an effective EX for competitive advantage*

Agile L&D

*A toolkit to improve organizational
learning and drive performance*

Natal Dank

First published in Great Britain and the United States in 2024 by Kogan Page Limited

2nd Floor, 45 Gee Street
London
EC1V 3RS
United Kingdom

8 W 38th Street, Suite 902
New York, NY 10018
USA

4737/23 Ansari Road
Daryaganj
New Delhi 110002
India

www.koganpage.com

Kogan Page books are printed on paper from sustainable forests.

© Natal Dank, 2024

The right of Natal Dank to be identified as the author of this work has been asserted by her in accordance with the Copyright, Designs and Patents Act 1988.

ISBNs

Hardback   978 1 3986 1327 0
Paperback   978 1 3986 1325 6
Ebook   978 1 3986 1326 3

British Library Cataloguing-in-Publication Data
A CIP record for this book is available from the British Library.

Library of Congress Control Number

2023952557

Typeset by Integra Software Services, Pondicherry
Print production managed by Jellyfish
Printed and bound by CPI Group (UK) Ltd, Croydon CR0 4YY

CONTENTS

FOREWORD

The modern workplace is continuously evolving. The future workplace will bring fresh and as yet unknown challenges, with external factors from the world around us influencing the business environment. Technology progresses at an exponential rate, with AI being the latest transformational technological movement. Market trends in all industries are shifting and changing faster than ever, which means organizations need to adapt and adjust to the ever-increasing rate of change to stay relevant and successful.

In this book, Natal explores the current landscape and the environment in which we live and work today in more depth. She brings to life the concept that the Agile mindset and way of working can deliver more impactful, timely and relevant solutions to business issues.

I've had the privilege of working with Natal over many years, in the pursuit of appreciating the value of Agile approaches and learning how Agile principles can enable more effective working practices across the various disciplines of Human Resources (HR). The publication of this book, focusing more specifically on Learning and Development (L&D), brings with it the opportunity for HR and L&D leaders to follow an approach that enables the introduction of Agile into their working practices.

It is an honour to write the Foreword as an introduction to Natal's latest work. Natal is an inspirational force behind the movement of Agile in HR and L&D and a proponent of the move away from traditional HR and L&D practices, championing a new world People Operating Model that is fit for the modern workplace.

In this book, Natal explores the notion of the L&D discipline being the pioneer of Agile within HR and people functions. Having begun my own HR career in L&D, and being fortunate to have had the opportunity to introduce Agile principles in multiple organizations, I can strongly advocate for the concept that L&D is an ideal space to experiment and experience Agile when starting out.

L&D is instrumental in the growth of skills within organizations, and with the ongoing scramble for talent, businesses need to be smart about attracting, retaining, and developing great people. There has been a shift towards skills-based recruiting and the concept of employee progression that is not just based on upward career ladders. This move towards experience-based career progression through project-based work and becoming more multi-skilled means L&D must be better recognized as a business enabler. To do this effectively, L&D needs to rethink its operating model in order to deliver the greatest impact, and this is where the Agile mindset and practices come in.

I have experienced first-hand the impact that Agile can have on L&D, with the speed of deliverables improving and the quality of the solutions provided being more in line with the business requirements. The concept of delivering in short iterations and making more informed decisions on the prioritization of competing business demands means that what L&D delivers has more impact and demonstrable value. Gleaning continuous feedback from internal customers at regular short intervals to stay close to any evolving needs results in greater overall abilities and being truly agile. In turn, this positions L&D as a trusted, credible and influential advisor in the organization. Leaders actively seek L&D's support and inputs as a strategic partner rather than the more traditional 'order taker', resulting in a highly engaged and motivated L&D department. I have seen this time and again in the teams I have worked with, and I can say with certainty that the shift towards an Agile mindset and working principles is truly groundbreaking.

When Natal shared with me her ambition to publish a book focusing on Agile in L&D, it felt like entirely the right step. Sometimes L&D can be seen as a costly 'nice to have' by business leaders but now, more than ever, L&D's role is imperative. With Agile principles at the heart of the L&D operating model, this is the time for L&D to stand out and shine as the area of HR that can have the most significant impact on business performance.

Nebel Crowhurst – Chief People Officer at Reward Gateway, former People and Culture Director at Roche and Head of People Experience at River Island

PREFACE

I must admit to being initially hesitant about writing a book focused on organizational learning and development. Despite a career that has included many L&D (learning and development), OD (organizational development) and talent roles over the years, I was concerned that readers might see me first and foremost as an HR (human resources) generalist because of my first book – *Agile HR: Delivering Value in a Changing World of Work*. I was conscious that many L&D professionals don't necessarily identify as being part of HR and, as I often did, sit within a business unit or external service provider that operates completely separately from any HR function. Such musings led me to fear that perhaps I lacked the thought leadership to represent this unique skillset. Maybe I just wasn't *L&D enough* any more...

I then realized I'd fallen prey to a legacy within the people profession of placing too much emphasis on job titles, functional topics and specialist silos. This is a legacy that I believe holds us back and I hope this book goes some way in overcoming it. In a complex, uncertain and ever-changing business environment all people professionals – whether L&D, OD, HR business partners or change managers – need to unite and collaborate as a strategic, people-centric, collective if we are to enrich the employee experience for the better of humans.

Also, if there is one area within the people profession that lacks clear definition or strict boundaries, it's probably the domain of L&D and OD. It's a real jumble and mishmash of capabilities, academic disciplines and project briefs. For example, at the time of writing this book, I was coaching an L&D Director who was responsible not only for all learning within the organization but also talent development, succession and the broader Agile transformation of the business. Another assignment saw a Head of Talent and Leadership for a large multinational insurance company tasked with innovating its executive C-suite onboarding and in doing so partner closely with recruitment, mobility and reward. I was also coaching a people leadership team on a monthly basis and the most critical strategic initiative in their portfolio was a project called Pay, Progression and Performance. This project essentially required every skillset from across the function and included learning, organizational development, talent, reward, HR business partnering, change management and people operations.

This tension of titles and competing remits versus the need to work collaboratively to solve complex problems within the people profession has shaped much of my career. With good humour I remember desperately wanting to be called the Head of OD rather than L&D in a previous role, because at the time I thought it was more progressive. I also assumed such a title better represented a job description that included performance, leadership and culture change as well as steering the organization's learning curriculum. I now appreciate that in the end it didn't matter what my title was. What mattered was my approach and how I collaborated with others. Interestingly, I also recall a constant struggle in that job to obtain enough capacity and talent to deliver large organization-wide initiatives. It felt like I was always negotiating to secure the right skills and stakeholder relationships necessary for the project to be a success, from people and teams already committed to other projects or targets. I think of what I could have achieved if I had known then what I know now. By forming a multidisciplinary Agile team around each problem to solve, I could have got so much more done!

This book, *Agile L&D*, is a combination of the following elements:

- An ode to my younger self leading L&D and OD teams, now armed with the knowledge that the discipline is ripe for Agile disruption. These teams are often the best to kickstart a broader Agile transformation within the people function or wider business.

- An update, refresh and enhancement of my thinking since the first book.

- Sharing of new tools, templates and step-by-step guides that I've crafted in collaboration with great L&D and people teams over the last few years.

- The point of view of a learning professional, whose consulting business is based on the ongoing need to coach, facilitate and design learning solutions.

- An understanding that some of the most pressing workplace challenges faced within organizations sit within the L&D and OD domain or at least require these skills to help solve them.

- A call to action to everyone working within, and in partnership with, the people profession.

Since writing the first book, the need for the people profession to embrace business agility has become even more urgent. Faced with business challenges never experienced before we need a transformational mindset and a related Agile toolkit or playbook to help us navigate this complex terrain. I hope that by the end of this book you'll agree that I'm still *L&D enough* for you, and you're ready to help in changing our profession for the benefit of people, profit and the planet.

ACKNOWLEDGEMENTS

This book is not only based on my own words but enriched with stories sourced from an amazing group of L&D and people leaders. Much of the real-world context and practical case studies in this book are thanks to them. The interviewees I would like to acknowledge and thank are:

Tracey Waters – former People Experience Director at Sky UK and now Group Leadership and Talent lead at a large Australian bank. Tracey was one of the first people leaders I know to embrace Agile and transform her team into a multidisciplinary innovative collective. These days I'm fortunate enough to call Tracey a friend and her achievements feature throughout this book.

Arne-Christian van der Tang – Chief HR Officer at TomTom, is a strategic visionary who has inspired me for many years both through the leadership of his function and his dynamic ideas on the future of work.

Amanda Bellwood – People Director at Tombola and former People and Culture Director at Sky Betting and Gaming – was one of my first clients and has generously given her time over the years to co-host numerous Agile HR meetups and events. Amanda continues to be a source of ingenuity, not to mention inspiring chats.

Nebel Crowhurst – Chief People Officer at Reward Gateway, former People and Culture Director at Roche and Head of People Experience at River Island – also very kindly provided the Foreword to this book and has been a close collaborator ever since working together back in her River Island days.

Eoin Cannon – business agility coach at Upwell Learning – regularly partners with me as an associate at PXO Culture. Eoin and I met at one of my very first Agile HR Meetups in London back in 2016 and we have remained friends to this day.

Cassie Soady – former Head of Culture and People Transformation at WooliesX and Chief People Officer for Digital Data, Analytics, Technology and Enterprise Operations at National Australia Bank. Cassie jokingly comments that I helped make her cool by co-hosting several Agile HR Meetups in Sydney. In turn, I have become more knowledgeable about Agile organizational transformation through Cassie and I love that she continues to push the boundaries of our profession.

David James – Chief Learning Officer at 360Learning and former Director of Talent, Learning and Organizational Development at Disney – is close to being L&D royalty and a true thought leader. David and I met when PXO Culture partnered with his previous company Looop, which was a trailblazer in building an Agile L&D business model. It was an honour to have David contribute to this book.

Greg McCaw – Chief People Officer at BKL and former Director of People Experience and DEI at Flutter. Greg and I first met when he worked with Amanda Bellwood at Sky Betting and Gaming and where they led some of the most groundbreaking people processes I've seen. Today, Greg helps me keep it real.

Jodie Pritchard – former Head of Learning at the large UK charity Citizens Advice and now Director of L&D at the children's charity Barnardo's – is the very essence of a great Agile L&D leader. It's a sign of the times that, despite having collaborated virtually for many years, Jodie and I only met face to face for the first time recently. I'm happy to report that Jodie is even better in real life!

Sara Sheard – Executive Director of Business Operations at Incommunities and former Deputy People Director at Mencap – is an amazing leader who goes out and turns your theory into practice. Sara is genuinely championing a new approach not just in how the people function operates but the whole organization.

Geoff Morey – Head of Colleague L&D at Macmillan Cancer Support – is again someone I've only ever met and worked with online, but it feels like we've known each other personally for years. We have the type of relationship where the coach learns just as much as the client.

Nicki Somal – experienced Agile HR coach and consultant, who partners with me at PXO Culture regularly as an associate. Nicki started as a Scrum Master in Tracey Water's team at Sky UK when they first went Agile. She then became an Agile coach for the broader organization and now fortunately shares her wisdom with me and other people teams through her consulting. Nicki's enthusiasm and positivity make even the most challenging scenarios fun.

Adam Hepton – former software developer and tech people manager who moved into HR and OD at Sky Betting and Gaming and then Tombola. Adam offers that much-needed outside-in perspective and his tremendous success in HR, despite a technical background, just demonstrates that thinking in job titles and functional silos often holds HR back.

Kate Walker – People Programme and Projects Lead at Arup. Kate invited her team to participate in one of my Agile HR bootcamps several years ago and we've stayed in touch ever since. Her team continues to grow and flourish in its Agile capability.

Danny Seals – founder of Knot, well-known HR innovator – and Vice President, Employee Innovation, Listening and Effectiveness at RAKBANK, graciously offered insights from his many years leading employee experience design and innovation teams. We also healthily disagree on the T-shape model.

Sarah Ford – Head of HR Innovation at Diageo – invited me to the launch of its new team and innovation model which fortuitously coincided with the writing of this book. Sarah's team is market leading and I've yet to come across another operating model like theirs. I have no doubt it will be a standard approach across people teams in the years to come.

Laura Keith – CEO of Hive Learning – is an excellent example of a courageous leader willing and able to use an Agile mindset to not only transform her team but continue to develop a market-leading gen-AI business. Thank you, Laura, for offering an insight into the future of L&D tech.

It's also important to thank my good friend and business collaborator Jane Weir, whose conversations always help me see things from a fresh perspective. Jane's reframing of the Agile Manifesto stars in Chapter 2.

Many ideas and frameworks are brought to life visually in this book by the fabulous art director, Tizano Pilustri. Tiz has been PXO Culture's illustrator and brand director from the start and I love his beautiful, inclusive and funky designs. I encourage you to check out his great portfolio at www.tiz-p.com.

Tom Haak, who has recently retired from the HR Trend Institute, definitely deserves a mention here as well. While we no longer partner closely in business, Tom's ideas, insights and controversial views have shaped many chapters in this book.

When you write books, it is inevitable that close relationships are negatively impacted. Tim Goodwin, my life partner, definitely bears the brunt of my anxiety and stress-induced meltdowns, and I'm forever in his debt. What's worse is that this time Tim was also recovering from a shoulder injury and surgery. Hopefully in years to come we'll be able to look back on this year with a smile.

I'm also terribly sorry to my dear sister, Eleanor Dank, for negatively impacting her Scottish holiday with book writing and Covid. Thank you for helping out and making it all ok. I love you.

To my two besties back in Oz, Nicole Henry and Kate McBean: your WhatsApp messages keep me sane, and your belief propels me forward.

And finally, a massive thank you to everyone I've worked with or has attended a webinar, learning event or conference over the years. You're the reason I'm able to write this book, because it's through you that I learn how to innovate our profession.

01

Delivering value in a new era of work

How we design work, upskill people and deploy teams have become intrinsically linked with modern business strategy. In the recent past, employee learning, career development and reskilling might have been considered employee perks or nice-to-have extras. Now they are strategic levers used in business to remain competitive in a disrupted and digitalized world. With the need to continuously adapt and respond to a complex business environment, companies seek a more fluid movement of people across the organization, better reflecting customer needs, market opportunities and capability requirements. Such a strategic approach requires a sophisticated interplay of learning, design, data, digital capability and people skills.

Our new work paradigm

The world of work has forever altered. In the post-pandemic era, it feels like we're reinventing what constitutes the workplace in real-time. *Unprecedented* now seems to be a standard business term, alongside phrases like social and economic turmoil, exponential change, rapid technological advancement and ongoing market disruption.

In today's workplace, it's common to hear business leaders discuss the need to solve complex organizational challenges never experienced before. Digging a little deeper, you discover that many of these challenges represent the very building blocks of the modern twenty-first-century organization – hybrid working, digitalization, artificial intelligence (AI), employee wellbeing, inclusion and ever-present skills gaps. Perhaps even more interesting is that many of these modern organizational building blocks are still in their infancy and have yet to entirely reshape our daily working lives. Just imagine how the workplace will look ten years from now as AI, robotics, and the metaverse forever alter our lives.

The need for business transformation to remain competitive is also felt worldwide and in all industries. For example, a recent global survey of 4410 CEOs across 105 countries by PWC reported that 40 per cent believe their company as it exists today will not be economically viable in ten years. Further, 60 per cent want to spend more time on business reinvention instead of execution (PWC, 2023).

While the short-term impact of the Covid-19 pandemic on our daily lives was unparalleled and largely undesirable, what the world of work is still grappling with is the more permanent change that was brought on by the rapid digitalization of the employee and customer experience. Almost overnight, pandemic lockdowns forced a mass social experiment with companies suddenly needing much of their workforce to operate online and remotely. While the choice around flexible and remote working was already on the rise before the pandemic in most developed countries, the office or factory floor was still very much considered the sole workplace. Now, many people (knowledge workers, at least) are just as likely to include the kitchen table or the local coffee shop in their description of where and how they work.

A McKinsey study suggests the pandemic sped up the digital enhancement of existing products and services or the creation of new ones by seven years, with an even more significant leap of ten years in developed Asia (McKinsey, 2020). A good illustration was a recent conversation with a human resources (HR) team from a global tech company exploring its EVP (employee value proposition) and what motivates a person to get up in the morning and go to work. In this conversation, people quickly rephrased the question as, '*What makes a person get out of bed and open their laptop cover each morning to log in to work?*'

The emerging hybrid working models are by no means one-size-fits-all, but what's clear is that team video calls and virtual brainstorming sessions are here to stay. The emerging models cover a broad spectrum, ranging from 'work from anywhere', remote-first strategies advocated by Slack, Spotify and Dell to office-only approaches at Goldman Sachs and Netflix. Despite this range, the flexibility trend is accelerating, with employees worldwide now working from home an average of one and half paid days a week, with countries like the UK and Singapore averaging two paid days (Aksoy et al, 2022). However, it's crucial to highlight that while the workplace is increasingly digital, many people still work in on-site jobs such as retail, hospitals, delivery drivers, warehouses and factories; it is even more of a reason as to why workplace solutions can't be one-size-fits-all.

This shift in where and how we get work done has blurred the boundaries that traditionally separated our working lives from our personal, home and social experience. As a result, we're witnessing a renegotiation of the employee–employer relationship. Whether we call it the great resignation, reshuffle or quiet quitting, the overriding theme is a more human employment deal and a re-evaluation of jobs, careers and our relationship with work.

Retrofitting out-of-date workplace models

These workplace challenges are both daunting and exciting. However, up until now, many organizations have simply retrofitted existing ways of working onto this new normal. Constantly debating the productivity levels of a person working from home versus the office fails to grasp the enormity of the shift in how we now interact and get work done.

Many of today's workplace practices are still rooted in a post-Second World War Tayloristic type of mindset. We formulate strategies centrally, and then roll them out over the organization with the aim that everyone becomes aligned. However, this emphasis on alignment and top-down strategy no longer reflects how workplaces function. The pandemic also served to demonstrate that a team is able not only to collaborate and innovate just as productively while working virtually but crucially can do so in more self-organizing and iterative ways.

Most learning and organizational development activities within businesses still reflect these old norms. This is a legacy of delivering projects or designing solutions from the top down, big bang and one-size-fits-all. Processes like job competency frameworks, talent boxes, succession plans and functional career pathways are now too rigid and static and unable to flex and adapt to the changing world of work. Instead, learning and development (L&D) and people professionals now need to understand the whole human experience of work if they want to craft more personalized and valuable outcomes.

Only by letting go of the traditional Taylorist, industrial mentality and embracing business agility can L&D and people professionals begin to co-create the answers to these complex organizational challenges. This is why I've written the Agile L&D playbook: to help you build these capabilities.

What Agile L&D is

Agile is a mindset and a way of working that gives you the tools and techniques to solve complex problems. This is why Agile is so well suited to the challenge of reinventing the modern organization: because the challenge is a perfect illustration of a complex adaptive problem. It's a complex business challenge with many possible solutions, which can be approached from multiple and, at times, competing perspectives, and once any solution is underway, begins to alter the very nature of the problem itself.

Business agility is not a new concept, but the pursuit of Agile organizational transformation is now synonymous with market survival. This is because the need to assess the strategic landscape quickly, experiment and test solutions to determine customer value and then pivot direction as required are now all expected activities just to stay in business, let alone take advantage of a volatile market.

In an effort to stimulate innovation and continuous improvement, business processes and operating models are becoming more iterative and adaptive. As a result, we're witnessing more fluid role-based networks, collaborative teams, integrated product lines, digital processes and flatter hierarchies. The Agile L&D playbook simply translates these same empirical, test-and-learn methods increasingly used in other parts of the business into the context of L&D and organizational development (OD).

At its core, the playbook applies a product mindset to organizational learning and development and guides you step by step through the product development lifecycle. It's a type of Agile project management that can be applied to any business problem linked to workplace learning or OD.

The Agile L&D playbook is based on five design principles:

1 **Product-led** – view the employee experience as your product made up of different component parts.

2 **Human-centric** – shape the employee experience like a customer journey full of moments that matter for our people and brand.

3 **T-shaped people in T-shaped teams** – deliver the employee experience through a collective, strategic, multidisciplinary delivery model.

4 **Experimentation** – co-create the employee experience in an evidence-based way through prototyping and testing.

5 **Deliver with impact** – ruthlessly prioritize and measure impact to ensure the employee experience delivers the value that matters most.

What the Agile L&D playbook does not do is replace the excellent knowledge and deep specialism you've already developed up until this point in your field of learning and organizational development. Instead, it aims to evolve and update your skills for the *now* of work. If the business context has dramatically changed, then it follows that the way you approach specialisms like learning and organizational development must also change.

It is probably good to note that while we'll explore different examples and case studies, this book doesn't prescribe solutions to implement but instead offers a toolbox of methods to help you co-create outcomes and deliver with impact. For our learning buffs, the playbook doesn't explore learning pedagogy or assess different teaching styles. However, we will cover numerous workplace topics and discuss a variety of OD and organizational learning case studies, ranging from leadership development to workplace flexibility.

Additionally, while we'll discuss the shift to a new skills-based approach within talent development, you won't be given a workforce planning template or talent matrix to fill in. Instead, you'll gain tools and techniques to research a business challenge, such as skills-based talent development, and use these methods to identify the right problems to solve and then prototype and test solutions at pace. If, after working this way, your solution just so happens to include a template or talent matrix, then the playbook would have helped you validate this solution for the context in which you work, rather than dictate the use of a template or matrix itself.

Why focus on Agile L&D?

L&D and its related discipline OD have traditionally operated in specialist silos. Standard models include:

- a standalone L&D or OD team working within a more extensive HR and people function
- a standalone L&D team working within a business unit, with no reporting line to HR
- individual single-topic owners covering standalone remits like leadership development or talent development
- functional specialists sitting within a centralized COE (centre of expertise or excellence)
- consultant, coach, designer or business leader working for an external L&D services provider.

It is also very common for businesses to buy L&D expertise from outside the organization and, after salaries and bonuses, learning budgets often constitute the most significant spend on people in a company.

In today's complex and rapidly changing world of work, this specialist siloed approach has led to several problems, as outlined here.

Too slow – taking three months or longer to design a learning programme or new competency model is simply too slow in the context of the rapid pace of change and innovation demanded across businesses.

Implementation risk – too often, the resulting learning programme or cultural change initiative is delivered as a big-bang, one-size-fits-all implementation. The problem is that we often don't know how valuable or useful a solution is going to be until people start to engage with it. The danger is that we only then discover the solution doesn't meet people's needs or fix the problem we were aiming to solve. It's also usually too late to make substantial changes because the solution is already fully implemented. At this point, the best we can hope to do is tweak the design and try to convince people to use it through communication campaigns or add more features in an endless battle to improve something that doesn't quite fit.

Waste – lots of activity but not enough measured impact. Siloed teams and single-topic owners imply standalone remits competing for time, money and resources, not to mention the cognitive load within a business to absorb organizational change. For example, it's common to find an L&D team working on learning programmes, a DEI (diversity, equity and inclusion) team working on diversity initiatives and a wellbeing specialist running stress management workshops all at the same time. In these situations, each team or expert focuses solely on their own objective or offering. The result is a huge array of deliveries into the organization, each of which might aim to solve a specific problem but ends up feeling disjointed and overwhelming for employees. Rather than focusing combined efforts on the most important problem to solve and doing one thing well before moving on, these competing remits limit the capacity people can allocate across different projects and reduces the impact of each individual initiative. Generally, silos lack the skill mix to deliver the whole end-to-end project and, even if the siloed team or individual owns the remit, they will need to borrow capabilities from other teams or experts, such as internal communications, tech support, talent development or reward, to deliver lasting and meaningful organizational change. All of this results in waste – lots of apps, intranet pages and emails detailing beautifully designed products and services that no one is using.

Can't do it all – doing one thing well rather than a series of mediocre projects demands ruthless prioritization not just within a silo but across remits. In today's workplace, everyone seems overwhelmed and held back by their endless to-do lists. You just can't do it all. To simplify the complex and deliver at pace, businesses must streamline strategy and planning to direct effort towards the most crucial challenges faced by the organization at that time. Then, if a new and urgent priority arises, people need a decision-making system to determine whether to say no, not now, or yes but only if this other thing is stopped first. To achieve such ruthless prioritization, you need the ability to compare the value and impact of each possible piece of work. You will also get more done and at a faster pace if you focus all the necessary skills on one thing at a time.

Evidence of impact – there's a pervasive myth that measuring learning and behavioural change is difficult. This legacy relegates most L&D and HR initiatives to be perceived as a cost rather than a strategic business investment in people. In turn, this damages the credibility of L&D and people professionals and leads to projects based on who has the loudest voice or is paid the most. Instead, it's time to embrace data and business metrics to understand the problem to solve, test possible solutions and measure what happens as a result. Sales, product management, tech and marketing do this all the time. Why can't L&D?

Experience of work – employee experience can be likened to a customer journey, full of moments that matter for each person as they navigate their career, team contributions and interplay of work with their personal and social lives. By its very nature, the employee experience is a joined-up, interconnecting series of touchpoints, interactions and activities. The ability to conceptualize the whole product is impossible for a siloed team or single-topic owner operating alone, not to mention the need to shape and personalize it.

We can't solve today's complex business problems by continuing to work in functional silos with competing remits. The good news is that the much-needed disruption of this outdated model has begun. Like other parts of the business, L&D and people teams are transforming how they collaborate and get stuff done by embracing agility. Powered by the Agile mindset and toolbox of working methods, a new type of people product team is forming within organizations ready and able to craft multilayered employee experiences.

As a result, the traditional operating model for L&D and people teams is quickly evolving. The individual topic owner or siloed learning team bogged down in large programme implementations is quickly being replaced with multi-functional teams skilled in capabilities like human-centred design, experimentation and data analytics.

With this transformation comes a demand for new skills, roles and working methods within the people profession. To help, Agile L&D provides the essential playbook to guide your transformation. This represents a new mindset in how we co-create organizational development and learning alongside a whole new operating model for HR, people and culture. It recognizes that functional expertise – L&D, OD, design, talent, workforce planning, change – can no longer solve the complex problems faced in the workplace alone, and it's time to do it together. In the Agile L&D playbook, we call this working as a T-shaped person in a T-shaped team.

Who is the Agile L&D playbook for?

The playbook is for people working in learning, OD, HR innovation, talent development and leadership development, as well as the people and HR leaders who help steer these teams. You'll also find this book extremely useful if you're a change management professional, HR business partner or people partner, Agile coach or anyone working as a product manager or owner in areas linked to HR, employee experience and people operations. Business leaders wanting to solve learning and skill gaps as well as external and independent consultants designing solutions in the learning and OD domain for organizations will also find the playbook relevant.

However, despite listing these different roles, the message is clear: we can't solve complex problems by working in siloed teams or as single-topic owners. The playbook recognizes that functional expertise – L&D, OD, design, talent, workforce planning, change, and reward – can no longer alone, solve the complex problems we face in the workplace. Instead, L&D and people teams must now collaborate as multi-skilled and multi-functional problem solvers. In this sense, the playbook also implies the end of the centre of expertise/excellence (COE) model as we know it.

From siloed specialists to T-shaped problem solvers

It follows that this evolution of the workplace demands a transformation of how you approach organizational development and learning. Having never experienced these organizational complexities before, L&D and people professionals lack a blueprint for how to solve these complex problems and require a new set of working principles to guide workplace learning and OD. I hope the Agile L&D playbook provides the tools to help steer your transformation.

References

Aksoy, Cevat Giray, Barrero, Jose Maria, Bloom, Nicholas, Davis, Steven J., Dolls, Mathias and Zarate, Pablo (2022) Working from Home Around the World, National Bureau of Economic Research (NBER) Working Paper No. 30446, September, JEL No. D22,E24,J20,L23

McKinsey (2020) How COVID-19 has pushed companies over the technology tipping point—and transformed business forever, McKinsey and Company, www.mckinsey.com/business-functions/strategy-and-corporate-finance/our-insights/how-covid-19-has-pushed-companies-over-the-technology-tipping-point-and-transformed-business-forever (archived at https://perma.cc/J6M9-LFA5)

PWC (2023) *PWC's 26th Annual Global CEO Survey*, www.pwc.com/ceosurvey#whats-the-half-life-of-your-business (archived at https://perma.cc/CQU8-UBRM)

02

Agile as a response to complexity

As I write this book, AI (artificial intelligence) and app products like ChatGPT have exploded onto the market. Within two months of launch, the ChatGPT app (aka GPT-4 by OpenAI) hit 100 million users and, at that point, was considered the fastest-growing consumer application in history (Heaven, 2023a). The response from potential competitors was just as epic. Google issued a 'code red' and recalled its founders Larry Page and Sergey Brin (Grant, 2023), Elon Musk led a group of 1000 cosignatories to pen an open letter calling for an immediate six-month pause on any AI development beyond existing capabilities (Hern, 2023) and the 'godfather of AI' Geoffrey Hinton has resigned from Google to raise public awareness of the threat to humanity (Heaven, 2023b). Yet, despite all this, perhaps the starkest warning of the existential threat posed by AI to humankind was the deep fake image of Pope Francis wearing a white puffer jacket going viral (Milmo and Hern, 2023). Suddenly all our fears of robots taking control through misinformation and manipulation were captured in this one single image.

The pace of change

Over the last century or so, technological advancements have mostly disrupted manufacturing, with automation and robotics steadily replacing blue-collar production-line jobs. This timeline started in 1913 with the birth of modern manufacturing when the Ford Motor Company replaced a team of workers with the car production assembly line and reduced build time from 12 hours per car to 90 minutes (Boisset, 2018). This trend has progressed through Toyota's quality circles (1950s onward) and Lean operations (1980s onward), for example, culminating in Tesla's gigafactories of today, which are the result of an engineering philosophy that obsesses over the design of the machine (the factory) that makes the machine (the vehicle).

Now, for the first time in modern business, we're witnessing the disruption of knowledge-worker jobs and the very essence of human creativity. The viability of whole professions, including L&D and the people profession, is now in question as AI and related technologies enter the workplace. Often labelled the Fourth Industrial Revolution (World Economic Forum, 2023), this new chapter in human development reflects mindboggling technological advancements that begin to make movies like *The Terminator and Blade Runner* appear scarily accurate. Described as a merging of the physical, digital and biological worlds, many technologies like AI seem to simultaneously represent an immense opportunity for humanity and potentially our ultimate peril.

Two examples illustrating this duality stem from the interviews undertaken for this book. The first saw AI used to automate the design of an L&D programme. Following several prompts, the learning platform was able to compile an entire curriculum alongside suggested activities and facilitator notes within minutes. It's this kind of scenario that is leading many in the L&D and people profession to highlight the potential threat of AI replacing their jobs. On the flip side, another team used AI to help them translate an extensive array of HR and workplace policies from English into a local language. In this example, HR business partners based in China were struggling to find time for strategic project work because of the need to answer numerous questions linked to policy that were only available in English. The use of AI in this case meant a time-consuming project was dramatically shortened and the outcomes greatly benefited the HR business partners involved. While in both examples there is still clearly a need for the L&D and people professional to be the final editor, these stories demonstrate how AI simultaneously benefits humans in the workplace while also posing a threat to their future job security.

Change and uncertainty have reshaped the workplace throughout time. Examples include the lasting impact of women entering the workforce at scale during the Second World War to produce arms on the assembly line, the socio-economic ramifications brought on by the oil crisis in the 1970s and the dot.com crash in 2000. Also, while the nationwide lockdowns and vaccine rollouts in response to the Covid pandemic were indeed unprecedented, society at large had experienced epidemics before, such as AIDS, Ebola and SARS. In many ways, humankind has been here before and experienced similar crises that served to reshape the subsequent era of economic development. However, it's the pace and insidious nature of modern-day change that makes organizational life feel so complex. There's something about today's entanglement of global supply chains, international finance, geo-political tension, climate emergency and technology that leads many to describe our current era as a true paradigm shift (see Figure 2.1). It's also this very complexity that drives businesses to seek out agility.

A short history of work

FIGURE 2.1 The paradigm shift

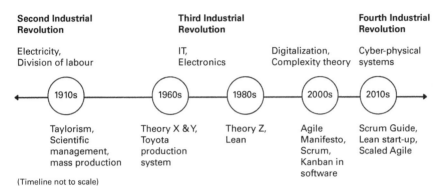

Second Industrial Revolution		Third Industrial Revolution			Fourth Industrial Revolution
Electricity, Division of labour		IT, Electronics		Digitalization, Complexity theory	Cyber-physical systems
1910s		1960s	1980s	2000s	2010s
Taylorism, Scientific management, mass production		Theory X & Y, Toyota production system	Theory Z, Lean	Agile Manifesto, Scrum, Kanban in software	Scrum Guide, Lean start-up, Scaled Agile

(Timeline not to scale)

It was the pace of change and increasing workplace complexity that led Tracey Waters (2023) to experiment with Agile methods with her team several years ago. For Waters, a pioneering HR and L&D Agilist and former People Experience Director at Sky UK and now Leadership and Talent lead at a large Australian bank, the team was taking too long to respond to business needs. 'We needed to find a way to get something into the hands and minds of our end users that would help them now, rather than in three months, six months, twelve months. And if you've ever designed a leadership programme that has taken twelve months, you know that that's not fast enough.' Waters also recognized a growing need to manage opinions with data. It wasn't enough to say you're the L&D expert in the face of competing business viewpoints. There was also a danger of designing a donkey product in an effort to please all stakeholders equally. Limiting waste was the next factor. 'I just saw so much waste, wasted time, wasted effort, wasted licences, wasted no-shows', and in a world of finite resources, such waste just wasn't acceptable. The final reason was silos and the need to move beyond the competing remits within L&D and HR based on functional topics. Throughout the book, we'll address each of these factors and demonstrate how an Agile approach can help you overcome these challenges within your own team and organization.

Birth of Agile

Agile began in software development over twenty years ago to manage risk in the context of uncertainty and develop products in an evidenced-based way. With the rise of the internet, customer choice exploded, and various developers started experimenting with different methods to better validate product design through testing and customer feedback before release. Prior to Agile, most projects followed a strict Waterfall approach. Waterfall is a project methodology that derives its name from visualizing project tasks cascading down a Gantt chart. In Waterfall, the whole project is planned upfront and project activities are broken down into linear sequential phases. Each phase of the workflow must be delivered before moving onto the next phase. While Waterfall may still suit environments with minimal dependencies and where your plans hold for the entirety of the project, it was increasingly recognized that a project plan now needed to adapt and even pivot direction in response to changing customer preferences, market forces or competition. As such, Agile developed as a direct response to the inflexible nature and slower pace of Waterfall projects.

The essence of Agile is to place your customer at the heart of everything you do and incrementally deliver value through a feedback-driven loop of *plan, do, review, adapt*. At its core is faith in people and their ability to solve complex problems by working together through a test-and-learn cycle. The key to adopting what is often referred to as the virtuous cycle and rapidly responding to customer needs is to work in multi-skilled teams rather than individual silos. By having all the skills necessary to design the whole solution, and complete every project phase, Agile teams can move faster and avoid being bogged down in handovers and dependencies. Moving at pace, Agile teams are trusted to self-organize and use visualization techniques to collaborate and make transparent, real-time decisions. As shown in Figure 2.2, Waterfall and Agile share the same project constraints, such as budget and time. However, in Waterfall, everything is planned upfront. All project work is then completed (represented by the shaded area), and the value (the box) is only realized when the project is delivered and the goal is achieved (the target). Conversely, in Agile, value is delivered early and often via multiple iterations of work. Following each value delivery, the plan is reviewed and adapted accordingly. Thus, as the project progresses, an Agile approach helps manage risk and potentially achieves the project goal faster by only focusing on the most valuable work in each iteration.

The skills to quickly assess strategic business needs, determine customer value and rapidly prioritize tasks in response to market forces are now crucial components of modern business. As a result, Agile has moved beyond the tech industry and now influences most business processes and organizational designs worldwide.

FIGURE 2.2 Waterfall method versus Agile

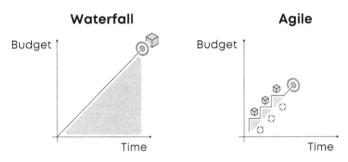

The start of Agile as a mindset and methodology is generally linked to the Agile Manifesto written in 2001 (Agile Manifesto Organization, 2001a). A collection of seventeen developers compiled the manifesto, including leading Agile figures such as Jeff Sutherland, Ken Schwaber, Alistair Cockburn and Mike Beedle, who realized there was a common thread to their various experiments and new ways of working. Today, Agile is essentially an umbrella term for an extensive, indeed unlimited, array of working practices that are all guided by the values and principles set out in the manifesto. As a result, tools and frameworks that enable these ways of working, such as Scrum and Kanban, are now commonplace, and we'll explore how some of these techniques are used within L&D and OD projects in later chapters.

First, let's explore the manifesto and translate it into the context of the L&D and people profession.

Agile Manifesto reframed

The four values

The manifesto is crafted around four core values (see Figure 2.3). The language reflects the context in which it was written and can seem quite 'techie' upon first reading. However, further exploration helps to unearth its positive approach to people and work.

There are two elements to each value, like two sides of a coin. Crucially, greater relative importance is given to the items on the left than those on the right. What's clever about the manifesto is that each value isn't an either/or proposition, rather it gives more weight or preference to certain items or procedures. Take the fourth value as an example. The need to follow a plan

FIGURE 2.3 Agile Manifesto original

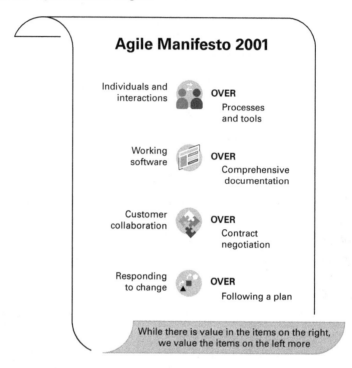

Agile Manifesto 2001

Individuals and interactions **OVER** Processes and tools

Working software **OVER** Comprehensive documentation

Customer collaboration **OVER** Contract negotiation

Responding to change **OVER** Following a plan

While there is value in the items on the right, we value the items on the left more

sits on the right because planning is an important business activity. However, in a complex, uncertain and ambiguous world, ensuring this plan can respond to change is even more important and, therefore, sits on the left.

We've all experienced scenarios where the items on the right took precedence in an organizational project, perhaps even to the exclusion of the items on the left. For example, one L&D leader interviewed for the book talked about an earlier project in their career that they now look back on with regret. This saw the development of a large organization-wide learning programme based on what they thought was a contemporary and groundbreaking concept. The entire programme was designed upfront to meet a self-imposed timeline. They then launched it to great fanfare without any prior testing, only to be told by participants upon release that it wasn't wanted or needed. In the end, the initiative simply fizzled out, and a lot of money and time was subsequently wasted. This is a great story that illustrates why the manifesto aims to balance your approach by allowing you to move between the two opposite ends of each value spectrum based on your context and customer needs.

FIGURE 2.4 Agile Manifesto translated

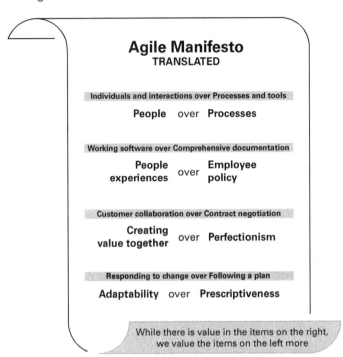

Agile Manifesto
TRANSLATED

Individuals and interactions over Processes and tools

People   over   **Processes**

Working software over Comprehensive documentation

People experiences   over   **Employee policy**

Customer collaboration over Contract negotiation

Creating value together   over   **Perfectionism**

Responding to change over Following a plan

Adaptability   over   **Prescriptiveness**

While there is value in the items on the right, we value the items on the left more

Figure 2.4 helps to reframe the manifesto in the context of L&D, OD and HR. This translation was crafted in partnership with Jane Weir, a leading HR agilist and close collaborator.

In the translated version, the first value becomes People over Process, a modern mantra for all people professionals. It's imperative that any process, system or programme you design helps people do their jobs rather than feel like an add-on that slows them down or doesn't immediately relate to day-to-day work. The goal is to build solutions *with* people rather than implement them *onto* people. Organizational processes need to have a reason and purpose; otherwise, it's just *process for the sake of process,* and people will quickly circumvent it. By designing a human-centric process, you place people at the heart of any value created.

A great example was a peer-to-peer rewards solution designed by Adam Hepton (2023), a former software developer and tech people manager who moved into HR and OD at his former employer, Sky Betting and Gaming. Using Agile principles, Hepton saw an opportunity to semi-automate a colleague's decision to recognize a peer's contribution as close to the point of need as possible. Hepton designed a bot that linked to a database of voucher codes and allowed people within the team to recognize another person's work with a small financial reward. When Hepton built the technical platform, the HR team at the time expressed concern that the system would be abused and suggested adding a collection of rules to manage behaviour. 'But as a people manager, I knew my people, and I knew they wouldn't abuse it, and I knew that if they did, they'd expect to be told off for it.' The solution was then introduced as an experiment without the additional policy or restrictions and a starting value of a couple of hundred pounds. The bot was a huge success, and the same platform is still used today by the organization ten years on, albeit with a few functionality enhancements.

The first translation then flows nicely into the second value, which translates into People Experience over Employee Policy. Here, the aim is to get an initial, perhaps smaller version of a programme, policy or process up and running to test and validate that it works before releasing it across the organization for people to use permanently. Too often, when faced with a problem to solve, L&D and people professionals still write the policy or design the entire programme first.

A good example has been the move to hybrid working for office-based companies following the pandemic. Many HR teams (albeit often at the behest of their executive team) rushed to define a new back-to-the-office policy that saw some organizations issue directives about which days people must be in the office. It was not surprising to witness a backlash among employees, coupled with debates about what constitutes work when in the office. Employees who were now forced to commute into the workplace only to sit on video calls talking to global team members reasonably questioned such policies. Organizations that instead approached hybrid working as a complex adaptive problem tended to see better outcomes by either testing different approaches first or, where possible, allowing teams to design the policy themselves. Chapter 10 details an excellent case study on how to take an Agile approach to this complex topic of workplace flexibility.

The third value becomes Creating Value Together over Perfectionism. This value is about how you co-create and use feedback from real people to validate your design and the resulting value delivered. When discussing agility, L&D and people professionals often talk about the fear of releasing products and services that are unfinished and far from perfection. But how does someone define finished and perfect? Ultimately, a product or service is only finished and perfect when people see value in it and they use it. It follows that the only way to achieve a sense of perfection and completion is to test before release and ask for feedback on solutions not yet finished.

It's also good to note that you should never test something that you don't think is at least valuable or worthy of feedback. Prototyping and testing are not about showcasing products or services that we can't be bothered to do properly. They're about testing early and often to ensure we're on the right track.

As stated by another people leader interviewed for the book, Greg McCaw, Chief People Officer at the professional services firm BKL and former Director of People Experience and Diversity, Equity and Inclusion at Flutter: 'Agile is one of the best things in your toolbox to create a more inclusive, equitable and diverse business.' For McCaw, an Agile approach ensures that L&D and people teams test the value of a product by understanding whether it solves the problem, something he feels is particularly important when designing DEI (diversity, equity and inclusion) solutions. Experimenting and scrapping what doesn't perform means you don't 'become entrenched and locked into big programmes of work that might not deliver positive outcomes'. McCaw also adds that Agile breaks the habit of buying off-the-shelf L&D and people solutions by quickly getting to the core of the problem and building better day-to-day experiences for different groups of people across the organization.

The fourth and final value becomes Adaptability over Prescriptiveness. To be prescriptive is to make rules or give directions. It can also reflect a legacy process, or an attitude of *this is how we've always done it around here*. A good example is an organization that recently issued mandatory management development training because of complaints raised about certain managers. While learning might still be an appropriate solution, any mandated approach will only ever result in most people being there because they must rather than because they see a purpose in it and helps solve a workplace problem. Also, mandatory learning doesn't target the specific instances of manager behaviour that led to these complaints. Instead, an Agile approach would research and investigate specific pain points and problems to solve at the point of need, which in this instance might be the circumstances and context that brought about the problematic behaviour.

'Do you have the acute ability to really identify problems and not identify them on your own, but identify them with others and through others, through deep empathy, mapping, getting the right type of insight, doing research, not relying on your engagement survey as your single source of truth and using that to really pinpoint the right problems and opportunities in a business? (Greg McCaw, 2023)'

The twelve principles

Supporting the values outlined in the Agile Manifesto are twelve principles (Agile Manifesto Organization, 2001b). These principles aim to guide your day-to-day practices when applying Agile. Below is a revised version of the original principles for an L&D and people context.

1 Delight the customer by delivering value early and often.

2 Welcome and incorporate changing people requirements at any stage of development.

3 Deliver value frequently by engaging in cycles of one to four weeks.

4 Collaborate across functions and skill silos.

5 Build projects around motivated individuals and trust them to get the job done.

6 Transfer information face to face, in person where possible.

7 Measure progress based on delivered value only.

8 Agile methods should promote a sustainable pace for all involved indefinitely.

9 Strengthen agility through continuous attention to excellence and improvement.

10 Simplicity is the art of maximizing the amount of work *not* done.

11 The best solutions emerge from self-organizing teams.

12 Reflect regularly on how to improve and then act on it.

Agile for L&D and people teams

Each L&D and people leader interviewed for the book was asked what Agile meant to them. The answers help to bring this somewhat hazy concept to life and place it in the context of the L&D and people profession.

Geoff Morey (2023), Head of Colleague L&D at Macmillan Cancer Support, started by describing a list of essential elements:

- the user at the heart of it
- being iterative
- responsive to needs
- about design that is useful and collaborative
- having the right people in the room

Morey then added that it was often easier to describe what Agile isn't and thinks that common misunderstandings of Agile often limit belief and commitment. Morey's subsequent list is based on how Agile is incorrectly used to describe being:

- fast (and while Agile does lead to speedier delivery, this pace takes time to be realized)
- unplanned
- spontaneous
- last minute
- chaotic

Morey concludes that many people confusedly see Agile as simply a bunch of tools, whereas for him, 'you can use all the Agile tools in the world and still not be Agile'.

Amanda Bellwood (2023), People Director at Tombola and former People and Culture Director at Sky Betting and Gaming, views Agile as a mindset and a move away from traditional L&D and HR practices where everyone operates in their own swim lane based on specialist silos and handing off tasks to each other. Instead, Bellwood describes Agile as having all the skills in one team. The outcome is 'you're all after the same deliverables, you're all on the same agenda'. This true one-team approach creates the necessary flexibility to be more adaptable and quickly respond to changing business needs because you're all in it together, making collaborative decisions.

'I think of it as a mindset, a set of principles, behaviours and practices,' states Danny Seals (2023), founder of Knot, and Vice President, Employee Innovation, Listening and Effectiveness at RAKBANK. 'It's about getting really close to the customer, our employees, and the business and understanding their pains, wants and needs.' Ultimately, Seals argues that Agile reflects how teams respond to the changing business landscape and continuously progress outcomes through iterative product design.

Returning to Greg McCaw (2023), who we met earlier in the chapter, 'Agile for me is also being comfortable with not being perfect.' McCaw highlights the proactive nature of Agile that helps teams continuously improve in an evidence-based way through experimentation and testing. 'In short, it really has to be the way that you think, act and behave every day.' Therefore, McCaw defines Agile as a mindset rather than a set of tools. For McCaw, the techniques associated with Agile are simply the enablers of the mindset.

Adam Hepton (2023), who we also met earlier, thinks people regularly embrace elements of agility in their everyday lives when trying new things and adapting to novel circumstances. 'For me, the practice of agility is something that we all do, whether we know it or not.' Hepton comments that many people break significant topics down into smaller, more manageable chunks to move forward in everyday life. Interestingly, Hepton adds that this natural agility seems to lessen once we're in the corporate workplace. For some reason, these things we do more naturally in our personal lives, such as pivot, learn, change, react and respond, suddenly become difficult once linked to KPIs and operational plans.

Eoin Cannon (2023), business agility coach and founder of Upwelling Learning, makes a distinction between Agile, with a capital *A* and agility, with a small *a*. Cannon describes Agile as a philosophy and a way of doing things. He then links agility to adaptiveness and the ability to successfully maintain a strategic direction, or north star, while adapting and evolving how you get there. Cannon observes that this is where people often go wrong with Agile because they interpret it as responding to change without the corresponding need to keep moving towards your north star vision. A key reason Cannon first embraced Agile working methods was due to frustration with how corporate projects were run. In his former role as a marketing manager working across large global drinks manufacturers, Cannon noted the length of time it would take to gather a cross-functional team and agree on a budget for any significant organizational-wide change project. This frustration would leave Cannon feeling like it almost wasn't worth the effort. For Cannon, the need for adaptiveness has been under-rated in the corporate world for a long time, but he thinks we're finally reaching the point where business leaders understand why it's critical.

So, how do these values and principles give someone an Agile mindset, I hear you ask? Let's turn to that in the next chapter.

Conclusion – five takeaways for L&D and people professionals

- Agile is a mindset and collection of working methods that helps you solve complex problems.
- Agile started twenty years ago as a response to a traditional Waterfall approach to project management that was proving too slow, inflexible and risky as the world of work became increasingly complex and uncertain.
- The Agile Manifesto sets out four values guiding your approach and is underpinned by twelve principles.
- The essence of Agile is to place your customer at the heart of everything you do and incrementally deliver value through a feedback-driven loop of *plan, do, review, adapt.*
- Agile shows up in how we think, act and behave each day.

References

Agile Manifesto Organization (2001a) Manifesto for Agile Software Development, agilemanifesto.org/ (archived at https://perma.cc/5KRG-AD2D)

Agile Manifesto Organization (2001b) Principles Behind the Agile Manifesto, agilemanifesto.org/principles.html (archived at https://perma.cc/55QX-3YV8)

Bellwood, Amanda (2023) Interview with Natal Dank, recorded 24 July

Boisset, Fabrice (2018) The History of Industrial Automation in Manufacturing, A3: Association for Advancing Automation, 24 May, www.automate.org/editorials/the-history-of-industrial-automation-in-manufacturing (archived at https://perma.cc/J2ZU-F73H)

Cannon, Eoin (2023) Interview with Natal Dank, recorded 12 July

Grant, Nico (2023) Google calls in help from Larry Page and Sergey Brin for A.I. fight, *New York Times*, published 20 January and updated 23 February, www.nytimes.com/2023/01/20/technology/google-chatgpt-artificial-intelligence.html (archived at https://perma.cc/XP3R-TWBP)

Heaven, Will Douglas (2023a) ChatGPT is everywhere. Here's where it came from, *MIT Technology Review*, 8 February, www.technologyreview.com/2023/02/08/1068068/chatgpt-is-everywhere-heres-where-it-came-from/ (archived at https://perma.cc/95YW-RCT2)

Heaven, Will Douglas (2023b) Geoffrey Hinton tells us why he's now scared of the tech he helped build, *MIT Technology Review*, 2 May, www.technologyreview.com/2023/05/02/1072528/geoffrey-hinton-google-why-scared-ai/ (archived at https://perma.cc/GJU9-K3EG)

Hepton, Adam (2023) Interview with Natal Dank, recorded 21 July

Hern, Alex (2023) Elon Musk joins call for pause in creation of giant AI 'digital minds', *The Guardian*, 29 March, www.theguardian.com/technology/2023/mar/29/elon-musk-joins-call-for-pause-in-creation-of-giant-ai-digital-minds (archived at https://perma.cc/RX9T-RK9B)

McCaw, Greg (2023) Interview with Natal Dank, recorded 23 June

Milmo, Dan and Hern, Alex (2023) From Pope's jacket to napalm recipes: how worrying is AI's rapid growth?, *The Guardian*, 23 April, www.theguardian.com/technology/2023/apr/23/pope-jacket-napalm-recipes-how-worrying-is-ai-rapid-growth (archived at https://perma.cc/E5UB-R5BZ)

Morey, Geoff (2023) Interview with Natal Dank, recorded 23 June

Seals, Danny (2023) Interview with Natal Dank, recorded 26 June

Waters, Tracey (2023) Interview with Natal Dank, recorded 26 July

World Economic Forum (2023) Fourth Industrial Revolution, www.weforum.org/focus/fourth-industrial-revolution (archived at https://perma.cc/U8CV-2EVP)

03

Grasping the Agile mindset

Whenever you ask someone to describe what Agile means to them, they'll tell you that it's all about mindset. But what is the Agile mindset, and how do you acquire it?

Tracey Waters, former People Experience Director at Sky UK and now Group Leadership and Talent lead at a large Australian bank, captured the essence of the Agile mindset in our interview (2023). 'Where it goes wrong for me is it's people not understanding Agile as a way of thinking and a way of working. They see the headings and the titles and the ceremonies, and they think that if they rename stuff, it will all magically happen. You have to actively break habits.' For Waters, Agile should feel a bit uncomfortable at first, like you're learning something new. 'Like if it feels familiar, you're probably not doing it right.'

One of the best explanations of the Agile mindset is by Simon Powers (2023a and b), an Agile thought leader and CEO and founder of AWA Global (Adventures with Agile), who uses three core beliefs and an onion to help people grasp this somewhat mythical and abstract concept.

Let's explore each belief first.

Complexity belief

It's about that ability to respond and adapt, which is so relevant to so many business problems, which are much more complex.
(Sara Sheard, Executive Director of Business Operations at Incommunities and former Deputy People Director at Mencap, 2023)

Believing that we live and work in a complex world might initially seem obvious until you dig a little deeper. Accepting that the modern business environment is a complex adaptive system also implies an acceptance that our organizational predictions, forecasts and plans are limited, if not sometimes flawed.

As brilliantly explained by Margaret Heffernan (2023) in her book *Uncharted: How uncertainty can power change*, with the onslaught of globalization, mass communication and rapid technological change, the modern world has moved from the complicated to the complex. A complicated environment is linear and predictable, able to be planned, managed and controlled, similar to a factory assembly line. A complex world is non-linear, fluid and volatile, and even the smallest of changes can lead to disproportional results. So, while we can generally be confident about many situations existing in a complex world, the ultimate outcome remains unclear (Heffernan, 2023). For example, while we can be confident that AI will impact the workplace, exactly how and which skills it will replace is hard to predict.

Cynefin®

David Snowden's Cynefin® Framework (thecynefin.co, 2023) is an excellent sense-making tool to help L&D and people professionals appreciate when and where complexity influences their work. Pronounced 'kuh-nev-in', cynefin is a Welsh word meaning place of multiple belongings and can be used to describe how our environment and experience (how we think, feel and act) are influenced by multiple and intertwined elements in a way that we never fully comprehend. The framework is made up of five domains, as outlined in Figure 3.1.

FIGURE 3.1 The five domains of David Snowden's Cynefin® Framework

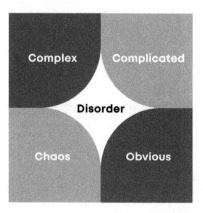

Crucially, most modern-day business decisions and organizational projects now sit within the complex domain. Here, it's necessary to experiment and work emergently to gather empirical evidence and move forward with data-driven decisions.

Interestingly, Cynefin® also helps to illustrate that most people, and at times whole organizations, have preferences when solving problems. As you explore the framework, consider which domain your organization prefers to operate in. For example, the legacy of specialist functions and expertise in engineering companies and banking means these organizations tend to favour the complicated domain where solutions can be predicted upfront through planning and analysis. In these organizations, tensions arise when the problem faced is complex, and these preferred working methods no longer suit the context.

Let's now explore Cynefin® (thecynefin.co, 2023) using onboarding as our example.

1 Obvious domain
   In this domain, best practice reigns as you sense, categorize and respond. Here, clear cause and effect exist, the environment is tightly constrained, and behaviour is predictable.

   o Obvious domain onboarding example: After accepting a job offer and returning a signed employment contract, a new employee's details are manually typed into the HRIS (Human Resources Information System, for example, Workday or HiBob). In this example, it doesn't make sense to experiment and test, and following best practices yields the most efficient result. Even if an error occurs, it can be readily solved by retracing the manual steps followed.

2 Complicated domain
   Here, you seek out good practice (as opposed to best practice) as you sense, analyse and respond. Generally, expertise is required to navigate a known selection of possible options that have been assessed and analysed upfront. This domain is characterized by governing constraints, tightly coupled.

   o Complicated domain onboarding example: Analysing, planning and liaising across different departments to agree on a list of tools that a new starter requires to begin their job. This list might include an office pass, laptop, access rights to specific drives and folders on a server, compliance checks or mandatory learning. The sequence of items or what needs to be included might vary from employee to employee, but it's generally known what's required. If not, requirements can be reassessed, and the process can be analysed and adjusted to maximize efficiency and support for the new starter.

3 Complex domain

When faced with complex adaptive problems, you must build emergent strategies to probe, sense and respond. In complexity, more is unknown than known, and everything is entwined with everything else. This means the outcome cannot be predicted upfront because the very act of solving the problem kickstarts effects that change the problem statement itself. Faced with multiple, sometimes conflicting, solutions, you must be ready to adapt plans and estimates and be prepared to pivot in response to uncertainty, ambiguity and an increasing rate of change (Powers, 2023b). The complex domain is characterized by enabling constraints, loosely coupled. The high level of uncertainty means you cannot seek out repetition, but you can seek out patterns to help you move forward.

  o Complex domain onboarding example: Designing and innovating the onboarding experience for a new starter. When creating an experience, the different touchpoints or moments that matter become central to the design. To understand how to enable and even delight people at different stages of the onboarding journey, you need to prototype, test and gather feedback on possible solutions. Even the onboarding journey itself could start and end at different moments depending on the organization or type of employee. For example, some companies develop solutions from the point of offer, while others align their onboarding with the first day on the job. Also, because different people require different skills, team connections and levels of authority, one-size-fits-all doesn't make sense, and the design requires you to research different personas and map the journey to personalize the experience for different workforce segments.

4 Chaotic domain

Chaos is a novel, unprecedented situation where you're forced to act, sense and respond. In this domain, you don't have time to experiment and test because very little is known, and immediate action is required to ensure people are safe. Only after this initial response can you begin to evolve emergent strategies to stop or limit the impact of the situation happening again. Chaos lacks any constraint and is de-coupled.

o   Chaotic domain onboarding example: The day before their start date, the new starter is contacted and instructed to stay at home because the country has gone into lockdown in response to a pandemic emergency. The new starter is told that the onboarding team will aim to send various tools, such as a laptop, to their home so they can start the job once more information is known. For now, the new starter should await a call from their manager to talk through expectations and devise a plan to begin the role virtually.

5   Disorder domain

This domain is the default when you don't understand what type of problem you are solving, and, therefore, utilize tools you're most familiar with. It's also what happens when we apply the wrong tools to the wrong problem, resulting in disorder and confusion.

o   Disorder domain onboarding example: An L&D team decides to deliver onboarding using a stand alone technical system. The new starter is asked to log in on their first day and complete the mandated process. However, given that the new starter doesn't have a laptop or is yet to be authorized for access, they sit at a desk confused and unable to act.

Implications of complexity

By believing in complexity, we question the traditional industrial structures and management styles that still characterize many organizations today. These conventional structures reflect the complicated domain and are based on hierarchical and bureaucratic separations between specialist functions, such as technology and finance or HR and communications. When faced with complexity, such organizational design proves too slow because information cannot be easily shared between specialist functions, nor the entire problem solved within a single siloed skillset.

A belief in complexity also challenges the sense of certainty and control that comes from KPIs, targets and business goals. This is a type of false assurance that, based on our predicted goal, the stated outcome will happen. KPIs and targets can only ever offer a pretend sense of security. However well intended, the certainty of business goals quickly changes as new information comes to light, unforeseen external forces take hold, or someone simply behaves differently from how you assumed they would.

This then highlights the tension within organizations seeking innovation and creativity. It's a pursuit that demands freedom for people to explore, get things wrong, experiment and, crucially, learn (Heffernan, 2023). To innovate, disrupt or adapt, companies need to embrace experimentation, failure and uncertainty, all of which present a risk that must be managed. Agile tools and techniques help us manage this risk by embracing the flow of up, down and around again. Agile shows us how to apply a disciplined test-and-learn approach so we can move forward by validating decisions as we go with empirical data rather than assumption or prediction. In turn, this helps to reduce risk and overall waste.

The implication is that to believe in complexity is to believe in an Agile organizational culture and operating system.

Most organizational change projects and learning initiatives sit within the complex domain, and Agile practices are the right fit. However, many L&D and people professionals question whether Agile is also applicable to operational processes and tasks that seem to fit the domains where good practice or best practice is applied. Does it follow that we don't use Agile in these situations? Let's explore this further.

First, an Agile mindset benefits everyone because we all live and work in a complex world. Next, it's about considering which tools best suit the problem you need to solve. So, an operations team would still use visualization techniques like a Kanban board (see Chapter 4 for more information) to manage the flow of work and prioritize tasks based on value. In this case, value generally reflects customers, service level agreements or business goals. The team would also benefit from committing to a cycle of *plan, do, review, adapt* to help them manage and continually improve their workflow. However, the team would use an agreed good practice when completing specific tasks that are visualized on the board and maybe even best practice for others. In this situation, it wouldn't be appropriate to prototype and test every time a team member undertook an operational task. However, as soon as the team recognized the need to innovate or improve the operational process and essentially update their good or best practices, the problem is now complex and an Agile approach of test and learn fits the scenario.

People belief

Feel safe enough to behave like no one is looking when everyone is looking. (Chris Hovde, Leadership and Culture Lead, Telia, at the HRcoreNORDIC conference, Copenhagen, 24 May 2023).

The Agile Manifesto's first value of 'Individuals and interactions over processes and tools' recognizes organizations as human ecosystems rather than machines (Agile Manifesto Organization, 2001). This mantra of people over process symbolizes the human-centred nature of Agile values and practices. To believe in people is to believe that humans sharing their skills, collaborating and learning from each other can solve the complex problems faced today. This belief in people is potent and gives us the optimism to experiment, fail and learn together. However, to be successful, the underlying culture needs to be one of trust. It requires a conscious focus on developing psychological safety within teams to ensure people feel able to speak up, disagree and challenge. Only through debate and exploration will teams find new and novel solutions.

We need to be our best selves and feel psychologically safe to give our best work. Regardless of the project, whether digital transformation or an operational restructure, success or failure lies with people. This need for a human-centred approach shouldn't be a surprise to L&D and people professionals. Trusting people as adults, being able to make real-time decisions and self-organizing to get the job done is the very definition of the commonly overused business term 'empowerment'. Autonomy and empowerment must be more than just words, however, for agility to succeed.

Adam Hepton, former software developer and tech people manager who moved into HR and OD at Sky Betting and Gaming and then Tombola, observes that it can often feel there is a need to execute the decisions of others, particularly senior leaders when working in L&D and people teams. However, Hepton (2023) encourages you to value your expertise and own any people decisions made. 'We are valuable. We do know what we're talking about. We can help. We can add value. We are not the harbingers of doom to enact others' unpopular decisions.' Hepton adds that it's vital to challenge unpopular decisions and ensure it is the correct action to follow. 'Any unpopular decision needs to be the right decision.' Working openly and transparently is critical, and even if you can't share all the details, you'll be able to explain why a decision was made. By believing in people and operating through a human-centric lens, L&D and people teams can proactively build an environment of trust and partnership across the organization.

The implication of this is that to believe in people is to believe that by trusting people to collaborate and self-organize, we can solve complex problems together.

Proactivity belief

The problem statement changes as we interact with it. It is necessary to learn as much as we can and as often as we can so that we are able to determine how the problem has changed and what we need to do next. (Simon Powers, 2023b, CEO and founder of AWA Global)

Interestingly, Powers (2023b) almost didn't include this belief but realized that without proactivity, people might lack a direction of travel when solving complex problems. Learning by doing and collecting feedback is fundamental to the empirical process. It underpins the emergent process because the way forward emerges as you learn more. This implies that simply applying Agile practices isn't enough. People need to be in a transformational state to move forward. In this state, people feel compelled to seek out improvement, feedback and lessons learnt and continuously gather insight on what works and what doesn't. It is this motion of continuous improvement that propels us forward when solving complex problems. The Agile cycle of *plan, do, review, adapt* is aiming to do this precisely and offers a simple but disciplined way of applying the proactivity belief day to day.

While the proactivity belief is based on positive intent, it can also leave people feeling vulnerable. Thus, it must co-exist with the other beliefs to mobilize people around a shared purpose and a pursuit of experimentation and learning when solving complex problems. Just because we can't predict the future doesn't mean we're helpless, but if we are to solve the vast complex problems faced by our organizations – skills crisis, climate emergency, AI – then we must embrace the opportunity to be creative, to experiment and explore (Heffernan, 2023). Otherwise, we remain at the mercy of uncertainty and change.

The implication is that to believe in proactivity is to believe that you can grow and improve through feedback and learning

The Agile onion

Now that you appreciate the Agile mindset, Powers' (2023a) onion helps you connect this somewhat abstract and intangible concept with the more visible and tangible tools and practices that make up Agile working methods.

FIGURE 3.2 Simon Powers' Agile onion

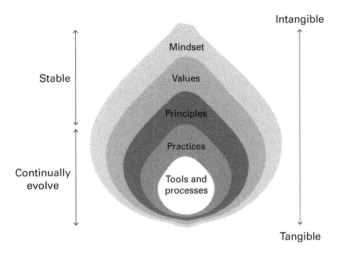

As depicted in Figure 3.2, the onion helps you connect the Agile mindset, otherwise known as being Agile, with the values, principles, practices and tools that make up the doing of Agile. The significance is that Agile is never just applying tools and techniques, and only by embracing the mindset and thus believing in complexity, people and proactivity will any of the tools and techniques make sense and, more importantly, work. As highlighted by Eoin Cannon (2023), business agility coach and L&D practitioner, 'While Agile with the capital A is a mindset, where I've moved on in my thinking is that it's not enough to say it's a mindset, there's way more to it. It's also all the things that go with Agile and support that way of working.'

Translating the mindset into business agility

Business agility implies scaling these concepts beyond an individual team and across a whole business. For some organizations, this might be as simple as the Agile mindset harnessing experimentation and cross-team collaboration. For others, it might entail the complete restructure of the entire operating model and related processes, often based on a scaled Agile framework like SAFe (Scaled Agile Framework, 2023, the most well-known model guiding organizational-wide business agility or Scrum@Scale, 2023), a model designed by Jeff Sutherland and based on the original Scrum Guide.

Cassie Soady (2023), former Head of Culture and People Transformation at WooliesX and Chief People Officer for Digital Data, Analytics, Technology and Enterprise Operations at National Australia Bank, has led many Agile organizational transformations and describes business agility as a spectrum made up of three phases. The first phase is all about leadership. Soady comments that it was this phase that saw her fall in love with Agile and is about 'how you turn command and control leaders into leaders that want to give people problems to solve, not solutions to implement'. In this phase, Soady would also include the activation of Agile practices within teams, the introduction of collaborative quarterly planning, identifying dependencies and connecting teams in an attempt to move beyond silos.

The second phase is when an organization starts experimenting with small-scale Agile delivery. In this phase, you aim to deliver a few important projects and initiatives using Agile. This might also involve setting up a cross-functional team or squad within one part of the business to act as a type of incubator or test case for the broader organization. The third and final phase is then moving into full-scale Agile or 'deep delivery' as Soady calls it, which involves the transformation of the entire operating model. For

TABLE 3.1 Characteristics of business agility

From	To
Rigid hierarchy	Fluid, collaborative and team-based networks
Jobs and functions	Skills and roles
Secrecy	Transparency
Discussions about people	Discussions with people
Product lines or functions based on product components	End-to-end product and customer experiences
Projects functionally led and with competing remits	Multidisciplinary teams aimed at simplification and removing waste
Top-down planning and forecasts	Open-sourced business portfolios and strategy
Annual cycles and budgets	Adaptive planning and iterative budgets
Trying to do everything at once	Ruthless prioritization based on true capacity
Top-down command and control	Team and personal ownership
Individual goals and rewards	Collective goals and rewards
Manager-led	Peer-to-peer and self-organizing
HR process and systems	Holistic employee experience

example, at organizations where Soady previously worked, this was characterized by squads, chapters and tribes (reflecting another common model known as the Spotify model).

Soady comments that too many organizations try to jump straight to phase three without first defining the problem to solve and gradually building capability and harnessing an Agile mindset by working through phases one and two. This leads her to suggest that most organizations should simply remain in the first phase and focus on evolving their leadership style. The aim is to connect business strategy with a strong sense of purpose throughout the organization and the delivery of value to the end customer. Soady views this as the most powerful way to build a shared vision and excite people to embrace Agile.

Whatever shape or form business agility takes within your organization, there is a collection of essential elements sparking this evolutionary change. Table 3.1 aims to capture the most important of these elements.

Conclusion – five takeaways for L&D and people professionals

- The Agile mindset is based on three beliefs – a belief in complexity, a belief in people and a belief in proactivity.
- To believe in complexity is to believe in an Agile organizational culture and operating system.
- To believe in people is to believe that by trusting people to collaborate and self-organize, we can solve complex problems together.
- To believe in proactivity is to believe that you can grow and improve through feedback and learning.
- Business agility implies scaling these concepts beyond an individual team and across a whole business.

References

Agile Manifesto Organization (2001) Manifesto for Agile Software Development, agilemanifesto.org/ (archived at https://perma.cc/J2HR-PS9E)
Cannon, Eoin (2023) Interview with Natal Dank, recorded 12 July
Heffernan, Margaret (2020) *Uncharted: How uncertainty can power change*, London, Simon & Schuster

Hepton, Adam (2023) Interview with Natal Dank, recorded 21 July

Hovde, Chris (2023) Leadership and Culture Lead, Telia, HRcoreNORDIC conference, Copenhagen, 24 May

Powers, Simon (2023a) Peeling Back the Layers of Agile: Understanding the Agile onion, AWA Global, adventureswithagile.com/understanding-the-agile-onion/ (archived at https://perma.cc/K5J6-DJS4)

Powers, Simon (2023b) What is the Agile Mindset?, AWA Global, adventureswithagile.com/what-is-the-agile-mindset/ (archived at https://perma.cc/S68R-F7JZ)

Scaled Agile (2023) What is SAFe?, scaledagile.com/what-is-safe/ (archived at https://perma.cc/Z2EA-83L3)

Scrum@Scale (2023) *The Official Scrum@Scale Guide*, scrumatscale.com/scrum-at-scale-guide/ (archived at https://perma.cc/6Z7S-KWSC)

Sheard, Sara (2023) Interview with Natal Dank, recorded 4 August

Soady, Cassie (2023) Interview with Natal Dank, recorded 30 June

thecynefin.co (2023) The Cynefin Framework, thecynefin.co/about-us/about-cynefin-framework/ (archived at https://perma.cc/G6RJ-2HW9)

Waters, Tracey (2023) Interview with Natal Dank, recorded 26 July

04

How to deliver value early and often

Value for the customer

The cycle of *plan, do, review, adapt* is the rhythm of Agile. It's a cadence that propels teams forward and drives a feedback-driven loop of continuous improvement. The source of this feedback is the customer, who sits at the heart of the cycle. The customer is crucial in Agile because it is their needs, problems to solve and feedback that define the value you deliver. This value then guides your work at each stage of the *plan, do, review, adapt* cycle (see Figure 4.1).

Value also constitutes what you're ultimately aiming for through your product or project vision and it's how you measure impact. It's helpful to think of a cycle as an iteration where you aim to deliver a slice of value and build an increment of your product. This means most teams aim to deliver increments each cycle that are considered done and can be used but are not

FIGURE 4.1 Agile cycle of plan, do, review, adapt

FIGURE 4.2 Agile cycle and Agile project

yet perfect. Over time, these value slices accumulate to the point where you achieve the overriding product vision and deliver the whole project (see Figure 4.2).

This Agile concept of incremental development is central to solving complex problems. By breaking the business challenge down into smaller, more achievable chunks of work, you can better prioritize where and how to start. Additionally, even if this starting point is to run a diagnostic or a short experiment, you're still delivering something of value, and your project is up and running. Most organizational challenges are multifaceted and hugely complex and it's common for L&D and people teams to feel overwhelmed with the scale of the problem to solve at the start of a project. For example, how do you create a learning solution that connects with people in a hybrid workplace? What constitutes employee wellbeing, and how do you improve it? There is no perfect solution to solve these types of challenges. Your only option is to break it down into component parts and get started.

David James (2023), Chief Learning Officer at 360Learning and former Director of Talent, Learning and Organizational Development at Disney, describes Agile as a 'commitment to adding real value incrementally without having to make big bets'. Agile draws on the critical components of data, experimentation and iteration based on feedback and other evidence to achieve this outcome. For James, such an approach is fundamental if L&D as a profession wants to move beyond a legacy of 'spend without impact', where output is based on assumed needs and plugging isolated skill gaps with generic content. Agile offers L&D a method to manage risk and reduce waste because you can't move forward unless you clearly define the problem to solve. You then require evidence of meaningful impact and a positive change in performance to deliver value.

Who is the customer?

For L&D and people professionals defining value based on the customer is a multilayered exercise, and it helps to view the customer through the lens of systems thinking (see Table 4.1). First and foremost, the customer is our people, the employees of an organization. Most L&D and people professionals feel comfortable talking about this customer segment and can measure impact with relative ease through metrics such as engagement feedback, career development and a sense of wellbeing. However, it's also important to be mindful that value needs to flow through to other customer segments for anything you create. For example, does your solution impact the business bottom line? Will it support the end customer, the people or organizations that buy or use your company's products and services? Lastly, have you considered other stakeholders in the design, such as suppliers, contractors, future talent, the broader community and, increasingly, our planet?

TABLE 4.1 Customer segments and value drivers

Customer segment	Value drivers
Business	• Market advantage
	• Revenue
	• Sales growth
	• Reduced costs
	• Productivity
	• Efficiency gains
	• Brand sentiment
	• Market growth in sector, industry or region
	• Return on funding investment
	• Healthy employee turnover

(continued)

TABLE 4.1 (Continued)

Customer segment	Value drivers
Enabler	• Health and safety measures • Self-service and straight-through processing • Managed compliance or regulatory risk • Controlled expenses • Reduced spend on 'fixes' • Workplace design and flexibility • Reduced complexity (e.g. in workload or systems)
Purpose-driven	• ESG standards – environmental, social and governance • Net-zero targets • Social contribution • Diversity, equity and inclusion • Community involvement at local levels • Charities and not-for-profit initiatives • External awards and certification
Employee	• Meaningful work and sense of achievement • Impact on end customer, product or service • Connection with purpose of organization • Career development • Wellbeing and mental health • Household financial stability • Personal growth • Performance support and useful feedback • Safety, both physical and psychological • Flexibility in how and where they work • Sense of inclusion and belonging
End customer	• Service quality and speed • Consistency • Market or brand growth • Connection with organizational purpose • Brand credibility • Product innovation • Resilient and reliable network or service • System or process simplicity • Low or fair cost • Personalization

Managing the risk of uncertainty or failure

Agility is about being responsive and adaptive in how we plan. This potential need to adapt the plan is why the Agile cycle is often one to two weeks in duration and generally not longer than a month. Too many factors can shift if you work (or go) beyond this timeframe. For example, even within a month, L&D and people teams might experience a change in budget, government regulation, negative or positive social media brand coverage, employee retention, talent sourcing, employee feedback, grievances, mergers and acquisitions, stakeholder needs, natural disasters, market movements, and the list goes on.

This is why it's imperative to keep the cycle short and regularly review the outcomes achieved alongside any changing circumstances so you can adapt the plan as needed. A good illustration was a story shared during the interviews of a person hired by an organization to help progress a large-scale project that, by this stage, was considered three years late. The narrator reflected that if an Agile approach had been applied, the project would have been abandoned by then, or something entirely different would have been released to iterate based on feedback and other data. Viewed this way, Agile is about testing early and failing quickly to save money and reduce waste.

Managing the risk and impact of change doesn't just relate to external factors. It could simply be that what you produce during a cycle fails or doesn't end up as expected. Perhaps people don't like it, it's not considered valuable, or it fails to fix the customer's problem. Rather than shy away from failure, the Agile cycle celebrates it. It is much better to learn fast and fail cheaply so you can quickly reprioritize or pivot direction than to slog away at something for months, even years, only to end in disappointment. Instead, by engaging in short, targeted iterations, you're better able to continuously evolve your product based on customer feedback and other data. For L&D and people teams, the empirical process of testing and learning results in the continuous and incremental enrichment of the employee experience.

Using Agile methods to reduce waste and manage risk are also critical factors for not-for-profit organizations, comments Geoff Morey (2023), Head of Colleague L&D at Macmillan Cancer Support. What Morey likes about Agile is that it encourages you to try new things and move into areas you wouldn't usually, confident that any potential risk is minimized by following a process of rapid experimentation and data-driven decisions.

As highlighted by Adam Hepton (2023), former software developer and tech people manager who now works in the HR and OD profession: 'There is no true failure other than one that you can't mentally recover from.' For Hepton, sometimes continuing with a doomed project proves more damaging than making the difficult call to end it early. Hepton observes that the tech teams he worked with previously were generally more willing to experiment and then quickly move on if the experiment failed, compared with the people teams he now works with. For example, in tech, they might work on something for a week and then test it with a small percentage of customers. If it didn't work, they would tweak it and test it again. If it still didn't perform, they would happily bin it and move on. Hepton encourages L&D and people professionals to be more accepting of failure as a helpful method to learn and validate outcomes quickly.

Minimal viable product

Test and learn underpins a central Agile concept: the MVP or minimal viable product. An MVP has just enough features to validate a design concept or engage early customers. It helps you test assumptions and explore whether a hypothesis is valid in the real world. It's effective when applied to the employee experience and organizational change because it invites people to co-create the solution with you. This helps to build more human-friendly outcomes and proactively builds trust in the solution. By collecting early feedback on an MVP, you also potentially avoid lengthy and unnecessary work on a design that isn't viable. Figure 4.3 shows an essential aspect of any MVP: it may not yet have all the product features, but it is a complete, functional delivery containing all the elements required in the final product; human-centric design, usable, reliable and functional. Figure 4.4 also illustrates this principle using the example of a chair.

Good enough for now, safe enough to try may sound easy, but it can be incredibly challenging in practice. Many L&D and people teams struggle with this concept due to the broader HR legacy of Waterfall and big-bang

FIGURE 4.3 Minimal viable product (MVP)

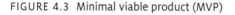
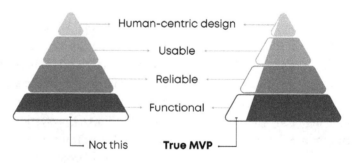

FIGURE 4.4 Incremental development and MVP

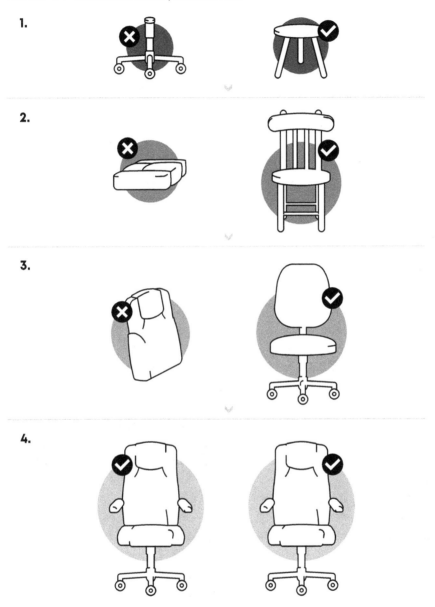

project implementations. Unfortunately, the concept of MVP often gets confused with unfinished or unpolished. For this reason, it's helpful to reframe MVP from a Minimum Viable Product to a Minimum Lovable Product. A minimum lovable product is released early but with style. The

MVP still needs to add value; it's just a smaller version of the whole solution or is initially only tested in one part of the organization. (See Figure 4.4.)

Geoff Morey (2023) from Macmillan Cancer Support embraced an MVP approach when delivering a significant management development project and testing a framework of eight commitments that would subsequently shape ongoing design. This saw Morey send a basic slide pack to twenty managers, asking them to comment on content, not style. Interestingly, he discovered this created a more inclusive approach for the people involved. A line manager who is neurodiverse and disabled thanked Morey because they didn't have to comment on accessibility and enjoyed how it was framed as an MVP. 'It just made it much easier for that person. But also meant that they were included.' As the project progressed, Morey and the team could be confident that important voices were heard and included in the design.

Prototyping and experimentation

To ease the sense of vulnerability when releasing an MVP, it's healthy to do a rapid prototyping stage first. Prototyping is an experimental process that helps you quickly and cheaply bring a design concept to life for people to experience and test. The aim is to gain feedback on whether the design concept works and is worth pursuing.

Prototypes can be made from cardboard cutouts, Lego, online whiteboards, Plasticine, short plays, and basic mock-ups of tech systems and simulations. There's an expression that if you're not slightly embarrassed by the standard of your prototype, you've probably spent too long working on it. Prototyping is a great way to validate whether a design idea has potential. There's essentially no limit on how many prototypes you can create and test, and the more you validate, the more possible solutions you can explore. We'll get into prototyping in more detail in Chapters 8 and 10.

Greg McCaw (2023) Chief People Officer at BKL and former Director of People Experience and DEI at Flutter, remembers how refreshing it was when he first joined a people operations team that was open and willing to experiment. At the time, McCaw saw an opportunity to innovate an existing reward and recognition process that seemed overly bureaucratic and clunky. He was pleasantly surprised when his manager instantly agreed to test it and assess the results. McCaw was so used to bottleneck decision-making in previous roles and the need for approval that he almost couldn't believe the speed at which he now moved. He was advised to set out what he wanted to test and a hypothesis, then gather ten willing participants to test it and sit down with these managers in a month's time to discuss the results. McCaw also reflects that the MVP approach was critical. To test it, he used tools already available, such as Slack, to create a basic mock-up of the system. In the past, he probably would have sought a much fancier off-the-shelf product to support the new approach without first establishing whether the proposed solution solved the problem.

What if you don't know the problem to solve?

It's critical at this point to connect Agile ways of working with design thinking and what's often called discovery work. It's not uncommon for L&D and people professionals to dive into a project without first clearly defining and prioritizing the problems to solve. This tendency in the people profession to start with the solution in mind can cloud judgement and often lead to confirmation bias, where people seek out data to support their perspective.

The strong opinions and assumptions held by business stakeholders, especially executive leaders, regarding L&D and people processes can further compound this issue. The danger is that everyone considers themselves an expert on employee matters because everyone has been an employee. If we add to the mix the plethora of off-the-shelf HR and learning digital platforms available on the market these days, all promising to save you time and money, it's not surprising that many of us fall into the trap of jumping to the solution first.

As the Chief HR Officer at TomTom, Arne-Christian van der Tang (2023) always reminds his team it's about 'falling in love with the problem, not the solution'. We'll explore in Chapter 9 TomTom's excellent case study of how it radically reimagined its operating model to deliver the value that matters most.

By applying *design thinking*, L&D and people teams are better able to move beyond these competing views or assumptions and develop a contextual design that suits specific organizational scenarios. Design thinking is deeply grounded in empathy and helps you explore the human experience of work. You can see from Figure 4.5 that it's also based on the test-and-learn

FIGURE 4.5 Design thinking and Agile

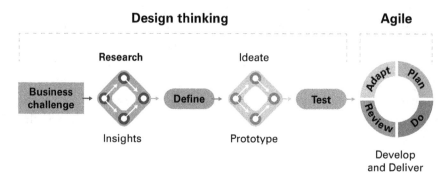

cycle and includes prototyping. Design thinking can be used at any time in your project, but it's instrumental at the start when you know the least about the problems to solve.

The design thinking sequence is based on divergent and convergent thinking, or the double diamond (Design Council, 2023). Divergence stops us from jumping to the first problem we find to solve (research) or the first solution we see (ideation). Convergence helps us concentrate on the most critical problem to solve now (insights) and focus on the best solution (prototyping) for our context.

When it comes to L&D and OD, it's best to see Agile and design thinking as interlinking methods. This is why human-centred design is one of the five principles in this Agile L&D playbook. Generally, a project's first one or two cycles are based on the design thinking sequence. Sometimes known as a discovery or a design sprint, this project phase might even involve a different group of people from the core team who deliver the remainder of the project. We'll cover design thinking in more detail in Chapter 8.

Sarah Ford (2023), Head of HR Innovation at Diageo, thinks this is where L&D and people teams have lost their way in the past. For Ford, there was a tendency to design things in a bubble, and we can effectively burst this bubble through design thinking. Design thinking is considered a core element in all the HR Innovation projects she oversees. Ford states that it's vital to hear the voice of the customer and gather direct employee feedback. She adds that 'It's not that hard to do. Normally, employees are really open to sharing what their frustrations are and what they feel. And it's a great way to involve them from the start.'

Scrum

Scrum is the most common framework used when running an Agile project and is based on focus, openness, respect, commitment and courage. The practices contained within Scrum are great for bringing the Agile cycle to life, helping teams self-organize and deliver value incrementally. Generally, when you observe a team engaging in Agile practices, the approach will contain elements sourced from Scrum even if they no longer follow the framework set out in the Scrum Guide.

The term Scrum stems from a comparison made between a traditional project team that operates like a relay race, where specialists pass sequential tasks to each other, and an Agile team that follows a rugby-style approach where a cross-functional team self-organizes and solves problems together to reach an outcome (Takeuchi and Nonaka,1986). Scrum originated in software development in the 1990s and follows the mantra of *doing twice the work in half the time* (Sutherland, 2015). Based on empirical process control, the framework advocates the principles of inspection, adaption and transparency to propel teams forward continually. The framework was developed over about a decade before being formalized as the Scrum Guide by Jeff Sutherland and Ken Schwaber in 2010. The Scrum Guide is regularly updated with the latest edition released in 2020 (Schwaber and Sutherland, 2023).

In Scrum, teams commit to delivering work incrementally within time-boxed periods called sprints. At the end of each sprint, there should be something of value to review with customers and stakeholders, known as a potentially releasable product increment. The team then uses feedback and other data gathered from this review to assess the value delivered so far, what they need to do next and how they might need to adapt existing plans. You'll notice the similarities with the Agile cycle and practices described earlier in this chapter, see Figure 4.6.

The Scrum framework is based on a 3-5-3 rule, which guides how teams self-organize and collaborate. This reflects:

- **Three team roles** – the development team who owns *how* the product is developed, the product owner who champions *what* to develop and the Scrum Master who coaches the team and supports their continuous improvement by helping them unearth and remove impediments slowing them down. See Chapter 9 and the section outlining essential Agile roles for L&D and people teams for more detail on each of these roles.

FIGURE 4.6 Scrum project

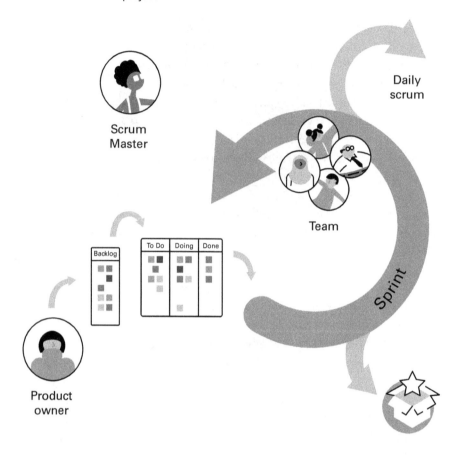

- **Five regular ceremonies or rituals** – sprints, sprint planning, daily scrum (also known as a stand-up or the more inclusive term, check-in), sprint review and sprint retrospective are events that help steer how the work gets done.
- **Three unique artefacts** – the product backlog, sprint backlog and product increment help visualize, manage and progress work.

All of these elements are further explored in Chapter 5 when we detail how Agile tools are used throughout the Agile cycle.

Kanban

Kanban is based on visualizing your work to support a continuous and healthy flow of work (as opposed to the time-boxed sprints in Scrum).

FIGURE 4.7 Kanban board

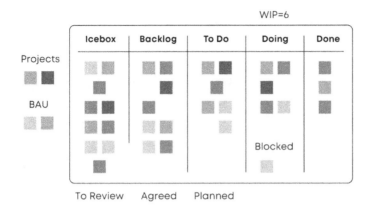

The framework centres around visualizing work on a board to limit work in progress and maximize efficiency through the principles of prioritization and continuous improvement (see Figure 4.7). Teams using Kanban focus on reducing the time it takes to move a ticket (or piece of work) across the board. While many L&D and people teams utilize Kanban to deliver a single project, it is also beneficial for teams responsible for BAU (business as usual) operational work or managing multiple projects simultaneously.

The origins of Kanban can be traced back to early visual ticketing systems used at Toyota in Japan to optimize JIT (just-in-time) manufacturing processes. These methods were then popularized by Taichi Ohno who evolved the Toyota production system and what became known as Lean manufacturing in the 1970s and 1980s. Then, in the early 2000s, David J. Anderson translated the Kanban principles into software development and in 2010 published *The Kanban Method*, which continues to steer most practices today (Kanban University, 2023).

Build your Agile toolkit

So, where do the frameworks of Scrum and Kanban fit in? Well, these frameworks help bring the Agile cycle to life. They also provide rigour and discipline to your approach. It's crucial, however, to select the right frameworks and techniques that suit your own needs, culture, values and, of course, problem to solve. Do this by selecting a specific framework or a selection of tools and deciding to run with it for an agreed period. As explored in Chapter 12, treat it like an experiment and assess outcomes based on a hypothesis to test and specific data points to track.

For illustration, Scrum is great when focused on one project, and the team can give one hundred per cent capacity. In these situations, applying the complete framework and committing to delivering product increments in sprints of two to three weeks is helpful. Then, use the first few sprints to practise getting each element working well.

Kanban is better suited, however, to situations where teams manage multiple projects at the same time or deliver BAU (business as usual) processes plus project work. For these reasons, many L&D and people teams use a Kanban board to visualize work, steer a continuous workflow and then add events and tools originating from Scrum.

For example, Agile HR coach Nicki Somal (2023) works with several teams within a people function that oversees L&D and people experience (PX) product design. These teams utilize a Kanban approach alongside a selection of Agile practices that stem from Scrum. The teams currently follow a monthly cycle and roadmap, supported by weekly planning sessions, two check-ins each week and a team retrospective at the end of the month. Somal provides the outside-in voice of experience in this example and mentors the Agile Champions who work within the teams. These Agile Champions are like Scrum Masters but use a different name because they're not following the Scrum framework. This approach allows Somal to operate and feed information to the enterprise level. In contrast, the Agile Champions feed information into the teams, ensuring consistency and a joined-up approach. As we will discuss in Chapter 9 the Scrum Master role is meant to be full-time. However, as with many L&D and people teams researched for this book, these Agile Champions work at 40 to 50 per cent capacity, with the remaining capacity given to project work.

As expressed by Kate Walker (2023), People Programme and Projects Lead at the well-known sustainable development consultancy Arup, 'you pick and choose, that's the beauty of it'. Walker doesn't believe in applying Agile as a rigid methodology or tick-box exercise and encourages teams to explore and experiment with different practices to discover what fits their context and supports effective team collaboration. The next chapter will help you decide which tools to use by describing each Agile practice in more detail.

Conclusion – five takeaways for L&D and people professionals

- Value drives the Agile cycle of *plan, do, review, adapt* and is defined by customer needs, problems to solve and feedback.

- The aim is to deliver value incrementally, slice by slice, starting with an MVP – minimum viable product – and then iterating a solution over time, validating as you go with data and customer feedback.
- For L&D and people teams, the customer is multilayered and represents the employee (our people), the business (bottom-line results), the end customer (people who buy or use the organization's products and services), and other stakeholders such as suppliers, contractors, future talent, the broader community and, increasingly, our planet.
- Viewing Agile and design thinking as interlinked practices is essential.
- Aim to build your toolkit of Agile practices, tools and techniques that best suit your context, needs, culture, values and, of course, problem to solve.

References

Design Council (2023) History of the Double Diamond, designcouncil.org.uk/our-resources/the-double-diamond/history-of-the-double-diamond/ (archived at https://perma.cc/GF4Z-5TS7)

Ford, Sarah (2023) Interview with Natal Dank, recorded 14 July

Hepton, Adam (2023) Interview with Natal Dank, recorded 21 July

James, David (2023) Interview with Natal Dank, recorded 2 August

Kanban University (2023) *The Official Guide to the Kanban Method*, kanban.university/kanban-guide/ (archived at https://perma.cc/2CVA-DY98)

McCaw, Greg (2023) Interview with Natal Dank, recorded 23 June

Morey, Geoff (2023) Interview with Natal Dank, recorded 23 June

Schwaber, Ken and Sutherland, Jeff (2023) *The 2020 Scrum Guide*, https://scrumguides.org/scrum-guide.html (archived at https://perma.cc/R6RD-H6G6)

Somal, Nicki (2023) Interview with Natal Dank, recorded 19 July

Sunderland, Jeff (2015) *Scrum: The art of doing twice the work in half the time*, Random House Business Books, London

Takeuchi, Hirotaka and Nonaka, Ikujiro (1986) The new new product development game, *Harvard Business Review*, January, hbr.org/1986/01/the-new-new-product-development-game (archived at https://perma.cc/4DJL-4Q7X)

Van der Tang, Arne-Christian (2023) Interview with Natal Dank, recorded 14 July

Walker, Kate (2023) Interview with Natal Dank, recorded 6 July

05

How to plan, do, review, adapt

No matter what tools and frameworks you use, the Agile cycle of *plan, do, review, adapt* guides your day-to-day work. It's also a great way to illustrate how to apply Agile practices to a project, team, function or whole organization. In this chapter, we'll use the cycle of *plan, do, review, adapt* to explain each practice. First, however, we need to understand the type of work we do.

Business as usual versus everything else

The type of work L&D and people teams undertake can be divided into two categories. The first is BAU – business as usual. These are the operations and tasks that power the daily employee experience for an organization. These include things like ensuring people are paid correctly and on time, onboarding a new joiner or issuing an employment contract when a person is hired. If these fundamentals don't happen, then people simply can't do their job. Also, even if many of these BAU operations are increasingly automated, most still require a few people to execute specific tasks in relation to each product and service.

The second category is everything else. Let's call it project work. Projects are temporary, unique and instigate some kind of change. If BAU runs the business, then project work evolves the business. It's essential to differentiate between the two categories. BAU is the specific operation or task necessary to deliver the product or service. Everything else is additional and not part of BAU. So, if you want to improve a process, streamline a workflow or change a template, it's a project – no matter how minor this change might be. One-off requests also fit into the project category. No matter how administrative or basic the request might seem, if it's outside the regular and repeated BAU process, it's additional and, therefore, project work.

You might be wondering why defining BAU versus project work is important. Well, if you want to prioritize, estimate and visualize workloads, it's critical to clarify the type of work it is, the effort required and who needs to do it. If it's BAU, you don't have a choice because it's a must-have and non-negotiable. However, if it's a project, you have choices. This distinction underpins how you plan and estimate work. For example, is there any capacity remaining for projects after completing BAU? If so, which project should you focus on first? Also, why is one project considered more important than another? And finally, what is the effort required to complete the project before moving on to the next project? You can only assess your capacity and prioritize workloads within L&D and people teams by answering these fundamental questions.

Let's consider how L&D and people teams get this mix of BAU and project work done. Essentially, there are three possible team types:

- Team One – undertakes project work only.
- Team Two – undertakes both BAU and project work.
- Team Three – undertakes BAU only.

In most cases, L&D and people teams fall into the Team Two category and undertake a mix of BAU and project work. Many argue that this can cause a lot of angst, confusion and inefficiency because it's challenging to get the right balance and often results in too much task-switching. Perhaps because of this, alongside the influence of agility within businesses, the Team One category is on the rise within the L&D and people profession. To achieve this hyperfocus on project work, these teams generally coordinate with an operations team who take on any resulting BAU processes or improvements within the function or broader business.

For these reasons, we'll now illustrate how Agile practices are applied at each stage of the *plan, do, review, adapt* cycle (Figure 5.1) using examples for Team One (project work only) and Team Two (BAU and project work).

Team One – made up of five T-shaped, multi-skilled professionals overseeing L&D and OD projects. In this chapter, we will track their main project focused on Career Development. The business challenge is to enhance career development and retain more people beyond 1.5 years.

Team Two – a people function of thirty team members. This function covers all L&D and OD projects plus HR business partnering, operations, reward and recruitment.

FIGURE 5.1 Agile cycle of plan, do, review, adapt

Plan

The *plan* stage is made up of the following practices:

- Define value
- Set vision
- Plan roadmap and release schedule
- Agree team roles
- Build backlog and portfolio
- Identify epics, user stories and acceptance criteria
- Prioritize backlog
- Estimate work.

Let's explore each further.

Define value

In Agile, all plans start with defining value – the why. Value forms the basis of your vision and guides your plan. By estimating the value, you can forecast a roadmap, expected milestones and probable deliveries. Value also guides your prioritization, how to build a backlog and your work commitments within a cycle.

DEFINE VALUE EXAMPLE

- **Team One** – embark on their career development project and business challenge of enhancing career development and retain more people beyond 1.5 years. Using the business challenge canvas (provided in Chapter 7) they identify a selection of value drivers for the project. For example, by increasing the number of internal hires, they will reduce recruitment costs and positively impact business value. An important metric to track will be the percentage of internal hires.

- **Team Two** – meet for their quarterly strategy session. Following the steps set out in Chapter 11 they identify business priorities, undertake an employee experience health check by assessing relevant data on their dashboard and consider existing gaps in culture and capability. From this they decide to use three company OKRs (objectives key results) as their value drivers for the subsequent quarter.

Set vision

A strong vision provides direction and helps people understand the bigger picture of what they are working on and why. The vision is a vital tool that helps to stop people getting lost in the day-to-day details. The aspirational vision aims to capture the promise of value to your customer groups – business bottom line, employees, end customers and key stakeholders. Use actionable words and write in the present tense when writing your vision. Be specific, don't generalize and don't get overly technical. Once you've drafted a vision statement, test it to assess if it's easily understood and sufficiently engaging with essential stakeholders or people experiencing the problem you want to solve. Also, don't be afraid to update your vision as the work progresses.

SET VISION EXAMPLE

- **Team One** – set the following vision for the career development project: *Help people achieve fulfilling careers, so they grow with us, do their best work and want to stay with us.*

- **Team Two** – agree an aspirational team vision: *Make our organization a life-defining place where people make an impact and can be the best version of themselves.*

Plan roadmap

It's important to be mindful of the longer-term, bigger-picture plan versus an immediate plan for a specific cycle. Cassie Soady (2023) is former Head of Culture and People Transformation at WooliesX and Chief People Officer for Digital Data, Analytics, Technology and Enterprise Operations at National Australia Bank. When interviewed for this book, she commented that she asked an Agile coach if it was still ok to plan long term when she was first introduced to Agile. Incorrectly assuming Agile is only about short-term planning is a common misconception.

A roadmap is a plan of action that illustrates the steps to reach your vision and aligns the team around a common goal. Roadmaps are high level, sometimes conceptual, and are particularly useful for managing stakeholder expectations and partnering with other business teams on when and how to release specific deliveries. For example, you're unlikely to release an MVP that aims to test a management development solution during the busiest quarter for a sales team or in a section of the business experiencing a restructure. Hence, a roadmap is never static and needs to respond to broader business needs, organizational changes and market fluctuations.

Often, employees complain of being overwhelmed by updates and initiatives communicated across the business simultaneously, often via multiple channels such as email, Teams, Slack and intranets. This problem of over-communication and mixed messages can reflect different teams within a function – L&D, reward, talent, DEI and so on – individually communicating about their siloed remits. It can become even more of a mess if we add messages from other support functions like compliance, legal and finance. A roadmap goes a long way to help remedy the problem and encourages all support functions to collaborate and, ideally, communicate as one.

PLAN ROADMAP EXAMPLE

- **Team One** – following some discovery work and a two-week design thinking sprint, the team highlight several problems to solve. Based on their value drivers they decide that the problem of making career opportunities more visible in the organization is the most important to focus on and have prototyped a marketplace website as the possible solution. The team then agree a roadmap by estimating the number of two-weekly cycles it will take to develop specific product features and release product increments or versions to various parts of the organization (see Figure 5.2).

FIGURE 5.2 Roadmap example

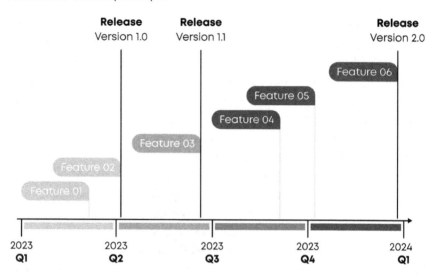

- **Team Two** – following their strategy session the team assesses BAU commitments that must be delivered over the coming quarter. They also estimate the capacity required across the team to deliver BAU and then assess what capacity remains. Based on the remaining capacity the team agrees how to approach the projects prioritized in their strategy and what is realistic to deliver that quarter. Next, the team maps out which days each week will be dedicated to project work and who in the team is working on what. They've decided to focus on three key projects and have formed a T-shaped team of four to five people for each project who dedicate 60 per cent capacity each week to work together. Teams decide which days of the week are dedicated project days and which days they focus on BAU and other commitments to limit task-switching. For now, they decide to document phases of each project based on the people experience (PX) product development lifecycle outlined in Chapter 7. For example, one week for the business challenge phase of a new project, followed by three weeks for the research and discovery phase. The function follows a cadence of one-month cycles (see Figure 5.3).

A FEW WORDS ON RELEASE PLANNING

Roadmaps tend to be high level and used for managing stakeholder expectations. So, it's often helpful also to detail a release plan estimating how long it will take to develop each project phase and when you expect to release

FIGURE 5.3 Portfolio roadmap

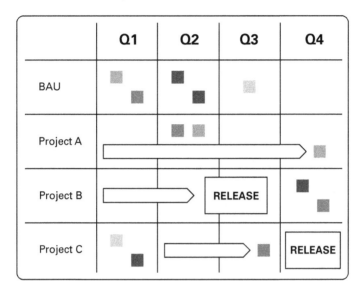

specific product features to your customer. Generally, this release plan is for the team only and you use it to guide decisions and update the high-level roadmap. For example, the release plan will estimate the length of time or number of cycles (and possibly even the backlog items you'll aim to complete) to develop an initial MVP or run an experiment in a section of the business. The aim is to divide the project up into deliverable product increments or big chunks of work. You'll also need to consider dependencies with other teams or product requirements, like whether customers need to complete a compliance task as part of the experience. Do a high-level release plan first without too much detail or specific features and then add in more detail as the project progresses.

Agree team roles

Use the T-shape framework outlined in Chapter 9 when forming new teams. Target the different skills needed to deliver the entire project or all the operational work. From there you'll want to select people to undertake specific roles within the team. Many teams rotate these roles over time or across different projects to help people gain new experiences and add to their T-shape. However, be conscious of ensuring consistency over a specific period or each project to allow the team to connect, build psychological safety and develop a healthy rhythm of work that helps to increase their velocity. See Chapter 9 for details of the essential roles for Agile L&D and people teams. For now, let's assume each team selects a PO (product owner if using the Scrum framework) or product manager (if not using Scrum) and Scrum Master (if using Scrum) or Agile Champion (if not using Scrum).

AGREE TEAM ROLES EXAMPLE

- **Team One** – Already have a permanent PO or product manager overseeing the team's ongoing backlog and each product vison. This role works across multiple projects and connects with other people teams to align release plans. They take a lead in managing stakeholders and sponsor expectations. Also, for the career development project they've invited a person from another team to be the Scrum Master / Agile Champion, who will facilitate important events such as the team retrospective.

- **Team Two** – have a person operating as an Agile delivery lead (see Chapter 9 for more detail) who coordinates roadmaps, expected delivery plans and backlogs across the whole function. This person connects with a PO or product manager for each of the three projects. The function also has a person who acts as a coach and works across all the teams. This person will be the Scrum Master / Agile Champion for every project team as well as facilitate events such as a team retrospective for the people working together on operational BAU work.

Build backlog

A backlog (see Figure 5.4) is one of the main tools Agile teams use to guide their work throughout the *plan, do, review, adapt* cycle. A backlog contains all the work that a team thinks it might need to do. It's a type of wish list that is regularly sense-checked and refined over time until it becomes a ruthlessly prioritized list of the most valuable things to do next. A backlog reflects the best knowledge and information the team has at the time. In this sense, it's a living thing, forever evolving based on the empirical data of experimentation, observation and feedback.

It's important to differentiate a backlog from a traditional Waterfall list of tasks or a Gantt chart. A backlog is not a detailed plan cascading down through handovers, but a list of items prioritized in the order of value that the whole team delivers together. Teams start working on the highest priority items first. These higher-priority backlog items are more detailed

FIGURE 5.4 Visualization board

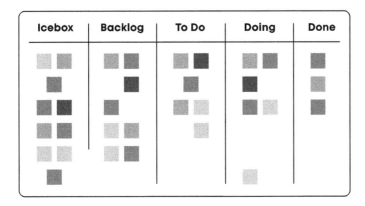

with specific tasks listed. Backlog items lower down the list are usually bigger and often vague because they don't need to be worked on yet. Once their priority increases, these bigger and more vague backlog items get refined and possibly broken down into smaller items to make them more manageable. Generally, higher-prioritized items in the backlog are planned in detail to task level. Tasks outline specific actions required to deliver the backlog item and who is responsible for what.

Backlogs are often visualized on a board, generally known as a Scrum or Kanban board. Items move from the Backlog column to the columns To Do (once planned in more detail and considered the next immediate thing to do), Doing (ongoing work) and Done (finished and checked against the DoD (definition of done) (see more on DoD in the *Do* section later on). Some teams also use an Icebox column to collect ongoing ideas and new requests. An Icebox column is regularly reviewed and, providing the team agrees, certain Icebox items are moved into the prioritized Backlog. It's worth mentioning, however, that many Icebox items remain a nice-to-do sometime in the future, which in reality often means never!

BUILD BACKLOG EXAMPLE

- **Team One** – get together for their first planning session and build a backlog for the career development project. First, they undertake silent brainstorming and each person records what they think needs to be in the backlog. The team then reviews what has been recorded and starts to sort and group all the possible backlog items. Next, they remove duplicates and merge some of the smaller backlog items that are more like tasks. After several hours they have a list of backlog items that they can now prioritize.

FIGURE 5.5 Portfolio

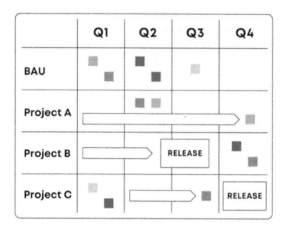

- **Team Two** – use a portfolio to visualize the three main projects alongside BAU deliveries across the entire function. Each project team then operates their own more detailed backlog, and the operations group uses a Kanban board to visualize BAU tasks and commitments (see Figure 5.5).

Epics, user stories and acceptance criteria

It's important to mention a few words on epics, user stories and acceptance criteria. These are terms that can sound like a foreign language to those new to Agile.

Epics – big chunks of work or topic areas within a project that can be broken down into smaller backlog items (or user stories). Epics help organize your backlog by supporting the creation of a hierarchy or categorization of information. Generally, an epic is delivered over a series of cycles, whereas a backlog item is completed within a cycle and generally within a matter of days. For example, Team One might include an epic entitled *1000 product experiment* under which sits a series of backlog items all aimed at designing and developing a good enough MVP to run an experiment with 1000 people for three months.

User stories – an alternative method of preparing backlog items. User stories represent a chunk of work written from the point of view of the customer who benefits from the end goal. User stories ensure your backlog reflects the voice of the customer and are an excellent method of helping people move beyond just discussing product requirements to consider the problem to solve and value to deliver. Each user story should be sized, independent, negotiable, valuable and testable. Generally, if you think it will take longer than a few days to get a user story done, then it is most likely an epic or needs to be broken down further.

User stories are written in the following format:

AS A *customer, stakeholder or persona*

I WANT *what or goal*

SO THAT *why or outcome.*

For example, Team One might write:

AS AN *employee who has been with the organization for a year*

I WANT *to find a new career opportunity*

SO THAT *I gain a sense of career progression and growth within the organization.*

Acceptance criteria – are often added to backlog items (or user stories) to indicate specific conditions or customer needs that must be met for the item to be considered done. Acceptance criteria refers to *what* is being delivered. The *how* is decided by the team as they self-organize and get work done. For example, acceptance criteria for the above user story could be that users can search for career opportunities based on recommended internal roles.

Prioritize backlog

Always remember to prioritize your backlog based on your value drivers first. Only after this should you estimate and size the backlog items. This ensures you don't prioritize backlog items based on the easiest thing to get done first.

In Chapter 11 we'll explore how to use the value versus effort matrix to prioritize strategy in order to decide on which projects to deliver.

A few other handy prioritization techniques include:

- **MoSCoW** – sort your backlog items into four categories:
  1 Must Haves: absolute minimum to get the product functioning.
  2 Should Haves: make the product usable or likeable but not mandatory. To decide, balance the value of delivery against the effort required to build them.

FIGURE 5.6 Value versus effort grid

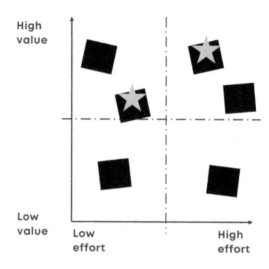

3 Could Haves: help delight your customers, though generally, impossible to deliver them all. Again, balance the value of delivery against the effort required to build them.

4 Won't Haves: these things simply don't add value at this stage or are considered unnecessary.

- RICE – a scoring system based on the following criteria:

  o Reach – how many people or events.

  o Impact – assessed against your value drivers and rated high, medium or low.

  o Confidence – your level of confidence that the impact will be realised rated high, medium or low.

  o Effort – estimated time, people required and complexity using a number or rated high, medium or low.

- Force ranking or sorting – compare each new item to other items in the backlog. It's generally advisable to invite people to prioritize items silently first, and then explore differences between team members.

- Dot vote – give everyone the same number of dot votes and invite them to distribute the dots on the backlog items based on potential value. Then step back, assess which items have the most dots and discuss.

Estimate work

Once the backlog is prioritized, how do you know the number of backlog items to commit to in each cycle of work? You do this by sizing and estimating your backlog items. The aim is to size backlog items relative to each other based on effort. In this context, effort is defined as the complexity involved to complete the backlog item, time and the number of people it takes to deliver the work, including any dependencies.

A common sizing method is T-shirt sizes – small, medium and large – or applying a number system often called story points. Once you've sized your backlog items, estimate how many can be completed in the next cycle of work. If you are following Scrum and using time-boxed sprints, this might be based on how many backlog items can be completed by the agreed date so you can deliver a releasable product increment or slice of value.

At the start of the project your estimates will be very approximate. It'll take a few cycles to improve your accuracy and ability to correctly estimate a realistic amount of work each cycle. It's also common to set a goal for each cycle in line with the work you've agreed to complete or product feature you're aiming to deliver.

ESTIMATE EXAMPLE

- **Team One** – use T-shirt sizes to size their backlog items and then estimate that they can complete seven backlog items in the next two-week cycle.
- **Team Two** – each month key people from the function meet to agree the delivery commitments across the whole function. This reflects their portfolio and roadmap and sizing discussion across the different project teams and operational tasks.

Do

The *do* stage is made up of the following practices:

- Pull-based work system
- Visualization of work
- Transparency
- Self-organization

- Check-ins
- Definition of done.

Let's explore each further.

Pull-based work system

The *do* stage is all about getting work done. The pull-based work system underpins the method, combined with the principles of self-organization and transparency. Various Agile thought leaders have wisely observed that teams need to '*stop starting and start finishing*'. To this end, the team commits to a certain amount of work each cycle or limits the work in progress according to their estimated capacity. They pull in new items only once they have finished previous and higher-priority backlog items. By focusing on a few items at a time, the aim is to be as efficient as possible and avoid multitasking. No one is pushing work onto the team. Instead, the team self-manages and pulls in the amount of work they feel comfortable with based on capacity and skills. To ensure everyone has clarity on the direction of travel, the team refers to the high-level vision and roadmap as they work.

Visualization of work

As mentioned in the *Plan* section earlier, teams use visualization boards to plan their work and track progress against the columns Backlog, To Do, Doing and Done. Most teams use digital tools, such as Teams Planner, Trello, Basecamp, Monday and Product Board, to track progress dynamically and support remote working. However, a few teams still use a physical board on a wall in the office with sticky notes as backlog items, particularly during the initial planning stage. In the *Build the Backlog* section, we saw that Team One used a Kanban board and Team Two a portfolio plus a Kanban board for each project and the operational group.

Transparency

Working this transparently can be a significant shift for L&D and people teams. In the past, a lot of HR work has been assumed secret or classified. Indeed, when working in an L&D role years ago, I sat in an HR function behind controlled access security doors. Needless to say, no one other than senior managers ever felt compelled to request access to come in and talk to us. While you must be mindful of protecting the details of a workplace grievance or employee complaint, most work can be openly shared within the team and with the broader business. Try using a code name for these specific backlog items if something is particularly sensitive. Working transparently helps people professionals be accepted as another part of the business rather than perceived as secret, compliance-driven fun police.

For example, a small people function uses a high-level portfolio board to update their executive team on progress and deliveries. Another HR director invites different people team members to present project updates and OKR deliveries to the executive because everyone in the team shares the same knowledge. In this example, it's been noted by the executive members how refreshing it is to hear from different representatives of the people team, not just the HR director.

Self-organization

An Agile team agrees on how to deliver their work. No manager is required to direct this work. Through collaboration, the team solves problems, explores alternatives and makes decisions. They test and validate directly with real people and adapt the plan based on collected feedback. The team also aims to continuously improve how they work collectively by assessing what they should do differently or better in the next cycle of work. In this way, the Agile cycle guides ongoing feedback and performance discussions. If successful, most Agile teams don't necessarily require additional layers of performance management systems to help them develop and achieve targets. It's already happening.

Of course, the organizational reality can be a little different…

Check-ins

With its origins in the Scrum framework, the check-in or daily scrum is generally a quick daily practice and micro-level planning session time-boxed to 15 minutes. It's quite common to call this ritual a stand-up; but because not everyone is physically able to stand up in a meeting, check-in is a more inclusive term.

In a check-in, the team visualizes the progress of work by tracking tasks, discussing and sequencing dependencies and raising issues that block progress, also known as impediments. Generally, the check-in is based on three core questions:

- What have you achieved in the last 24 hours or since the previous check-in?
- What will you focus on in the next 24 hours or agreed period?
- What blockers (impediments) are affecting your ability to progress your work?

While I'm a big advocate for quick daily check-ins no matter the team type, many L&D and people teams working across multiple projects and BAU deliveries at the same time find slightly longer, less frequent check-ins, every few days or weekly, a better fit.

CHECK-IN EXAMPLE

- **Team One** – undertake daily check-ins of 15 minutes as part of their two-week cycles.
- **Team Two** – run a weekly check-in that the entire function can dial in as part of their monthly cycle. In the check-in the team refer to the portfolio and share updates alongside any blockers, challenges and new urgent priorities that can't wait for the next monthly planning session. All of the project teams within the function also have bi-weekly check-ins for their specific project.

CHECK YOUR CHECK-INS

In a recent coaching session, a team complained that their weekly check-ins had become laborious operational update meetings where everyone felt compelled to provide detailed step-by-step updates. In these meetings people also added new work to the board despite the team agreeing commitments monthly. The team's manager felt they had slipped back into a traditional operational meeting. Instead they only needed a quick overview about what was on track, what was blocked and how they could keep things moving forward. If you see any of your check-ins veering off towards this painful operational update, have the courage to call it out in the next team retrospective and agree a new format and behaviour expectations.

Definition of done (DoD)

The DoD (definition of done) is a list of overarching requirements, delivery expectations and non-negotiables guiding the entire project. These are guiding principles that ensure quality, efficiency and good design, and shouldn't be confused with impact metrics for the project.

Essentially, the DoD determines if backlog items can be moved into the Done column on your visualization board. The DoD generally reflects factors like the project vision, constraints, specific workplace tools to use, company guidelines and compliance or regulatory needs. The DoD evolves as the project progresses and is often agreed following team retrospectives. For example, following a few cycles of work the team might decide to add something to the DoD, such as the need to use a specific template or save files on a certain tech platform.

DOD EXAMPLE

- **Team One** – have a DoD that states all materials must be designed according to company brand guidelines.
- **Team Two** – have a function-wide DoD that states all products must reflect the organizational values and be tested before released.

Review

The *review* stage is made up of the following practices:

- Review what – the product
- Review how – the team retrospective.

Let's explore each further.

Review what – the product

The *review* stage is divided into two parts. The first focuses on the product or *what* the team achieved through the most recent work cycle. The aim is to inspect the slice of value delivered and gather the necessary data to understand what to do next. The product review is a vital component of the Agile feedback loop and often reveals unexpected findings that help evolve and adapt the backlog, roadmap or vision.

Product reviews also demo specific product increments or project outcomes to key customer groups, such as senior executives or intended users. The earlier we get feedback and validation from real users, the better. As a result, teams often discover new insights or have assumptions proved wrong during a product review.

REVIEW WHAT EXAMPLE

- **Team One** – run a product review every two-weeks and assess the outcome of work completed during the cycle. Generally, the review involves the team presenting and reviewing the completed backlog items with the PO or product manager. When a significant product feature has been delivered the team invites people from the business to give feedback. For example, when the team were ready to go live with their *1000 product experiment,* they invited key stakeholders to the review.

- **Team Two** – host a monthly review looking at different products or deliveries worked on, but not necessarily finished, during the monthly cycle. The aim is to review unfinished work as much as possible. People nominate different teams to showcase work and cover anything from the three projects or BAU operations. The session is hosted online and anyone from the function can dial in and offer feedback.

Some L&D and people teams find it helpful to run reviews quarterly with different parts of the organization to showcase deliveries and achievements. Instead of running a review for every project, they combine these into a more extensive review and gather feedback to inform their overall portfolio of work. This is an excellent method to regularly check in with the broader organization, understand that you're working on the right things and reprioritize your roadmap and backlog if needed.

Review how – the team retrospective

The second element of the *review* stage is the team retrospective. This explores *how* you worked as a team by assessing behaviours and working methods. Often known as the retro, this vital ritual invites the team to share stories and explore different perspectives on how each person experienced the last work cycle. The discussion explores team dynamics and behaviours to improve communication and collaboration. It's also an opportunity to assess the team's application of different tools and techniques to visualize and prioritize work, measure the team's velocity (rate of work completed), assess productivity and discuss any significant impediments that are slowing the team down.

Of course, this is a lot to cover, and teams generally focus on specific themes that may have caused tension or slowed work down during the cycle. It's also impossible to solve everything at once, and the best approach is to prioritize one improvement action based on the retro for the following work cycle, otherwise you risk taking on too much. Creating the capacity and space in the next cycle to apply the improvement action is just as important as agreeing on what it is.

To help build psychological safety, and stop the discussion from becoming a blame game, the retro code is: *What happens in Vegas, stays in Vegas.* The neutral, objective role of an Agile coach or Scrum Master is critical here. Even if you don't have such a role in the team full-time, it's incredibly beneficial to invite someone from outside the team to facilitate the retrospective. Many teams ask someone from another team within the same function or perhaps an Agile coach or Scrum Master from another part of the business to conduct the retro. Over time, we want teams to become comfortable talking about mistakes, failure and personal learning, which are fundamental building blocks of psychological safety.

REVIEW HOW EXAMPLE

- **Team One** – run a team retrospective every two-weeks for 30 minutes, facilitated by the Scrum Master or Agile Champion. In each retrospective they agree on one improvement to take into the next cycle of work. For example, the team updated their DoD to include that a backlog item should only move into the Done column providing at least two people have reviewed the acceptance criteria to ensure it's *definitely* done.

- **Team Two** – across the function each project team runs a monthly retrospective as well as the operational group. Then once a quarter the function hosts a combined retrospective in line with their quarterly strategy and planning session. These sessions also lead to new DoD items, such as an agreement that nothing is released into the business without first being showcased at a monthly review, so everyone is across it and not caught out if asked a question by an employee.

A few extra words on the review stage

The *review* stage is critical in the Agile cycle because it drives forward the notion of continuous improvement. All too often, it slips when teams feel time-pressured. Feeling vulnerable and open to criticism or negative feedback can also lead to teams shying away from the *review* stage. Receiving and discussing feedback can be confronting, and people can only strengthen their feedback muscles through regular practice.

Adapt

The *adapt* stage is made up of the following practice:

• Backlog refinement.

Let's explore this further.

Backlog refinement

Adapt is the final stage of the Agile cycle. Armed with feedback and other data from the product review plus one improvement from the team retrospective, it's time to return to the backlog and consider what needs to change. Known as backlog refinement, it's vital to apply rigour and discipline to this step. It's common for people to confuse Agile ways of working with not having a plan or changing the plan at will. Instead, the opposite is true, and any change must be supported by evidence and team agreement. Striving for excellence is also why the cycle is relatively short. The goal is to work just long enough to deliver a slice of value and collect data that validates you're on the right track, but not so long that it becomes increasingly costly to pivot direction if the evidence proves otherwise.

A few different actions might be taken at the *adapt* stage. It may be deemed that the whole initiative is going in the wrong direction, and a complete change is required. More commonly, it leads to movements in the backlog as different items are prioritized up or down, removed or added. Subsequently, the roadmap and, at times, the vision requires an update.

Additionally, the adapt stage is an opportunity to discuss whether to end or kill the project or product. It may be that, despite several experiments, the evidence demonstrates that it's just not worth pursuing. Alternatively, you may deem that a sufficient amount of value has been delivered, and your time is now better spent on the next big problem to solve. Knowing when and how to end work is a challenging but critical capability that guides successful prioritization and capacity planning.

Many teams combine the backlog refinement discussion with the next planning round for the following cycle. If you do this, be conscious of clearly separating the *adapt* stage from your *plan* stage so the two don't become blurred and people get confused about what has changed and what hasn't in the next cycle.

ADAPT EXAMPLE

- **Team One** – refine their backlog every two weeks following their product review and team retrospective. This then leads into a planning session for the next two-week cycle.

- **Team Two** – host a monthly *adapt and plan* meeting, where the Agile delivery lead coordinates with the PO or product managers, the Scrum Master or Agile Champion and other key points of contact for the portfolio such as HR business partners. In this session critical priorities and delivery goals are agreed for the monthly cycle ahead.

Conclusion – five takeaways for L&D and people professionals

- No matter which tools and frameworks you decided to use, the Agile cycle of *plan, do, review, adapt* guides your work both at the team level and across the people function.

- To plan and estimate commitments it's critical to divide your work into two categories: 1. Business as usual (BAU); 2. Everything else, which we call project work.

- Only prioritize and estimate project work commitments once you've assessed the remaining capacity after delivering the BAU work each cycle.

- For teams managing both BAU and project work a monthly cycle, involving a monthly adapt and plan session, weekly check-ins and monthly reviews and retrospectives, is a good fit, especially when combined with quarterly strategy and roadmap sessions.

- A team retrospective is essential for building psychological safety and harnessing a culture of continuous improvement.

Reference

Cassie Soady (2023) Interview with Natal Dank, recorded 30 June

06

The Agile L&D playbook – an introduction

It's a wonderful thrill when someone approaches me at a conference clutching my first book, *Agile HR: Delivering value in a changing world of work* and asks for a signature. The book is usually full of sticky notes, personal notes and dog-eared pages. While these moments are very special for me, they also reinforce the value of a practical toolkit and the need for handy templates, tips and step-by-step guides to help you through your Agile adventure.

A genuine advantage is also gained by distilling topics into a few key essential elements. This approach aids learning and crucially accelerates your application of skills. That's why this playbook is based on five core design principles. These principles reflect years of experience working with L&D and people teams and helping transform working methods to deliver the value that matters most. These principles also reflect an update on ideas, concepts and, of course, the business and organizational context since writing the first book. Additionally, even though the five design principles are applicable across the whole people profession, the playbook was lovingly compiled with my L&D and OD peers in mind.

The five principles were also inspired by experiences collaborating with two important and pioneering leaders, both of whom are on the list of great people interviewed for this book. The first is Tracey Waters, who started applying Agile to L&D and then the broader remit of people experience at Sky UK at a similar time to when I started to host Agile HR meetups in London. Tracey and her team were regular attendees, and their work provided excellent case studies for other participants to learn from. One aspect of their work that I greatly admired was a collection of design principles the team formulated based on experimenting with different working methods. These principles acted as a definition of done, guiding their project methods and shaping the solutions created. The principles also seemed to successfully capture what applying the Agile mindset to L&D and OD meant. For example, one principle was the need to digitize solutions where possible to eliminate or decrease any future administrative burden for the team or someone else within the business. Inspired by Tracey and her team, I began to help other teams formulate their own design principles and much of this work is now reflected in the five principles outlined in this book.

The second source of inspiration was working with Arne-Christian van der Tang and the TomTom people team over the past years. While much of this journey is documented in the excellent case study in Chapter 9, one of the main activities that remained with me was again formulating a series of design principles to guide the team's Agile transformation. In this example, the design principles not only steered the new ways of working but, perhaps more significantly, they acted as a statement to the team that the transformation was based on positive intent and human-centred values. Interestingly, the TomTom design principles also reflected what was happening in the broader business at the time and the need to reimagine the organizational strategy in response to an increasingly complex marketplace. As a result, I felt it essential to continue that same performance orientation and business-led approach when crafting the five design principles for this Agile L&D playbook.

So, what are the five design principles?

Principle 1 is product-led

Product-led invites you to view the employee experience as your product – made up of different component parts such as recruitment, onboarding, career growth, team performance, feedback, internal mobility, exit and alumni. Being product-led represents a fundamental shift in perspective within the L&D and people profession that will help transform your work. It also implies the need for a few new working methods. The first constitutes a new delivery model centred around the ability to identify, prioritize and solve business challenges in a multidisciplinary way. Crucially, this represents a move away from a traditional operating model within L&D and people teams based on specialisms and functional silos towards multiskilled professionals working as strategic collectives. To be product-led also demands more effective methods in the way L&D and people teams define, articulate and measure the value their product delivers across the organization. Finally, the principle of working product-led encourages L&D and people professionals to become product managers in how they approach their work. To help with this, Chapter 7 walks you through the product development lifecycle and demonstrates how to apply different tools when solving L&D and OD challenges.

Principle 2 is human-centric design

In Chapter 8, you'll explore how to shape the employee experience like a customer journey full of moments that matter for your people and brand. As mentioned in earlier chapters, design thinking and Agile tools are intricately linked. To help you get comfortable with this topic, Chapter 8 starts with the philosophy of human-centric design, and then outlines a selection of excellent design thinking tools to help you empathize with the employee experience and research business problems in an evidence-based way.

Principle 3 is T-shaped people in T-shaped teams

As mentioned in the first principle, product-led, it's time for L&D and people teams to embrace a new collective, strategic, multidisciplinary delivery model. This new team structure is crucial if we are to solve the complex problems faced within organizations, and it forms the basis for how you deliver the employee experience as a holistic product. But don't let this new operating model scare you. It's a natural progression from where the profession is today. The T-shape framework celebrates all the great experience, skills and knowledge you've gathered over the years. Moreover, the teams I work with rave about the T-shape model because it helps people proactively develop their careers in a modern, contemporary way. I hope you find the T-shape framework just as useful.

Principle 4 is experimentation

Co-creation was a term I started to use when first introduced to Agile ten years ago. The reason is that it captured the very essence of what it meant to build the employee experience through the lens of our people, our customers, and in collaboration and direct partnership with the broader business. I've now come to appreciate that co-creation only happens if you are willing to experiment and test. L&D and OD topics are full of opinion, speculation and assumption. If L&D and people professionals are to be credible business partners, they need data to back up any recommendations and decisions impacting the organization. By embracing an experimental approach and learning how to prototype and test, you'll become the corporate scientist who backs decisions with data. This includes learning how to write a hypothesis to test – for example, what is the impact on team performance if people undertake a specific learning programme? The goal is to rapidly and safely test our ideas to gain early feedback and validation rather than sinking valuable time into programmes and processes that ultimately don't work.

Principle 5 is to deliver with impact

You can't do it all, right? One of the main challenges L&D and people teams set out to solve when embracing Agile is to develop an effective method to prioritize and get their gigantic wish list of things to do under control. Intriguingly, the answer lies in applying rigour and discipline in how you define and measure the value your employee experience product delivers across the organization. To help you achieve this outcome, Chapter 11 looks at how to identify the right business problems to solve and how value guides your L&D and people strategy. Next, you'll drill down into measurement and explore different ways to track ongoing results. Deliver with impact is also the final design principle for a reason, because to do it well, you need to combine all the elements explored in this book. Delivering with impact means becoming data-obsessed in the pursuit of ongoing and continuous marginal gains.

So, let's get into it!

07

Principle 1: Product-led

One of my first L&D roles was as a training consultant at a small London-based company that specialized in business skills and management development for financial markets professionals. As a relatively inexperienced facilitator, I suddenly found myself tasked with educating primarily older businesspeople. To survive, I quickly learnt the art of effective facilitation alongside a repertoire of examples to illustrate the various learning frameworks that made up each workshop. All the usual generic content was covered, such as situational leadership, the change curve and even Maslow's hierarchy of needs. Conscious of meeting the brief, I mastered delivering all the pre-agreed topics and activities within the time allocated. At the end, people would record their action plan by answering, 'What's the one thing that you'll do differently as a result of your learning today?' The success of the event, not to mention my training capability, then rested solely on participants filling in a paper-based survey, known in the industry as the happy sheet. It was considered job done if I emailed the client a proud collection of high scores. Usually, I never saw any of these learners again. I now cringe just thinking about this time in my career, but it's an excellent reminder of why the people profession needs the Agile L&D playbook. Too often, activity, output and scores on a happy sheet get confused with value. To understand and measure value, you must first know the problem to solve. Until then, you only have output and a lack of hard evidence that the activity has made an impact.

From output to outcomes

Interestingly, I'm not alone in regretting past career moments now that I've embraced an Agile approach. When asking the L&D and people leaders interviewed for this book what Agile meant to them, many described it as a refreshing and much-needed change to what they did before. David James (2023), Chief Learning Officer at 360 Learning and former Director of Talent, Learning and Organizational Development at Disney, calls Agile 'the antidote'. Agile is a timely remedy to an unhealthy tradition within L&D and people functions of focusing on content and activity rather than business value. James describes this shift as a move away from an outdated 'learning mindset', where learning itself is the goal, towards a performance orientation that aims to directly affect how work is done. A good example is his frustration when reading LinkedIn posts about curiosity being the most critical factor in learning. For James, curiosity might be a helpful indicator of an individual's learning motivation, but it will not fundamentally shift business results. Instead, to deliver business value, you need to unearth problems in the flow of work and target the skills, knowledge and behaviours that help solve these challenges.

For Danny Seals (2023), founder of Knot, an employee experience design and innovation consultancy and Vice President, Employee Innovation, Listening and Effectiveness at RAKBANK, the path to agility began with a realization that L&D was a 'broken system'. Through a desire to push traditional boundaries, Seals discovered the benefits of human-centred design and began to appreciate that solving business problems was very different from delivering a typical L&D solution. Once you let go of the assumption that learning is the answer, it just becomes another business challenge to solve. The outcome might still be related to learning, but it could also be as simple as providing new workplace tools that help get the job done. Without a relentless focus on the end user and what they need to be great at their job, there is a danger of just creating output rather than outcomes.

Goeff Morey (2023), Head of Colleague L&D at the large UK-based charity Macmillan Cancer Support, also talks about agility shifting his perspective. With Agile L&D, teams start to base their work around the objective and the problem to solve instead of the objective being moulded around the team and their functional remit. Too often, you end up with an eLearning solution if you task the eLearning specialist with the business need. For Morey, the ultimate aim for an L&D team is to improve the organization's performance, albeit primarily by developing people, skills and teams. Once he embraced Agile, Morey recognized the team had previously been too focused on learning itself rather than creating targeted outcomes based on the problems to solve. 'We just said, here's a problem, here's the L&D fix and let's crack on.' Morey viewed this as waste, even if the L&D solution got rave reviews, because it lacked evidence of impact. Considering Macmillan is a not-for-profit organization, he was particularly keen to eliminate that waste. Now, by placing the user at the heart of their design and continuously validating that the solution fixes the problem as they iterate, the team naturally explores a wider range of possible outcomes, some of which may not even be typical L&D solutions. As Morey points out, the solution shouldn't be based on whether you're an eLearning specialist or a great workshop facilitator. Instead, it's about what will make the biggest difference for the customer in the end.

This recognition of wasted effort and time, not to mention wasted licences over the years for unused learning tech solutions, were also reasons for Tracey Waters (2023) to switch to an Agile approach when working with Sky UK as Director of People Experience. Instead of solving the problem now, her team would take months to design a solution that was often too late to have the necessary impact. Waters recognized a need to move beyond this siloed L&D thinking and embrace a data-driven, iterative approach.

Delivering value by solving shared problems and challenges sits at the heart of Agile L&D. This represents a distinct move away from a tradition of L&D and people strategy presented as a type of wish list detailing a multitude of deliveries over the next twelve months. Many readers will recognize this strategy wish list and how the goals are often just titles, such as talent retention, leadership development or high engagement. To demonstrate that these strategic goals are being met, another list is compiled, this time detailing all the activities and new initiatives delivered each quarter. This traditional focus on output means L&D and people teams will always be on the back foot when measuring and articulating the value delivered to a business. People strategy is about knowing the problems to solve, not just the projects or processes to deliver. For example, why might a topic like talent retention constitute a strategic goal? Do you need to retain key people within a business-critical team, or perhaps the organization requires new data science or genAI skills to stay competitive in a changing market? By describing the problem, you can better research and experiment with possible solutions. More importantly, you can begin to track whether the problem is being solved and, thus, measure the value delivered.

What is product-led?

In a podcast exploring what L&D can learn from product management, Owen Ferguson, Chief Product Owner at Mind Tools for Business, defines a product as something that creates value for a group of people with a shared challenge or problem, which in turn creates value for the organization (Ferguson, 2021). If it's a commercial product, then it's about selling something and the value is realized through outcomes such as revenue, loyalty or generating sales for a related product. Conversely, suppose it's an internal organizational product, such as an L&D solution. In that case, the value is realized through outcomes like productivity, reducing costs or retaining talent. Using this definition, it follows that to be product-led is to focus one hundred per cent on the value you deliver to your customer. In this sense, it becomes more than just building products people love. Instead, it's an overarching organizational strategy and structure where every component part is integrated and organized around delivering delightful product experiences. To do this, organizations require deep knowledge and ongoing communication with the customer to anticipate and respond to their continuously evolving needs. The product is no longer just one part of the customer experience; it becomes the experience (Chernov, 2019).

The concept of a product-led business reflects the massive growth of online digital products and businesses over the last decade. As a result, the associated role of product management is now standard across most companies despite being a relatively new field compared with other functions like marketing and sales. Melissa Perri (2018) is the founder of the Product Institute and author of *Escaping the Build Trap*. The '*build trap*' is when businesses become too focused on delivering product requirements rather than understanding what problems to solve for customers. Perri describes the product-led approach as a direct response to this phenomenon. With direct similarities to the L&D and people teams described earlier in this chapter, many businesses also struggle with measuring value and end up tracking activity by default. For Perri, a product-led organization thrives on being laser-focused on solving customer problems, is experimental by nature and oriented around outcomes, not output.

Onboarding illustrates a shared customer problem that L&D and people teams often need to solve. Anyone who starts a new job requires a certain amount of knowledge about their team, the company values, business strategy and how their contribution fits. They also need a range of specific tools to get started, like ID badges, laptops and logins. By conceptualizing onboarding as a holistic product experience and a shared challenge to solve, it's easier to grasp that it requires multiple component parts to delight the customer (the new starter). So, while doing the company's compliance eLearning or reading the handbook might be an important regulatory need, it doesn't necessarily solve the broader onboarding problem for the customer. They will still need other component parts like work buddies, job shadowing and team lunches to feel welcomed and productive from day one. Moreover, if the onboarding problem remains unresolved, new starters don't just talk about the missing laptop or mandatory eLearning. Instead, people generally describe the overriding experience as an emotional state, such as feeling lonely, unloved or bored. For these reasons, it's increasingly common to see onboarding designed as an end-to-end journey, starting from the moment of offer and incorporating a range of component parts and touchpoints to accelerate a sense of belonging and connection for the new starter.

The people experience product

To be product-led is a shift in how the L&D and people function builds, executes and measures business value. By working product-led, you switch into a value-driven Agile mindset. Through this lens, the employee or people experience becomes our product and is conceptualized as a holistic journey comprising many different components, such as attraction, recruitment, hiring, onboarding, workplace facilities, career development, team performance, career progression, pulse feedback surveys, exit and alumni. Each element combines to make up the total sum of a person's experience at work.

It's a perspective that Sarah Ford (2023), Head of HR Innovation at the global drinks manufacturer and industry giant Diageo, expressed when sharing her story for this book on why she embraced Agile. Ford's take is that people don't just buy products and services; they buy experiences. Ultimately, they're buying something to make their life better in some way. Ford expressed how Agile HR and L&D share this goal. 'It's putting people first in the same way, so it delivers better outcomes' (Ford, 2023).

Ford's resulting HR innovation model reflects this product-led vision of creating value through product experiences that solve shared employee problems. To illustrate, the team target prioritized business challenges directly sourced from employees through a technique called 'product playgrounds'. These timeboxed design sprints draw on a combination of tools such as employee listening, group ideation, prototyping and user testing to quickly generate and refine new L&D and people products.

For example, a recent product playground allowed the team to experiment with genAI (specifically ChatGPT) to enhance employee letters, one of which was a parental leave letter written in a celebratory tone that proved a hit with employees. Product playgrounds have also been used to improve the employee experience of international transfers, and a current project is focused on redesigning secondments to be more skills-based and flexible. The innovation team is also targeting specific demographics like Gen Z or 50+ by inviting these groups to user test product ideas and people strategy. The team have found their work with Gen Z employees instrumental in helping them future-proof product designs, considering this group is expected to grow within the company from the current 6 per cent to 30 per cent by 2030.

As Ford concludes, up until now, innovation has been misunderstood within many L&D and People teams as something for technology to use when building a new tech tool or for marketing when designing a new brand. But there is no reason why it can't work in HR. If brave enough, it becomes a catalyst to help the function think differently and zero in on meaningful work (Ford, 2023).

In her book, *Built for People: Transform your employee experience using product management principles*, Jessica Zwaan (2023), Chief Operating Officer at Whereby, applies a product-led approach to envision the employee experience as a type of product subscription. To illustrate, Zwaan describes activities like joining a company, contributing to its culture and growing a career based on their values as representing some of life's most significant purchasing decisions. 'It is a subscription to an experience, an opportunity and a path in life.' As a result, Zwaan advocates for the people function to operate as product managers overseeing the employee experience product.

Intriguingly, this concept also links to the term 'product-led growth', attributed to Blake Bartlett from the venture capital company OpenView (Poyar, 2022). Product-led growth describes an organizational model where the product itself drives sales and thus grows the business. By building a product that solves shared problems, customers want to use it. They are then encouraged to upgrade or buy more through features like a 'freemium' product, self-guided tours and automated upselling and onboarding. Using this interpretation, a product-led people experience is about fuelling business growth through people's capability, collaboration, ideas and performance. Many companies even try to get the product itself to drive future growth and talent acquisition through features like a great EVP (employee value proposition), culture and candidate referrals.

By viewing people experience as your product, you can better define, measure and deliver value as an L&D or people function. First, the people experience product becomes a differentiator in the market and represents how an organization attracts, retains and grows its people. Second, the people experience product represents people's capabilities and how an organization sources, grows or deploys skills to achieve strategic outcomes. Finally, the people experience product constitutes a sense of purpose and engagement. The aim is to create an environment where people want to give their best work, which can be measured through employee feedback and other metrics. As highlighted by Arne-Christian van der Tang (2023), Chief HR Officer at TomTom, as a leader, you need to be ready to adopt a product mindset yourself. 'What does that mean for me as a leader in HR, if employees and candidates and anyone we interact with, if we perceive them as customers?' What product should we build for them, and how do we make it delightful so they keep coming back? You need to determine what your customers love and incentivize them to do their best work.

Delivering the people experience product

Applying a product-led approach implies that L&D and people teams must work as an integrated collective that can anticipate, track and respond to the continuously evolving needs of customers. The system also requires time and skill to understand the users of the people experience product, unearth their pain points and engage in rapid experimentation to solve their problems. When operating product-led, keeping the product running becomes as essential as improving or innovating new features. You can't just launch new things. Equally important is the ability to track, maintain, improve, innovate, replace or even kill off different products and services based on data and evolving customer needs. This calls for a product management approach that oversees all the various products and services that make up the people experience. In Chapter 5, we called this the portfolio, and it can be managed at a team or functional level depending on your organizational size and setup. In Chapter 9, you'll explore an example in the TomTom T-shape team case study.

The need to build a new product-led organizational model within L&D and the people function is also gaining traction among leading HR commentators. Labelled 'systemic HR' by Josh Bersin, influential HR thought leader, the aim is to coordinate the people function like an integrated operating system. 'We need to rethink HR as a "system," not a set of "services" or "offerings," and we need to interconnect them together in a solution-oriented, real-time way' (Bersin, 2023). Crucially, Bersin advocates a complete re-engineering of HR's culture and structure. It's not enough to just use Agile tools like design thinking and Kanban if the profession wants to be fully integrated and work strategically. Like earlier examples in this chapter, Bersin (2022) describes this shift as a need to focus on employee experience, not just output. 'The idea, put simply, is that we can't just design jobs and work practices; we have to look at employees' total experience at work' (Bersin, 2022).

For years, Myles Runham (2023), Senior Analyst at the Fosway practice and digital learning expert, has been championing (or howling as he puts it) for L&D to embrace a product-led approach. Inspired by the fantastic disruption and innovation achieved in digital technology businesses over the last decade, Runham (2021) encourages all L&D professionals to learn from product management. To do this, L&D and people teams require a solid understanding of technology, the broader business and the ability to monitor ongoing user behaviour and feedback. By applying the same product management practices used by other business teams, like tracking conversion rates, frequency of use, number of uploads and viewing times, you can experiment and design at pace rather than wait for significant ROI (return on investment), a proof point that only happens at the end of the project.

Perry Timms (2023), founder of PTHR and leading author on HR transformation, also argues for product management to play a central role within his HR.3 model for the profession. For Timms, a product-led approach is essential to use digital technology to catalyse better workplace outcomes. 'We need our people to work with HR teams to get the products right. And create the Ikea effect of loving something you've built that has purpose and value.'

One word of warning at this point, however. Many HR functions have taken this need for product management as a reason to create a separate and individual employee experience team. While this has some positives, there is a danger that employee experience becomes yet another competing remit and functional silo, especially in cases where the employee experience team manages specific component parts like feedback surveys or wellbeing. These topics then sit separately with other groups working on related L&D or talent development issues. As explained in Chapter 9, working in T-shaped multidisciplinary teams is crucial, no matter the topic. Ultimately, to work product-led equates to a complete mindset shift within the people function that moves beyond traditional job titles and COE (centre of excellence) domains to operate as a multidisciplinary, problem-solving collective.

Also, if you're wondering, this collective approach still applies to a people professional working in an individual L&D role or small OD team. No matter what your team structure, the message remains that you can't solve complex business challenges alone or in a functional silo. Managing your work using a portfolio is vital whether you work in an individual role or a small team. You can also collaborate and link up with other people across the business to build a holistic people experience product approach.

So, how do you work product-led and deliver business value?

First, it's about embracing the other design principles outlined in this book – human-centred design, working as a T-shaped person in a T-shaped team, experimenting and delivering with impact. Then, to guide specific projects and product design, you can use the people experience (PX) product development lifecycle, which we'll explore next.

People experience product development lifecycle

The PX product development lifecycle, see Figure 7.1, is a framework that helps you build valuable people products and reflects years of helping L&D and people teams apply Agile tools and techniques. If you delve into product management within other business teams, you'll likely find similar tools. However, the PX product development lifecycle has been translated into your specific people experience context.

One thing to note is that during this section, we'll refer to the project as the work that results in a product being delivered. So, the project is the work (which links back to our definition of BAU versus project work in Chapter 5), and the product is the outcome. Also, don't assume the lifecycle is linear, and you can only use certain tools at specific times. As you progress through the lifecycle, always overlay the work with the ongoing Agile cycle of *plan, do, review, adapt.* You also need to be mindful of keeping product experiences alive. So, even if you've transitioned into the final product maintenance phase, you might need to immediately step back into the research and discovery phase to evolve the product in response to new data.

Possibly the most significant difference between the PX product development lifecycle and other more standard project management tools is the clear separation between phase two, research and discovery, and phase three, agreeing scope and backlog. One of the most common mistakes across all the people teams I've worked with is a tendency to formulate the whole project scope and backlog before they confidently know the problem to solve. Often, this results in highly detailed PIDs (project initiation documents) and committing to rigid timelines too early and when you know the least about the business challenge. Separating the research and discovery phase from other phases helps to manage this issue.

FIGURE 7.1 People experience (PX) product development lifecycle

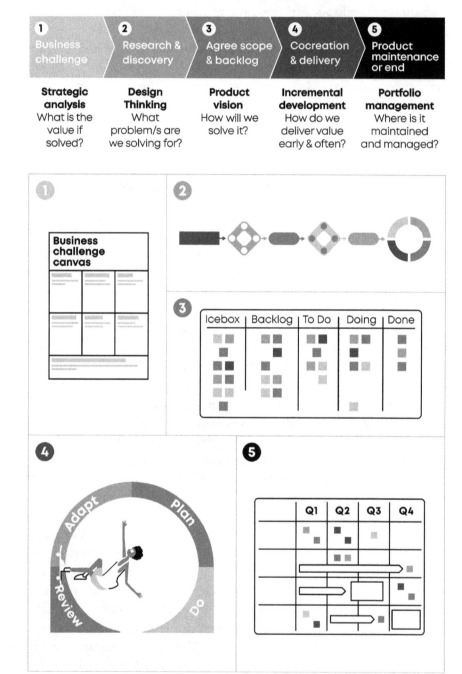

① Business challenge	② Research & discovery	③ Agree scope & backlog	④ Cocreation & delivery	⑤ Product maintenance or end
Strategic analysis What is the value if solved?	**Design Thinking** What problem/s are we solving for?	**Product vision** How will we solve it?	**Incremental development** How do we deliver value early & often?	**Portfolio management** Where is it maintained and managed?

However, this separation implies a need to gain sponsor sign-off or critical stakeholder buy-in at the initial business challenge phase and again when agreeing on scope and backlog. Why? Because they represent two very different decision points. The first is prioritization, deciding which business challenges to focus on compared with other problems to solve within an organization. The second is agreeing or gaining commitment around the product vision and high-level project roadmap. At this stage, you'll also need to estimate some critical elements such as budget, expected timelines, dependencies and the timing of product releases. However, in highlighting these two major touchpoints, it shouldn't be assumed that you never check in again with your sponsor or important stakeholders – quite the contrary. A healthy Agile project embraces the ongoing cycle of *plan, do, review, adapt* and uses the product review as a vital checkpoint throughout the co-creation and delivery phase.

Another point is that the term sign-off might seem overly bureaucratic for Agile, but it's essential to be realistic. Most L&D and people professionals need to agree on a few basics with an executive team, HR director or perhaps even a people portfolio manager (see Chapter 9 for more information on this role) before starting a project. These are crucial decisions, and an outside-in perspective is essential. You need sufficient data and evidence about what, why, how and when to move forward at each point. So, even if you can call most of the shots yourself or work within a self-managed team, clarifying these two major decision points with stakeholders and business representatives is a healthy practice to follow.

Let's now work through each phase in the PX product development life-cycle.

Phase 1: Business challenge

PURPOSE

Strategic analysis to understand why the business challenge is worth pursuing and investigating in the first place. For most teams this step involves building a business case and short pitch to gain stakeholder approval or sponsorship. You should also assess the value versus effort in undertaking this business challenge compared with others. You need to be confident that this is the right challenge on which to focus time, money and resources.

The key to building a great business case is to determine the value drivers for the project, see Table 7.1. The value drivers will guide future

TABLE 7.1 Example value drivers

Employees seek	Impact on business bottom line
• Meaningful work and sense of achievement • Impact on end customer, product or service • Connection with the purpose of the organization • Career development • Wellbeing and mental health • Household financial stability • Personal growth • Performance support and valuable feedback • Reduced complexity (e.g. in workload or systems) • Safety, both physical and psychological • Personal choice • Flexibility in how and where they work • Sense of inclusion and belonging	• Market advantage • Revenue • Healthy employee turnover • Sales growth • Productivity • Efficiency gains • Reduced costs • Economic growth within sector/industry • Controlled expenses • Return on funding investment • Managed compliance risk • Brand sentiment (positive reputation) • Self-service and straight-through processing • Increased workforce capacity for customer products and services • Reduced spend on 'fixes'
End customers seek	**Purpose and social value**
• Service quality and speed • Consistency • Market or brand growth • Connection with organizational purpose • Brand credibility • Product innovation • Resilient and reliable network or service • System or process simplicity • Low or fair cost • Personalization	• Environmental and conservation – ESG • Net-zero targets • Social contribution • Diversity, equity and inclusion • Community involvement at local levels • Charities and not-for-profit initiatives • Good workplace governance

prioritization and articulate and measure impact as the project progresses. At a minimum, aim to define value drivers in these three areas:

• **Business value:** Strategic value, such as creating new opportunities or a competitive advantage, impacting on the business bottom line, and reducing costs.

- **End customer:** The customer who buys the products and services that the overarching business produces or the customer the organization supports, such as the community in the case of a not-for-profit organization.
- **Employee:** Our people, which is generally measured through feedback, retention and brand advocacy metrics.

Also, see Chapter 11 for more information on tracking value.

WHAT QUESTION DO YOU NEED TO ANSWER?
What is the value if the business challenge is solved?

STEPS
Gather data for your business challenge.

1 Initial investigation of existing metrics, market research, plus business and people data. Remember, we're not proposing the solution yet but exploring the overarching business problem or issue.

2 Identify value drivers and possible metrics (see Table 7.1).

3 Describe your customers. Keep this high level for now; you'll do more in-depth customer research in the next phase.

4 List your project constraints, such as any regulation or compliance needs and other factors like budget, time and team capacity.

CONSTRAINTS

Don't let constraints dictate or limit your approach. Instead, focus your work on solving the customer problem, eliminating pain points and creating a great user experience. Just because you need to meet specific compliance needs or work within a set budget doesn't necessarily mean you need to limit the design. Many teams find that recognizing the upfront constraints encourages them to think beyond the norm and be even more innovative.

TOOLS

The **business challenge canvas** (Tables 7.2 and 7.3) is a great tool to use at the start of any project. Many L&D and OD professionals also use it to guide conversations with business stakeholders when scoping out problems to solve. It's generally an excellent approach to complete the canvas in

TABLE 7.2 Business challenge canvas

Describe the current business problem and impact on the organization (for example, cost, risk or lost opportunity).		
Business value Value to business bottom line if problem solved.	**End customer value** Value to end customer if the problem is solved.	**Employee value** Value to employees if the problem is solved.
Metrics How will we know we've succeeded?	**Metrics** How will we know we've succeeded?	**Metrics** How will we know we've succeeded?
Who are our customers (specific employee segments and/or stakeholders impacted by the business challenge)?		**What constraints** do we need to consider (for example, risks, restrictions, non-negotiables or compliance needs)?

TABLE 7.3 Example of a career development business challenge

Describe the current business problem and impact on the organization (for example, cost, risk or lost opportunity).

Challenge: *Enhance career development and retain more people beyond 1.5 years.*

Problem:

- *After two years in a position, it is more straightforward for employees to find a job at another company than to navigate a fulfilling career in the current role.*
- *Nearly 80% of new hires are external, with 55% leaving within the first two years.*
- *Unhappiness in the current role and lack of career progression were two top reasons for leaving.*
- *Internal hires are hired 70% faster, perform better and are more likely to stay – but bi-annual survey feedback suggests it's hard to find and negotiate new job opportunities.*

Impact: *Lower levels of expertise and experience within the organization. Recruitment and onboarding costs to replace leavers.*

Business value	End customer value	Employee value
• *Cost savings – higher % of internal hires impacting bottom line results* • *Sustained productivity – higher % of internal hires means people are up to speed in new roles faster* • *Higher performance – skills growth over time with improved retention means better performance*	• *Reliability – consistent quality and service delivery* • *Improved customer relations, especially for high-value clients requiring senior expertise* • *Knowledge and experience through lateral moves and promotions brings fresh thinking to our products and services*	• *People can easily find and apply for new career opportunities* • *User-friendly internal candidate experience* • *Sense of career fulfilment and growth within organization* • *Recognition for skills and expertise*

(continued)

TABLE 7.3 (Continued)

Metrics	Metrics	Metrics
• *Reduced recruitment and onboarding costs by %* • *Tracked productivity rates* • *% internal hires* • *% job moves*	• *Increase in NPS by %* • *High-value client loyalty maintained* • *Higher innovation rates by %*	• *Increased retention rate beyond 1.5 years by %* • *New hire engagement (6 and 12 months)* • *Exit interview data*
Who are our customers (specific employee segments and stakeholders impacted by the business challenge)?	**What constraints** must we consider (for example, risks, restrictions, non-negotiables or compliance needs)?	
• *The main target group is employees up to line manager level that fall within the tenure of 1.5–3 years, which is when most people leave.* • *People within business units where career development is cited as a significant reason for leaving the company.* • *Need to also test for gender, ethnicity, disability or sexual identity differences within the target group.*	• *Need to build a solution using an existing budget.* • *If utilizing any government funding for skills development, must meet specific compliance requirements.* • *Consider existing Learning Management System (LMS) within any solution.*	

collaboration with key stakeholders or ask them to validate what you've written once prepared. For example, in a recent executive leadership onboarding project, the product lead used the canvas to guide their initial exploratory discussions around the intended project with relevant HR directors, HR business partners and other support function heads (like compliance and legal). From these discussions, the Head of Compliance nominated themselves as the overriding project sponsor to champion the product across the company.

Phase 2: Research and discovery

PURPOSE
At the research and discovery phase, use design thinking (Figure 7.2) to unearth the user problems and rapidly prototype and test possible solutions. In all the case studies covered in this book, a distinct discovery phase was undertaken before the project moved into a longer co-creation and delivery phase. While some might fear that this phase slows things down, it can be

FIGURE 7.2 Design thinking sequence

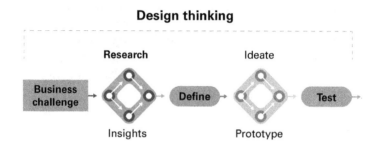

completed relatively quickly and knowing the correct problems to solve saves time. Moreover, providing you have an effective method of monitoring data, the phase can be as simple as assessing the latest user behaviour metrics and running an experiment to test a hypothesis.

Many teams time-box this phase into a one-to-four-week design or discovery sprint. The reason for time-boxing is twofold. The first is that it's easy to over-analyse and get lost in research. The second is that you're still validating whether this business challenge is worth the effort being invested. Hence, you want to move quickly into experimentation in case current assumptions are wrong.

We'll cover the research and discovery phase in more detail in Chapters 8 and 11. For now, let's understand the core elements.

WHAT QUESTION DO YOU NEED TO ANSWER?
What problem/s are we solving at the research and discovery phase?

STEPS
See Figure 7.2.

1 Research (divergence)

   a. Deep dive into the user experience and explore business needs.

2 Insights (convergence)

   a. Discover patterns, gather findings and prioritize moments that matter for the customer.

   b. Compile user research and record business insights.

3 Define

   a. Identify the most critical problem to solve first.

   b. Write problem statement/s based on user research and general findings.

4 Ideate (divergence)

   a. Brainstorm, challenge assumptions and conceptualize solutions.

   b. Assess ideas using a value-versus-effort grid.

   c. Choose solutions to prototype.

5 Prototype (convergence)

   a. Develop prioritized solutions and set a hypothesis to test.

   b. Build prototype/s.

   c. List data and other evidence to collect during the test.

6 Test

   a. Invite real users to test prototype/s.

   b. Gather feedback and data on what worked and what didn't.

   c. Assess the validity of the hypothesis and recommend next steps.

TOOLS

See Chapter 8 on human-centred design for tools covering the steps from research to ideate.

See Chapters 10 and 11 on experimentation for tools covering the steps prototype and test.

Phase 3: Agree scope and backlog

PURPOSE

Now you're ready to build your product vision and undertake an initial estimate of the project scope and expected roadmap. Once you've done some product strategy and visioning exercises, have your first go at building a project backlog. It's okay if it's messy and vague at this stage. The main objective is to identify how best to start delivering value. As mentioned before, you'll need to touch base with and gain sign-off from any sponsors or critical stakeholders. Budgets will also need to be agreed upon. Ideally, aim to secure an iterative budget, where additional funds can be released based on specific proof points and value realized as the project progresses.

WHAT QUESTION DO YOU NEED TO ANSWER?

How will we solve it? As detailed in our scope and backlog.

See Figure 7.3. to agree scope and backlog.

1 Set a product vision and strategy.

2 Build a backlog.

3 Prioritize the backlog.

4 Discuss scope, planning and budget with sponsor or key stakeholders.

5 Agree on the initial roadmap and release plan.

6 Set a definition of done for the project (see Chapter 5 for more information).

7 Identify the future owner – once the product is realized, where will it go and who will maintain it (for example, does it stay within the same team or move to an operational team)?

8 Consider scalability needs – most solutions can't be a one-off and must be repeatable. Also, based on the target customer group and business requirements, will you need to scale the solution to cover the whole organization?

9 Identify dependencies with other business teams.

10 Complete any necessary vendor, IT support or procurement processes (or have these flagged for future actions during the next phase).

TOOLS
See Figure 7.3, Project scope one-pager.

Phase 4: Co-creation and delivery

PURPOSE

Now, the project shifts gears, and you move into incremental development. Some teams even execute this stage with a different group of people. For example, in most case studies in this book, a smaller group undertook phases one to three. Then, they expanded the project team to include a broader mix of skills for the co-creation and delivery phase.

From this point, it's essential to be disciplined in applying the Agile cycle. Decide on your cadence and agree when each Agile team ritual – planning, product review and retrospective – will happen in each cycle. Then, stick to it. It's advisable to practise the same cadence, for example two-week cycles and fortnightly team retrospectives, for at least three cycles before making

FIGURE 7.3 Project scope one-pager

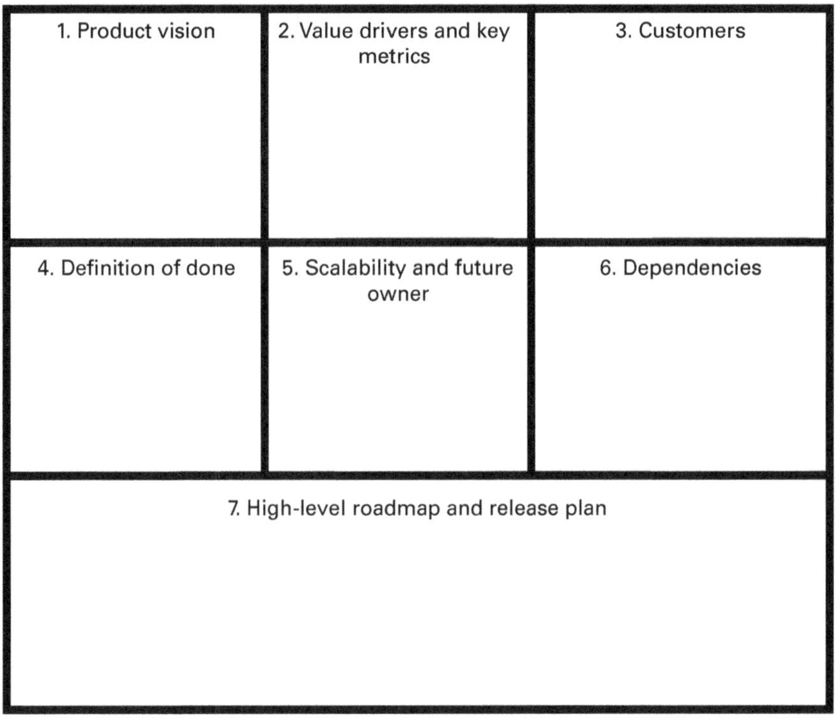

1. Product vision	2. Value drivers and key metrics	3. Customers
4. Definition of done	5. Scalability and future owner	6. Dependencies
7. High-level roadmap and release plan		

significant adjustments. Remember, it's okay for this phase to constitute an experiment still. For illustration, the executive leadership development case study, which is covered in Chapter 11, moved into this phase when running the main experiment, following initial prototyping using pen and paper. Generally, you'll transition into this phase once an experiment becomes more sophisticated or you need to test product features rather than just a proof of concept.

It's also critical to mention a few words on team capacity at this stage. Many teams try to do too much and commit to multiple projects plus BAU work simultaneously. This makes it incredibly hard to deliver value because the constant task-switching harms productivity. This dilemma also links back to why it is essential to consider a new organizational model for your team or function similar to the TomTom case study in Chapter 9. The aim is to focus on one problem to solve at a time. If a restructuring isn't possible at this stage, another option is to carve out blocks of time in the diary where people come together for a focused sprint. During these project sprints, people usually work on the project between 10am and 3pm, so there is time in the day to catch up on emails and other activities. Another option is to commit to specific whole days in the week when the project team comes together to get work done. However, don't just do various rituals like a team retrospective on these days but commit to actual project work, even if this work is individual. All other work commitments remain untouched on these days. This approach also effectively manages the expectations of others, who learn not to ask for anything else on the designated project days.

WHAT QUESTION DO YOU NEED TO ANSWER?
How do we co-create and deliver value early and often?

STEPS
To create and deliver.

1 Agree on specific team roles, like product owner/manager or Agile delivery lead (see Chapter 9 on T-shaped teams for more information).

2 Revisit the backlog and adapt it for any changes agreed in the earlier phase.

3 Decide on your cadence, for example two-week cycles, and when each team ritual will occur, such as fortnightly planning, reviews and retrospectives.

4 Sync diaries.

5 Agree the cadence with the user test group involved in experiments or product reviews.

6 Agree on key stakeholders who should attend future product reviews.

7 Agree on future owner involvement and any intended handover process.

8 Identify specific skills needed and determine whether you need to invite people to join particular cycles of work to contribute capabilities from outside the team.

9 Size and estimate backlog items.

10 Plan and start the first cycle of work.

11 Set up a primary method to track team velocity.

12 Start tracking any relevant metrics or user behaviour data.

13 Complete any necessary vendor, IT support or procurement processes as you move into the MVP stage or you scale up the product.

14 Release your first valuable increment and then go again!

FIGURE 7.4 Backlog

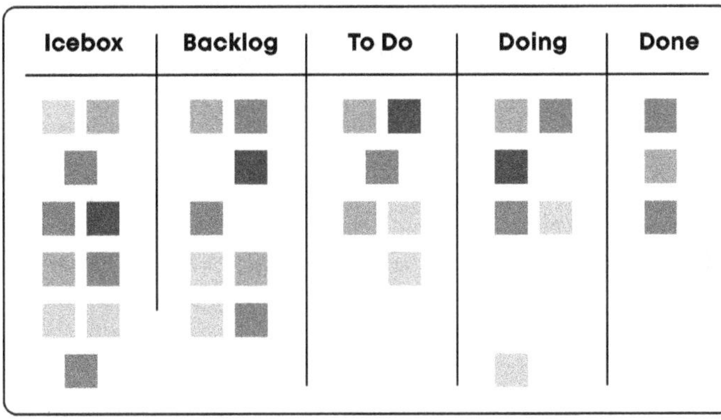

Icebox	Backlog	To Do	Doing	Done

TOOLS

To co-create and deliver use a backlog as shown in Figure 7.4.

Phase 5: Product maintenance or end

PURPOSE

The final phase concerns portfolio management and understanding how the product will be maintained alongside other component parts of the people experience. Depending on the size and type of product, this might happen within a few weeks following the co-creation and delivery phase or months later. Some teams will need to partner with an operations team or someone who manages BAU tasks, like an L&D coordinator. For others, future product maintenance may remain with you because your role covers design and ongoing product management. Ideally, this handover would have been discussed and planned during phase three when agreeing on scope and backlog. It's also critical to design products in such a way that reduces future administration and that are digitally automated as much as possible. Don't create more work for yourself or others further down the line.

There may also be situations where the product now ends. For example, if it was linked to a specific event, or the problem has been resolved, and ongoing product maintenance is not required. If so, wrap it up, celebrate success and move on to the next business challenge.

WHAT QUESTION DO YOU NEED TO ANSWER?

Where is the product maintained and managed?

FIGURE 7.5 People portfolio

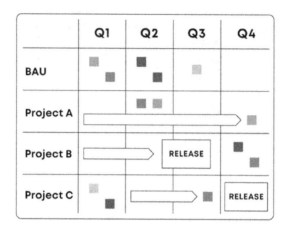

STEPS

1 Agree on handover, BAU transition or ongoing owner of the product.

2 Move the product into ongoing maintenance and wrap up the project.

3 Celebrate success.

4 End the product if no longer required or value realized.

5 Update the people portfolio to reflect new owner and product status.

6 Move on to the next prioritized business challenges to solve.

TOOLS

To visualize or to end a product, use a people portfolio as shown in Figure 7.5.

Conclusion – five takeaways for L&D and people professionals

- View the employee (or people) experience as your product, which is conceptualized as a holistic journey comprising many different components, such as attraction, recruitment, hiring, onboarding, workplace facilities, career development, team performance, career progression, pulse feedback surveys, exit and alumni.

- By viewing people experience as your product, you can better define, measure and deliver value as an L&D or people team.

- Products deliver value by solving a shared problem for the customer – you need to clearly identify and prioritize the problems that your people experience product will solve.

- The people experience (PX) product development lifecycle is a framework that helps you build valuable people products and reflects years of helping L&D and people teams apply Agile tools and techniques.

- By working product-led, you switch to a value-driven mindset.

References

Bersin, Josh (2022) *Irresistible: The seven secrets of the world's most enduring, employee-focussed organizations*, Ideapress Publishing, Washington, DC

Bersin, Josh (2023) Redesigning HR: An operating system, not an operating model, https://joshbersin.com/2023/03/redesigning-hr-an-operating-system-not-an-operating-model/ (archived at https://perma.cc/R7XV-MN8A), published 1 March, updated 10 March

Chernov, Joe (2019) Becoming Product Led: What it means and how to get there, LinkedIn, 20 May, www.linkedin.com/pulse/what-means-product-led-organiza-tion-joe-chernov/ (archived at https://perma.cc/SR2Z-8GT3)

Ferguson, Owen (2021) *The Mind Tools L&D Podcast*, hosted by Ross Dickie and Ross Garner, Documentary Special: What can L&D learn from product management?, 22 June, https://podcast.mindtoolsbusiness.com/250-documentary-special-what-can-ld-learn-from-product-management (archived at https://perma.cc/Y8KL-C2BQ)

Ford, Sarah (2023) Interview with Natal Dank, recorded 14 July

James, David (2023) Interview with Natal Dank, recorded 2 August

Morey, Geoff (2023) Interview with Natal Dank, recorded 23 June

Perri, Melissa (2018) Escaping the Build Trap, Productized, YouTube, 11 December, https://youtu.be/DmJXpI7OJuY (archived at https://perma.cc/S5MZ-UHSL), filmed as part of the Productized conference

Poyar, Kyle (2022) Inventing Product-Led Growth: How PLG went from an idea to the biggest trend in software, OpenView Venture Partners, 2 May, https://openviewpartners.com/blog/inventing-product-led-growth/ (archived at https://perma.cc/A9W9-2U8Q)

Runham, Myles (2021) *The Mind Tools L&D Podcast*, hosted by Ross Dickie and Ross Garner, Documentary Special: What can L&D learn from product management?, 22 June, https://podcast.mindtoolsbusiness.com/250-documentary-special-what-can-ld-learn-from-product-management (archived at https://perma.cc/SZ75-EUK2)

Runham, Myles (2023) Still howling about product management for L&D, 21 February, https://mylesrunham.com/2023/02/21/still-howling-about-product-management-for-ld/ (archived at https://perma.cc/9KUS-5DP2)

Seals, Danny (2023) Interview with Natal Dank, recorded 26 June

Timms, Perry (2023) Why we need a new model for HR: part 3, people as product, *HR Magazine*, 16 June, www.hrmagazine.co.uk/content/comment/why-we-need-a-new-model-for-hr-part-3 (archived at https://perma.cc/88B2-GHPC)

Van der Tang, Arne-Christian (2023) Interview with Natal Dank, recorded 14 July

Waters, Tracey (2023) Interview with Natal Dank, recorded 26 July

Zwaan, Jessica (2023) *Built for People: Transform your employee experience using product management principles,* Kogan Page Limited, London and New York

08

Principle 2: Human-centred design

'If only we chose an easier business challenge to solve' is a common phrase when working with a new L&D or people team. 'But what would you solve instead?' I often reply. If this is the most critical issue for the business right now, it can't be delayed. Why don't we make a start by applying some trusted human-centric design methods and see where we end up?

The shift that transpires from this point is fascinating. Once the team embraces a human-centric design process, they start to relax. Now it's all about solving problems for others and the business rather than themselves. The pressure to have the perfect solution immediately at hand starts to fade. The team empathizes and understands the shared human experience by flipping the perspective. Through this research, they gather insight and meaning that helps them move forward and make decisions. It still might feel difficult and unclear, but a sense of comfort builds as people begin to trust the process, a kind of certainty that the tools and data will continue to propel you forward.

Despite the workplace existing because of people and their interactions, it's easy to start from competing angles – revenue, cost, power, regulation – when solving business problems. A human-centric approach doesn't deny that these other factors greatly influence the context in which we operate, and each element must be considered when solving organizational challenges. However, I've come to appreciate that the philosophy of human-centred design and the related design thinking tools offer L&D and people professionals a way of navigating this uncertain and complex environment. It's a method that helps you build desirable solutions from a human point of view and, crucially, products that are feasible and viable for your business and organizational context.

When first faced with the enormity of a business challenge, many teams express frustration and confusion. Most feel overwhelmed with the task ahead and start to over-analyse. In all these situations, by applying some of the tools outlined in this chapter, nearly every team I've worked with starts to see a path forward.

Let's now explore what human-centred design looks like in practice and why the philosophy of solving shared human problems in the workplace is a common thread throughout the five design principles in the Agile L&D playbook.

What is human-centred design?

Human-centred design implies that no matter the problem, all solutions start and end with a deep empathy for people and their unmet needs. Viewed in this light, human-centred design becomes an overarching philosophy guiding Agile L&D. Human-centred design flips the perspective. By seeking to understand alternative viewpoints, you're better able to create purpose-built solutions that delight and add value to the employee experience. Rather than designing solutions based on your own experiences and assumptions, you immerse yourself in your customer's shared problems, needs and desires. It is a powerful approach to problem-solving used within businesses to resolve workplace challenges or design commercial products, as well as in government and not-for-profit organizations to address significant societal challenges like poverty or social justice.

Many L&D and people leaders interviewed for this book saw human-centred design philosophy as the common thread connecting the five design principles in the Agile L&D playbook. 'You're there to enable people to succeed. So, you've got to start with people,' states Tracey Waters (2023), who pioneered Agile HR as the People Experience Director at Sky UK and now leads Leadership and Talent at a large Australian bank. For Waters, the very essence of Agile L&D and OD is 'about recognizing that the whole purpose for designing products and services is to remove pain points and to make life and work easier, more fulfilling, and achieve objectives and goals quicker'.

For Jodie Pritchard (2023), former Head of Learning at the large UK charity Citizens Advice and now Director of L&D at the children's charity Barnardo's, Agile helps L&D and people professionals operate through a human-centric lens. You remain the expert, but rather than starting from a 'tell' position based on your experience and opinion, you shift into a place of seeking to understand other people's needs, aspirations and challenges. 'I'm still an expert, but to design impactful solutions, I need to be flexible, adaptable and really understand the people I'm delivering to.' This shift in perspective was so inspiring for Pritchard that the first time she was introduced to Agile was a 'light bulb moment' and at the time, she thought 'Why on earth have I never worked like this before in all my years as an L&D professional?'.

Additionally, for Sara Sheard (2023), Executive Director of Business Operations at the UK housing trust Incommunities and former Deputy People Director at the large charity Mencap, discovering human-centred design led to a big *aha* moment. Sheard realized that until that point, many HR and L&D solutions had been based on assumed best practice. Outcomes were driven by the needs of the people team rather than the needs of the business. While the user had always been involved, it was usually via a survey and only considered one part of a longer, separate design process. Conversely, human-centred design interweaves the user throughout the whole project.

In her current role overseeing tech support and organizational change alongside the people and culture function, Sheard highlights the risk of teams losing touch with this core human-centred design philosophy when applying Agile working methods. In her experience, there is a potential for teams to become too focused on the project methodology of Agile rather than the shared human problem the project needs to solve. While this might sound like a contradiction, it was a common issue also mentioned by other leaders interviewed for the book. This is a good reminder that the purpose and reason for embracing agility must remain at the forefront of any initiative.

Agile is more than just applying tools and techniques to deliver a project faster. To realize value, it is critical to stay grounded in the users' experience and continuously iterate towards the goal of making people's working lives easier. By infusing your work with the philosophy of human-centred design, it's easier to stay true to this core purpose and remain focused on delivering customer value.

Sensemaking

Much of human-centred design can be linked to the practice of sensemaking. David Snowden, who we met in Chapter 3 when exploring the Cynefin® Framework and an influential figure in the theory, describes sense-making[1] as 'how you can make sense of the world, so you can act in it' (Rebel Wisdom, 2021). As Snowden explains, sensemaking helps you gather enough data to move forward and act because knowing everything about a situation is impossible. In highly complex and uncertain situations, sensemaking provides a process through which you build situational understanding and awareness in order to make decisions (Klein et al, 2006). Sensemaking also challenges the notion that one perspective is sufficient to understand the complexities of human and organizational life. Instead, you can compile a series of insights with explanatory possibilities by unearthing the different stories, views and framings of meaning that people assign to organizational outcomes (Centre for Public Impact, 2022). While Snowden himself might question the linear nature of human-centred design, in my experience, it's a critical skill that helps L&D and people professionals discover patterns and make sense of organizational behaviour and outcomes.

For Eoin Cannon (2023), Business Agility Coach and experienced Agile L&D consultant, the emphasis on understanding the customer through ethnographic research was a key attraction to Agile. As an ex-marketeer who transitioned into L&D, Cannon saw immense value in applying Agile and human-centric design within organizational learning and development. 'Understanding why people did what they did' was central for Cannon: 'Let's really get into their heads rather than just assuming we understand them.' Cannon likens many of the human-centric design tools explored in this chapter to methods used in marketing to examine consumer profiles and customer journeys or touchpoints. 'I always felt that HR and learning needed more of that, and Agile provided that way of zeroing in and starting with the users, that was very attractive.' Cannon comments that a great marketeer strives to deeply understand why people behave as they do and how they interact with their social environment. 'I think L&D professionals are typically very focused on the content, and they don't always think if you give somebody something here, what's their frame of mind? What's their association around it?' For Cannon, human-centric design helps L&D and people professionals examine the environment and ecosystem in which people operate, assisting the profession in moving beyond a traditional focus on content and output.

Moments that matter

As Cannon suggests, much of what we're exploring in this chapter reflects practices borrowed from customer experience and marketing. A good example is the increased focus within HR and L&D on moments that matter, critical snippets of time that create a lasting impact on our people. The concept originates from customer experience as 'moments of truth' or points in a customer's journey when they form an impression of your product or brand. It follows that if customers are delighted with every interaction, they are unlikely to quit the product or brand in favour of a competitor (Interaction Design Foundation, 2023a).

Bridger and Gannaway (2021), in their book *Employee Experience by Design: How to create an effective EX for competitive advantage*, describe these as emotionally charged moments that have a disproportionate impact on a person's experience and engagement with an organization. These can be further broken down into the categories of:

Specific moments – for example, the first day in a new role.

Regular moments – like performance or salary conversations with your manager.

Created moments – such as team or employee recognition.

Broken moments – that may happen daily or through routine, for example searching for digital content on a Learning Management System (LMS), which can quickly escalate into something more significant when a person has a poor user experience. (Bridger and Gannaway, 2021).

All these moments that matter combine to make up an overriding employee journey, which might constitute a day in an employee's life, part of their career or perhaps reflect a specific employee process.

Generally, a moment that matters equates to a problem to solve or a pain point to fix for employees. Again, this can be linked to another marketing concept called *jobs-to-be-done*. This theory equates customer needs to jobs customers want to complete with the products and services they buy (Ulwick, 2017). We already know many of these moments that matter or jobs-to-be-done within the employee journey. A good example is a new team manager joining an existing team. This is a significant moment that could quickly become negative not only for the manager, who might feel out of their depth and lacking experience, but also for the team, who may start to mistrust the manager's intentions or question their ability. Focusing on the job-to-be-done makes it clear that the manager requires specific skills and tools to help them build a sense of belonging and shared purpose within the team. Usual development actions for this moment that matters include the team co-creating a shared vision and mission with the new manager alongside a series of career conversations focused on what each person wants to achieve and contribute to the strategy. The benefit of human-centred design is that you can consciously target these moments that matter to deliver value and delight people.

Solving shared workplace problems and targeting moments that matter also help L&D and people teams transcend pre-set processes or limiting assumptions that often restrict learning and OD design. For example, recognizing that customer needs were evolving led Agile HR coach and consultant Nicki Somal (2023) to experiment with agility in her former L&D role. 'It's about how we're satisfying our customers, how we're co-creating with our customers and making sure that we're delivering what the customer wants and not what we think they want.' Somal saw that digitalization had started to provide learners with a level of choice and real-time access never experienced before in the workplace. As a result, the way people consumed learning was fundamentally changing. For example, when solving everyday problems, people are now more likely to 'Google it' or watch a TikTok video than to reach for an instruction manual. This realization led Somal to question the traditional L&D rulebook and experiment with new ways to design and deliver learning at the point of need. Somal challenged the long-held assumption that workplace learning had to be delivered through face-to-face sequential programme cohorts, which she felt only served to remove people from the flow of work. Instead, she began to explore how to provide real-time access to different learning solutions, both digital and in person, at the time the learner experienced the problem rather than asking them to wait for a scheduled training course.

From this, it's clear that a key benefit of human-centred design is the ability to consciously target moments that matter. As a result, you accelerate performance outcomes by solving the problem at the point of need.

Connecting human-centred design with design thinking

At this point, you might be wondering if human-centred design differs from the process of design thinking, which was introduced in Chapter 4 and Chapter 7. In essence, the two go hand in hand. Human-centred design represents the core philosophy guiding your work, and design thinking provides the specific tools and processes that help you achieve your creative goals. Design thinking is a series of discrete but interrelated activities that a human-centred designer applies when solving a problem. While the design thinking process is rarely linear in practice, it is generally depicted as a sequence that starts with researching and building empathy with the human experience and ends with ideating and prototyping user-centric solutions (see Figure 8.1). Tim Brown (2019), former CEO and now chair of the famous design agency IDEO, describes design thinking as a human-centred form of innovation aiming to combine the needs of people with the possibilities of technology and the conditions necessary for business success. As mentioned in Chapter 4, design thinking is based on divergent and convergent thinking.

FIGURE 8.1 The design thinking sequence

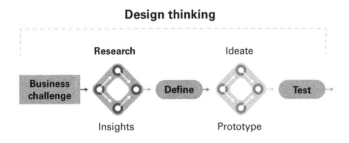

FIGURE 8.2 Author interpretation of design framework sourced from Interaction Design Foundation (2023b)

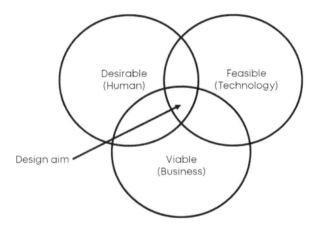

An interplay of desirability, feasibility and viability

As suggested at the beginning of this chapter, organizational design must account for multiple factors and reflect your business environment and customer needs. The aim is to design a desirable product for people that is feasible with the tech available and viable within the organizational context in which you operate (see Figure 8.2).

First, a product is valuable if it satisfies people's desires and helps them solve problems. The majority of the design thinking process focuses on this human element of desirability by testing ideas and validating hypotheses directly with users.

Toward the end of the design thinking process, you must determine whether building and distributing your product is technically feasible. This is the technology element. Do you have the capability within your team or organization to design and deliver the product and the distribution channels to deliver the product to your customers?

The third element is financial and tests whether your product is viable within your business context. In a commercial environment, this is determined by the amount people are willing to pay to buy the product. In an organizational context, it's whether people use it and find it valuable.

Some practitioners also include usability as part of this validation process. Usability is considered a second level to desirability and a component of the user experience (Interaction Design Foundation, 2023c). Once you've determined that the solution solves the customer's problem, usability tests whether it's easy to use and relatively intuitive. It also assesses if it operates as expected in the user's context and meets people's needs.

Interestingly, Dom Norman, professor emeritus at the University of California, co-founder of the Nielsen Norman Group and former Vice President of Apple, now broadens this framework to apply to humanity as a collective, not just individual users (UX Design Institute, 2023). Norman argues that this wider lens is necessary to challenge businesses and organizations to design for a better world, not just for profit. In the face of the climate emergency and the need for more sustainable practices, design must benefit the planet and community where humans operate rather than just delight people with aesthetics or functionality (UX Design Institute, 2023). For example, how can product design help people live a better life? Can products positively contribute to the sustainability of our planet? How are they made? Can they be repaired? Can they be reused? How are they disposed of? These are all crucial questions for L&D and people professions as you help businesses transition towards net-zero and ESG (environmental, social and governance) goals.

Balancing people needs with business needs

In a recent conversation with a chief people officer at a large pharmaceutical company, the need to act from a human-centred point of view was questioned. Their concern was that companies are forced to make tough decisions linked to financial and business outcomes, often detrimental to people, for example a restructure that reduces headcount and costs, resulting in layoffs or people forced to apply for a role elsewhere in the company.

My argument is that even in these situations, you can solve the problem in a human-centred way. Decisions can be communicated transparently, and the resulting restructuring experience can be empathic and caring. Restructures and similar business processes should be seen as components of the overall people experience (PX) product, just as much as the more likeable processes such as career development or engagement surveys. There is the opportunity for people who exit the organization to remain advocates of your brand, and those who stay continue to contribute critical skills to the business.

A good illustration was a senior HR business partner at a large bank who steered a department through such a restructure using many tools we'll explore in this chapter. The function was a newly formed digital team within the organization that had scaled too quickly. Specific skills needed to be utilized differently, and some roles were made redundant. The HR business partner guided the management team through a human-centric design exercise. First, they built personas (which we'll cover shortly) to represent employees who would stay or exit. They then mapped out the intended restructuring experience and explored what would happen for each persona. The exercise challenged the managers to think beyond the process. In particular, the managers developed a deeper appreciation of how their one-to-one conversations would impact each team member. People leaving needed to exit with respect. The decision reflected skills and headcount and was not personal. Conversely, explaining why the skills of those who stayed were valued and how they would be supported and secure in their future role was essential. Clearly, a new vision and team-working agreement should be quickly formed to build a sense of belonging and future direction.

What's interesting about this story is that many organizations ask their managers to act empathically when overseeing a restructure. Some are even given a script to follow. However, in this example, managers wrote their own scripts by flipping the perspective and applying human-centric design. Furthermore, these scripts were designed to solve a shared problem rather than simply executing instructions or reflecting a manager's good nature.

Short history of design thinking

Many attribute the philosophy of human-centred design and the related design thinking process to the design consultancy IDEO, founded in 1991 (IDEO, 2023a). It's probably more accurate to say that IDEO successfully brought what was previously a scientific framework used within engineering and architecture into the mainstream of business and product design (Dam and Siang, 2023; Baytaş, 2021; IDEO, 2023b).

The academic roots of design thinking can be traced back to the 1960s when various thinkers and universities set out to solve human and environmental problems by applying a scientific approach to design. During this time, Horst Rittel, a leading design scientist, first coined the term 'wicked problem', which many still use today to describe complex and multidimensional challenges requiring a design methodology to solve (Dam and Siang, 2023; IDEO, 2015). At the same time, Professor John Edward Arnold at Stanford University linked creative thinking and design theory with innovation and a human-centred approach (Francis, 2017). Additionally, in the 1969 book *The Sciences of the Artificial*, the Nobel Prize laureate Herbert A. Simon referenced design as a way of thinking and a theory of human problem-solving.

While these ideas continued to evolve throughout the 1970s and 1980s, it would take IDEO's founding to make it accessible to all. IDEO represented the coming together of three thought leaders in design at the time. David Kelley, who studied at Stanford and later set up the design school Stanford d.school, joined two British designers, Bill Moggridge, who designed the first laptop through the company ID2 and Mike Nuttall, who founded Matrix Design in Palo Alto (Francis, 2017). Later, in the 2000s, IDEO was led by Tim Brown, who many view as instrumental in elevating the agency's reputation and global influence through clever branding and social media blogging.

Today, some argue design thinking has reached an almost religious fervour within modern business due to very successful information and marketing campaigns by agencies like IDEO (Baytaş, 2021). Regardless of your position, even the sceptics would argue that design thinking is a potent tool that has propelled multimillion-dollar businesses worldwide, such as Airbnb, Oral B, Netflix and Uber Eats (Han, 2022).

How – design thinking and related tools

First, it's helpful to refer back to Chapter 7 and to consider where we are in the PX product development lifecycle (see Figure 8.3).

As emphasized on numerous occasions already, while it's useful to visualize the lifecycle and design thinking sequence as linear to demonstrate flow, this also becomes problematic because it fails to capture the stop, start, forward and back nature of design work. Generally, you'll use design thinking at the research and discovery phase of product development. However, this is not exclusive and many of the tools we'll explore next can be used at every PX product development lifecycle stage.

FIGURE 8.3 PX Product development lifecycle

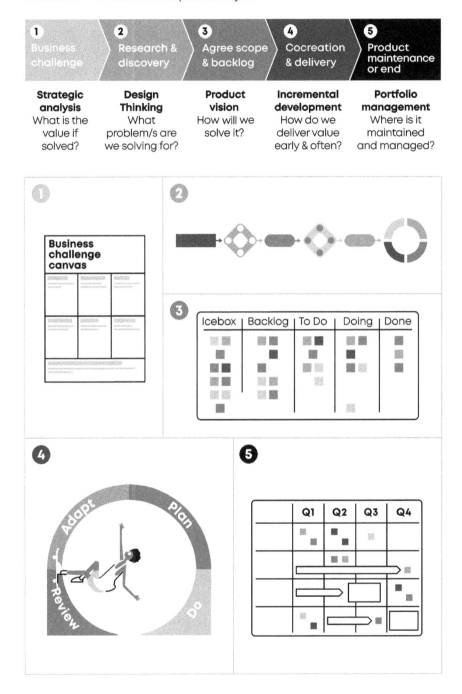

As mentioned in Chapter 4 and Chapter 7, it's helpful to note that many teams time-box this phase in one-to-four-week design or discovery sprints. These sprints might even involve a different group of people than the team who later design and deliver the product. Treating this phase as a time-boxed sprint highlights the need to turn insight into experimentation and action at pace. Too often, L&D and people teams suffer from analysis paralysis, overwhelmed by the enormity of the topic and the data collected. Complex workplace issues like wellbeing and career development often contain multiple elements and require myriad solutions. Rather than debating whether a specific solution suits different types of employees or business areas, a time-boxed sprint encourages you to test these outcomes through real-time experimentation instead of hypothetical discussion.

This section will focus on the following design thinking steps – Research, Insights, Define and Ideation, see Figure 8.4. This complements the section in Chapter 7 on the Business challenge step and feeds into Chapter 10 – Experimentation – which covers the final two steps – Prototype and Test.

Research

Working evidence-based and applying critical thought are vital modern business skills for L&D and OD professionals, increasingly recognized by professional bodies like the CIPD (the UK's Chartered Institute of Personnel and Development). In today's world of mass communication, social media and rampant conspiracy theories, your personal experience and opinion are not trustworthy on their own. Sourcing data and other evidence also significantly heightens your professional gravitas and commercial credibility in the eyes of your stakeholders and business leaders. If you want a seat at the table, you need to back up what you say with data. The CIPD (2023) outlines

FIGURE 8.4 The design thinking sequence

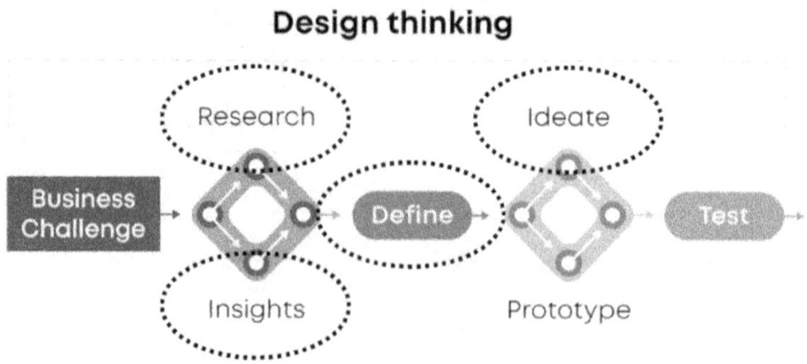

four main types of evidence for people professionals to explore when researching business challenges.

1 People and organizational data – consider internal data, such as retention or employee feedback and external data, such as customer net promoter scores or product sales. Also, be aware of whether you are looking at 'hard' data, such as employee turnover, versus 'soft' data, such as perceptions of company culture and job satisfaction.

2 Internal and external stakeholder feedback – internal stakeholders include employees, managers and business leaders. External stakeholders include end customers (who buy the organization's products and services), suppliers, investors and shareholders.

3 Scientific and professional literature – source relevant case studies, academic journals, and publicly available research to further interrogate, support and assess internal findings.

4 Expertise and judgement – seek input from other L&D and people professionals, business leaders, specialists and consultants (CIPD, 2023).

At a minimum, you should source information from three of the following research methods. A typical mix from this list includes designing and validating customer personas that represent example user profiles, mapping out and assessing an existing employee journey, and combining insights gained with existing people and business data, such as turnover, exit interviews and sales reports.

PERSONAS

This a tool that helps you empathize and identify different customer needs, preferences and pain points (see Figure 8.5 for a template). Personas are essentially fictional characters representing a reliable and realistic version of our customers. While they can be fun to create, it's essential to base the information on actual qualitative and quantitative data. Always test and validate personas with real people. Of course, aiming for an exact match and capturing every employee's unique aspects is impossible. Instead, the goal is to be confident that any potential design will meet around 80 per cent of a persona's needs. L&D and people teams often undertake a series of interviews with employees and stakeholders before building the personas. Generally, four to six personas that explore the most critical workforce segments are sufficient for most projects. (See Figure 8.6 for an example.)

FIGURE 8.5 Persona template

	Characteristics	Career or work goals
	2–3 keywords to describe personal attributes and distinguishing features	2–3 personal goals. What do they want to achieve in their career or role?

Name

Realistic but fictional

Role or skills

Capability and contribution

	Pain points	Personal needs
	2–3 business challenges or frustrations faced when getting things done	2–3 essentials in life to feel satisfied or content

What they say

A quote that sums up their personal style

Mini life story

Short sentence or bullet points describing their personal or career background

FIGURE 8.6 Example persona using template

	Characteristics	Career or work goals
	Sociable. Chatty. Humorous.	To become a workplace coach. Mentor others.

Name

Henrik

Role or skills

Customer services, new hire.

	Pain points	Personal needs
	Prescribed customer service scripts. Strict workplace rules.	Sense of team belonging. To feel loved by the customers.

What they say

I'm a people person

Mini life story

Amateur actor outside work. Loves customer services and has worked in similar roles for 15 years. Excited about working for an innovative tech start-up.

Be careful to challenge biases and develop personas that reflect diversity in nationalities, cultures, religions, sexual orientations and physical abilities. In some projects, teams consciously build personas representing minority or disadvantaged groups to explore alternative experiences. The goal is to explore the employee experience and test any possible solution from multiple perspectives. Constructing personas that represent extreme users can also yield interesting results.

Many L&D and people teams develop a collection of personas to use continuously across all project work and to sense-check the design of processes and systems. Personas can also help you prioritize which areas of the business or employee groups to target, for example where the most significant pain point exists.

EMPATHY MAP

An empathy map can be used in many different ways, and it's often useful to combine this with other tools like personas and journey mapping (see Figure 8.7) to explore the entire employee experience. An empathy map captures what a user says, does, thinks and feels in the flow of work or when they engage with a specific product or service. To do this, create a layout on a whiteboard or digital tool and populate four columns based on your observations or interview notes using the following categories:

- **Say:** quotes or defining words used by the person.

- **Do:** actions or behaviours observed.

- **Think:** what the person might thinking and what this tells you about their beliefs.

- **Feel:** emotions they might be feeling or expressing.

Once you've completed those, identify the person's needs – consider their emotional or physical necessities – and document your insights on the empathy map.

FIGURE 8.7 Empathy map and persona

Persona		Say... about business challenge	Do.. about business challenge	Think... about business challenge	Feel... about business challenge	Insights
	**Sara the Thinker** I'm customer-led and love to plan. I don't miss a thing and crave detail, accuracy and simplification in everything I do.					
Pain Points	Data inaccuracy. Vague instructions and unorganized steps.	Quotes or defining words	Actions	Questions	Emotions	Identified needs, necessities and insights
Needs	Streamlined processes. Effective knowledge management systems.					
Roles	Leader, line manager, technical expert or advisor.					

JOURNEY MAP

A journey map helps you to think systematically about how a person moves through the steps or touchpoints of a process or product lifecycle. A journey map can capture multiple observations or experiences. It might represent an employee lifecycle, a process such as onboarding or how a product is used day to day, for example how a person engages with an internal digital learning system. You can base the journey map on observations and interviews, or even better, ask the user to map it with you. Once done, look for patterns and unexpected outcomes and ask why certain events or actions occurred. From this, you'll gain insight into the moments that matter to support and pain points to solve.

EXPERIENCE MAP

An experience map combines the journey map approach with the empathy map (see Figure 8.8). The aim is to capture and visualize a person's complex interactions with an experience or process linked to a product or service.

FIGURE 8.8 Experience map example

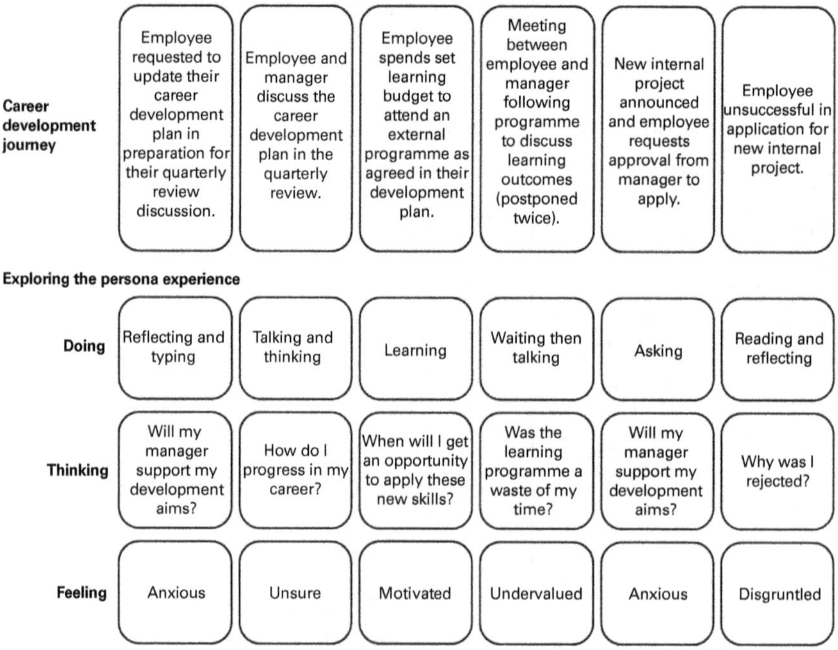

Career development journey: Employee requested to update their career development plan in preparation for their quarterly review discussion. | Employee and manager discuss the career development plan in the quarterly review. | Employee spends set learning budget to attend an external programme as agreed in their development plan. | Meeting between employee and manager following programme to discuss learning outcomes (postponed twice). | New internal project announced and employee requests approval from manager to apply. | Employee unsuccessful in application for new internal project.

Exploring the persona experience

Doing: Reflecting and typing | Talking and thinking | Learning | Waiting then talking | Asking | Reading and reflecting

Thinking: Will my manager support my development aims? | How do I progress in my career? | When will I get an opportunity to apply these new skills? | Was the learning programme a waste of my time? | Will my manager support my development aims? | Why was I rejected?

Feeling: Anxious | Unsure | Motivated | Undervalued | Anxious | Disgruntled

The approach helps us build empathy and understand the steps or milestones of this journey. Therefore, it's perfect for discovering, capturing and exploring moments that matter in the employee experience.

HUMAN-CENTRIC INTERVIEWS

Great human-centric interviews contain powerful questions encouraging people to share their wants and needs. Invite people to share stories by starting with statements like, *'Tell me about a time when...'*. The aim is to develop empathy with the user's experience and explore different frames of meaning. It's also good to look for non-verbal clues to assess people's reactions to questions and gauge feelings. When conducting the interview, remain neutral and don't suggest answers. For these reasons, working in pairs or using voice or video recording equipment to help capture all the information is a good idea.

Tips for preparing:

- **Brainstorm questions:** Write down all the potential questions you can think of, or, even better, do this as a team so you can build on each other's ideas. Aim to frame questions in a human-centred way. For example, rather than ask, 'How can we minimize our high employee turnover?' try something like, 'How can we engage people to develop careers with our business?'

- **Categorize:** Identify and group questions into themes or subject areas.

- **Order:** Once you've categorized your questions, sort them into an order that allows the conversation to flow most naturally. This helps to structure the interview for the user.

- **Refine:** Now do a final review and remove any questions that seem too similar, are now redundant or appear out of place in the order you've created.

I LIKE, I LIKE, I WONDER IF

This framework was referenced by several people interviewed for this book and I often use it to collect feedback. Ask the person to offer two things they like or appreciate, followed by one thing that is either a question, something not considered, or another perspective or criticism. This format is commonly used in focus groups to explore current issues and when testing products through an experiment.

OTHER HELPFUL RESEARCH METHODS

These can include the following:

- **Pulse checks, surveys and employee experience metrics** – these are some of the most favoured sources of information for the L&D and people professional. The key, however, is never rely on one source.

- **People and business data** – start by accessing what your organization already tracks. By knowing the problem to solve and questions to explore, you can usually access a lot more data than at first assumed available. Only consider setting up methods to capture new data points after integrating existing data.

- **Digital tracking** – such as how many people open an email, search for something on a website or view a digital video.

- **External research** – an excellent source of information, but always check if an article or report confirms the accuracy and validity of the data provided. Also, seek out peer reviews, listed research methods and references.

Insights

At the insights step, you engage in sense-making, as described earlier in this chapter. The aim is to seek out patterns, explore assumptions, alternative frames of meaning and build organizational and situational awareness of the business challenge. Insights are also about capturing the moments that matter or jobs-to-be-done. The overriding goal of this step is to converge on specific themes and problems to solve from your research findings. While most teams compile vast lists of insights at this stage, it is helpful to group and distil the information into two to six key themes. You can then use each theme to form the basis of a problem statement in the next step: Define.

GALLERY WALK OR ONLINE MURAL

Stick all the data you have collected throughout the research step, such as interviews, personas and people analytics, on a large whiteboard (physical or online). Then, invite your team to explore the data and ask them to record insights and moments that matter on sticky notes as they review the information – once done, ask people to sort and group these insights into clusters.

BEWARE BIASES

To help our brains process large amounts of information, we naturally create mental shortcuts to make decisions. Unfortunately, this also means we're prone to bias. Even the 'best practice' concept leads to a bias where you favour examples from market-leading organizations. As discussed throughout this book, let's challenge ourselves to move beyond this best practice one-size-fits-all mentality and continuously test and validate for our organizational context. Common biases to look out for include: .

- **Confirmation bias** – a common bias when researching organizational issues, where you seek information confirming your existing beliefs or initial assumptions.

- **Conformity bias** – often referred to as 'groupthink' or 'herd behaviour', this is a tendency to conform with other views within the group and why it's necessary to always encourage silent brainstorming as part of any design thinking process.

- **Authority bias** – the tendency to overvalue the opinion of an individual or organization perceived as an expert or authority figure. Within Agile circles, the term HiPPO – highest-paid person's opinion – is common.

- **Patternicity or the illusion of causality** – a desire to see patterns and assume causal relationships by connecting the dots even when there is random noise (CIPD, 2023). In other words, confusing correlation and causality.

Define

At the define step, we translate all the great insight gained from our research into targeted problem statements written from our customers' perspectives. Ultimately, a project is an extensive list of problem statements you have identified as essential to solve based on your initial business challenge. You've broken the large, complex business challenge into manageable chunks and different problems to solve. From this list, you'll prioritize the issues to focus on first and why, while others will remain in the icebox for later or perhaps never at all.

Each problem statement can be likened to a hypothesis, which we cover in more detail in Chapter 10. Each hypothesis aims to describe what the problem is and what the impact of solving the problem would be for specific customers. A great problem statement has the following qualities:

- It provides focus and frames the problem with clarity.
- It acts as a reference when assessing competing ideas and solutions.
- It inspires the team to act.
- It stops the tendency to attempt to design solutions that are all things to all people.
- It guides your next steps of prototyping and testing.

Writing a powerful problem statement takes time. It's useful to write a few different versions and test these with colleagues or people experiencing the problem you want to solve. A common mistake is to assume a specific solution within the statement. For example, the problem statement '*How might we make career opportunities more visible?*' assumes career opportunities are available but allows the designer to be creative in making these visible within the organization. Too often, L&D and people professionals write a problem statement more like '*How might we make career opportunities more visible by improving the internal application process?*' Now, they're stuck exploring only one component of a more extensive and potentially more creative solution.

'HOW MIGHT WE' QUESTION

The 'How might we' format is easy to use and effective. Placing 'how might we' in front of statements focusing ideas on specific solutions and user needs.

For example, 'How might we build a more diverse mix of senior leaders in the organization over the coming two years?'

POINT OF VIEW STATEMENT

[*User*] needs to [*user's need*] because [*surprising insight*].

For example, 'Layla, the new hire, needs a mentor because she has great skills to offer but lacks the organizational knowledge and connections to get the job done quickly'.

WHAT'S THE POINT?

A type of checklist that asks and answers: What's the point? Who says? What's new? And, so what?

For example, 'Great career development harnesses business success; employees say it determines whether they stay with the company beyond one year; we can realize greater innovation by ensuring our people continually grow their skills, giving us a competitive advantage in the market.'

Ideation

Solving complex problems requires radical, out-of-the-box thinking. But this rarely comes naturally and demands high levels of psychological safety within teams. Most innovative ideas aren't sourced from one perfect idea from a sole thinker. Instead, innovation reflects a collaborative process where a group of people build on and combine a range of ideas to develop a concept to prototype gradually. Indeed, facilitating good ideation sessions is a critical L&D and OD skill.

It's helpful to combine ideation with the next step in design thinking – Prototype, which is covered in more detail in the next chapter. Working back and forth between idea generation and basic prototyping is very effective. You might sketch the idea out on paper or an online tool like Miro as a rough prototype, which tends to generate additional ideas that help you further develop the design concept.

The ideate step aims to think big (deferring judgement and opinions) and then use prioritization techniques to select the best ideas to prototype. While there are many ways to prioritize, each idea needs to be assessed based on its potential value against the initial business challenge, alongside factors like the effort required, available budget or financial and regulatory risk.

Giving the ideate step time is crucial. Allowing people to explore their ideas before converging on what you will prototype is vital. The key is to avoid people jumping to conclusions, being influenced by groupthink, or opting for obvious solutions that reflect preferred comfort zones.

SILENT BRAINSTORMING

The benefit of allowing people to think and generate ideas privately before sharing them with others cannot be stressed enough. Not only is this essential for different personality types and neurodivergence, but it's also important for people to explore their thinking before being influenced by what others contribute. In all workshops and ideation sessions, I create space for people to brainstorm individually, for example writing as many ideas as possible on sticky notes within a time-boxed period before inviting the group to discuss and share ideas.

GROUP BRAINSTORMING AND CROWDSOURCING

There are a lot of techniques that work well once the group starts to share and build on each other's ideas. For example, you can challenge the group to record a specific number of ideas before integrating them, knowing that the more they are forced to brainstorm, the more unconventional people's thinking becomes. You can also introduce constraints (what if you had no budget?) or remove all parameters (what if you spent as much as you like?). Inviting others from across the business to join the ideation session is also beneficial, opening it up to a broader organizational audience or even the public through a crowdsourcing platform.

STORYBOARDING

This technique straddles ideation and prototyping in many ways, but it's mentioned here because it's a fantastic method of helping groups bring ideas to life (see Figure 8.9 for a template). One of the easiest ways to do this is to

FIGURE 8.9 Storyboard template

Storyboard your idea or prototype

1. **Experiment name** – Give the idea or prototype a name.

2. **Hypothesis** – What are you testing and what do you think will happen as a result? For example, if you do x, then 10% of users will do Y.

3. **Success metric** – What data needs to be collected and assessed to determine the result?

4. **Storyboard** – Create a four-step-sketch using the table below to describe the solution using pictures and words.

Current state	**Step 1**
Step 2	**Outcome**

divide a large piece of paper or online whiteboard into a two-by-two grid. Then, challenge the group to storyboard their idea in four steps. In the first quadrant, draw images that represent the current state. In the next quadrant, describe the solution to be designed or built. In the third quadrant, describe how it would be implemented and experienced by customers. Then, in the fourth quadrant, describe the outcome and how the product solves the problem.

PRIORITIZING IDEAS TO PROTOTYPE

While exploring innovative concepts and alternative solutions is great fun, you must converge and decide which ideas to prototype and test.

Using a value-versus-effort grid is an effective method for figuring out how impactful each idea is using metrics identified at the business challenge stage against what is possible regarding capacity, resources, budget and organizational complexity. Before using the grid, it's essential to clearly define the value and effort criteria, which we'll cover in more detail in Chapter 11.

Most teams still need to apply a voting or sorting system even after using the value-versus-effort grid. Always ensure these approaches are linked to data points and metrics to make them as objective as possible. Inviting other business representatives into the conversation alongside potential customers of the intended product is always invaluable in helping to accelerate this stage.

Let's return to the example business challenge used in Chapter 9 and apply some of the design thinking tools outlined in this chapter to the same scenario.

A Business Challenge

- Enhance career development and retain more people beyond 1.5 years.

B Research

The team undertake the following research to explore the business challenge further:

- Analyse existing attrition, recruitment, diversity and engagement data.
- External research (for example, the team explored case studies sourced from Harvard Business Review and Gartner).
- 25 human-centric interviews, including extreme users (people who are extremely satisfied or dissatisfied with career development).

C Insight

The team identified the following insights from the research conducted above:

- It is difficult for employees to develop a career within the organization and easier to find a job at another company after 2 years.
- Career opportunities exist, but people don't know how to find them.
- Internal hires are hired 70% faster, perform better, and are likelier to stay.

D Define

Based on their insights, the team formulated the following problem statements:

- How might we make career opportunities more visible in the organization?
- How might we help people feel more stretched and challenged?
- How might we help people help others?
- How might we make supporting careers appealing to managers?

The team then prioritize the problem, 'How might we make career opportunities more visible in the organization?' Chapter 10 will explore how to prototype and test a possible solution.

Inclusive design example

'Humans are not a monolith. We all have our own individual experiences,' states Greg McCaw, Chief People Officer at the professional services firm BKL and former Director of People Experience and Diversity, Equity and Inclusion at Flutter. McCaw (2023) considers human-centred design as a great DEI tool and an approach that doesn't require a huge upfront data exercise because it quickly moves into the lived experiences of humans in the workplace. It also helps manage the temptation of fancy off-the-shelf DEI products, which won't necessarily solve the underlying problem.

A good example was when McCaw and a previous team started to plan for Pride and decided to go beyond just the celebration. Instead, they wanted to drill down to the day-to-day micro experiences of LGBTQIA+ people. Using design thinking tools, they designed a trans persona. Then, they mapped out their recruitment experience, including all the different touch-points, such as brand awareness, that can limit applications from the very beginning. This led to a series of problem statements to solve for trans candidates in the recruitment process. One outcome was reviewing the language used throughout the process and how to support the hiring manager to have a great conversation with a trans candidate, such as using the correct pronouns. 'What design thinking and human-centred design brought to that conversation was we all really started to empathize with that persona, and it challenged us to think beyond our own lived experience to create a better recruitment process.' They then applied the same approach across LGBTQIA+. Interestingly, off the back of this work, the team created an allyship playbook to help people day to day. This outlined why pronouns are important and the nuances of language and shared lived experiences of the LGBTQIA+ community.

Conclusion – five takeaways for L&D and people professionals

- Human-centred design helps you build desirable people products that are also feasible and viable for your business and organizational context.
- To realize product value, it's essential to stay grounded in the users' experience and continuously iterate towards the goal of making people's working lives easier.
- Human-centred design helps you build more inclusive and equitable solutions by empathizing with the lived experience of work, but watch out for bias.
- A key benefit of human-centred design is consciously targeting moments that matter and accelerating performance outcomes.
- At a minimum, you should source information from three different research methods, for example designing and validating customer personas that represent example user profiles, mapping out and assessing an existing employee journey, and combining insights gained with existing people and business data, such as turnover, exit interviews and sales reports.

Note

1 David Snowden uses a hyphen – sense-making – where other scholars write it as one word.

References

Baytaş, Mehmet Aydın (2021) The story of design thinking, Design Disciplin www.designdisciplin.com/the-story-of-design-thinking (archived at https://perma.cc/XYW5-8BAD)

Bridger and Gannaway (2021) *Employee Experience by Design: How to create an effective EX for competitive advantage*, Kogan Page, London

Brown, T. (2019) *Change by Design: How design thinking transforms organizations and inspires innovation* (revised edition), Harper Business, London

Cannon, Eoin (2023) Interview with Natal Dank, recorded 12 July

Centre for Public Impact (2022) What is sensemaking?, 13 January, www.centreforpublicimpact.org/insights/what-is-sensemaking (archived at https://perma.cc/E2JT-7S8K)

CIPD (2023) Evidence-based practice for effective decision-making, 25 July, www.cipd.org/uk/knowledge/factsheets/evidence-based-practice-factsheet/ (archived at https://perma.cc/TMY3-H4AE)

Dam, Rikke Friis and Siang, Teo Yu (2023) The History of Design Thinking, Interaction Design Foundation, www.interaction-design.org/literature/article/design-thinking-get-a-quick-overview-of-the-history (archived at https://perma.cc/WB4T-CBN4)

Francis, Dexter (2017) The Roots of IDEO's Design Thinking Process, LinkedIn, 30 January, www.linkedin.com/pulse/roots-ideos-design-thinking-process-dexter-francis (archived at https://perma.cc/HYQ4-CWE6)

Han, Esther (2022) 5 Examples of Design Thinking in Business, Harvard Business School Online, 22 February, https://online.hbs.edu/blog/post/design-thinking-examples (archived at https://perma.cc/TJY3-KZQR)

IDEO (2015) *The Field Guide to Human-Centered Design*, IDEO.org, San Francisco

IDEO (2023a) What's the difference between human-centred design and design thinking?, https://designthinking.ideo.com/faq/whats-the-difference-between-human-centered-design-and-design-thinking (archived at https://perma.cc/CL36-29J9)

IDEO (2023b) Design thinking defined, https://designthinking.ideo.com (archived at https://perma.cc/R248-7SRB)

Interaction Design Foundation (2023a) The Moment of Truth: Build desirable relationships with users and customers, www.interaction-design.org/literature/article/the-moment-of-truth-build-desirable-relationships-with-users-and-customers (archived at https://perma.cc/WGF3-3LG7)

Interaction Design Foundation (2023b) From Prototype to Product: Ensure that your solution is feasible and viable, www.interaction-design.org/literature/article/from-prototype-to-product-ensuring-your-solution-is-feasible-and-viable (archived at https://perma.cc/3AQ4-SXBW)

Interaction Design Foundation (2023c) Usability, www.interaction-design.org/
      literature/topics/usability (archived at https://perma.cc/9M25-4MQB)
Klein, G., Moon, B., and Hoffman, R. R. (2006) *Making Sense of Sensemaking 1:
      Alternative perspectives*, IEEE Educational Activities Department, https://doi.org/
      10.1109/MIS.2006.75 (archived at https://perma.cc/R7R6-6N3T)
McCaw, Greg (2023) Interview with Natal Dank, recorded 19 July
Pritchard, Jodie (2023) Interview with Natal Dank, recorded 20 July
Rebel Wisdom (2021) Sensemaking & Complexity, Dave Snowden, Rebel Wisdom
      YouTube channel, 22 September, youtu.be/JiVbrj3byJY?si=A1ndGoUIoi_
      HmfhY (archived at https://perma.cc/7DPP-7SU6)
Sheard, Sara (2023) Interview with Natal Dank, recorded 4 August
Somal, Nicki (2023) Interview with Natal Dank, recorded 19 July
Ulwick, Tony (2017) Jobs-to-be-Done: A framework for customer needs, Medium,
      6 January, jobs-to-be-done.com/jobs-to-be-done-a-framework-for-customer-
      needs-c883cbf61c90 (archived at https://perma.cc/HU96-AT3Y)
UX Design Institute (2023) Design for a Better World with Don Norman, YouTube,
      18 August, www.uxdesigninstitute.com/blog/design-for-better-world-don-
      norman/ (archived at https://perma.cc/LG5Y-JLSZ)
Waters, Tracey (2023) Interview with Natal Dank, recorded 26 July

09

Principle 3: T-shaped people in T-shaped teams

When four different emails from the same business function land in an employee's inbox in the space of 48 hours, you know that business function has a coordination problem. This example might sound extreme, but it's not uncommon. Many HR and people leaders interviewed for this book mentioned embarrassing moments like this as their catalyst for change and the need to embrace Agile.

The recognition that siloed functional teams and competing remits slow down organizations is not unique to the people profession. As we've seen in earlier chapters, a central Agile principle is to have all the skills in the team to get the whole job done. The benefits of team collaboration have long been discussed in business literature, and its potential to eliminate waste makes it central to Agile and Lean methodologies. It's estimated that up to 50 per cent of knowledge gets lost in every handover between functions and skill silos (Poppendieck and Poppendieck, 2006). Organizational context and tacit knowledge are difficult to pass on through an email or diagram. The need to explain specific customer needs or stakeholder requirements slows projects down because of repeating information each time a task is handed over.

As mentioned in Chapter 3, attempting to manage and control a project where one person does their bit and then hands over responsibility to the next person reflects an outdated model based on a linear and predictable business environment. In today's increasingly complex organizational context, this conveyor belt approach adds risk because it just needs one component to break and the whole project stalls.

'Kill the silo' was a key objective for Arne-Christian van der Tang (2023), Chief HR Officer at TomTom, when moving to a new people team model, explored later in this chapter. However, this structural change to the HR operating model was not carried out in isolation and reflected a broader organizational redesign across the business to be more product-led and customer-focused. As highlighted by Van der Tang, it's increasingly important for people teams to mirror the same 'go to market' strategy characterizing the broader business. 'The whole notion of organizing our own dedicated product team is so very close to what we do as a company,' comments Van der Tang. 'If you think about how HR has been structured until now, we often haven't reflected the business structure. We've been even more siloed than the business, and then we go out, and we try and help them break down their silos when we have so many of our own.'

A product-led organization is built around outcomes rather than just delivery (Perri, 2018) and focuses on how to continually improve and evolve the product experience rather than just different component parts. A considerable crossover exists here with the employee experience of an organization. If L&D and the people function want to deliver impact led by employee experience, they require product teams to work closely with customers and respond in real time. It follows that if the L&D and people team are designing solutions to enable a product-led and customer-centric strategy within an organization, it's only logical for the team to be structured similarly to the broader business.

In this chapter, we will explore how T-shaped people in T-shaped teams allow you to move beyond the siloed legacy existing within the L&D and people profession and deliver product-led impact. It also heralds a new structure and mindset for the people function, crucially offering an alternative to the traditional Ulrich model, the adherence to or misuse of which still hinders many L&D and HR teams today. It's also a vital rethink about how to build L&D and people professional careers and develop the necessary skills to solve the significant complex challenges faced in the workplace today.

Breaking the L&D and HR siloed legacy

Over the last decade, the people profession has debated how best to update the traditional Ulrich model that has essentially monopolized HR's functional structure since the 1990s. The Ulrich model divides HR into three core components: HR business partners (HRBPs), HR shared services and HR COEs (centres of excellence). In this model, L&D and OD professionals sat one step back from the customer as specialists within the COE. In practice, this often resulted in a handover conveyor belt between the HRBP, who was responsible for identifying a business need, the COE, who was then tasked with designing a solution, and then back again to either the HRBP or HR shared services to implement it. If global versus local business needs were also included and many COE teams launched programmes and services based on their own topic remits, the model got overloaded and bogged down in complicated and competing deliveries. It also often resulted in confusing messages for the broader business as numerous initiatives were launched at the same time, all hitting the inbox simultaneously.

Gartner (2023), a leading research and consulting firm, also advocates re-engineering the HR operating model, and was referenced by several leaders interviewed for this book as influencing their team restructures and capability development. The Gartner model is similar to Josh Bersin's 'systemic HR' (2023), as mentioned in Chapter 7 and reflects today's push for agility, customer-centricity and operational synergies within the people profession. To achieve this collective approach, Gartner argues that approximately 40 per cent of the function should collaborate as a dynamic, multi-skilled, and cross-functional problem-solving pool, tackling business challenges in an Agile and prioritized way. Strategic business partners and what's called a 'next generation' Agile and significantly streamlined COE then work alongside this problem-solving pool and a robust operations and service delivery team (Gartner, 2023). Interestingly, the Gartner model has given some people functions already experimenting with Agile methods licence to take the next step and restructure their team model. In this chapter, we'll explore a few, including TomTom, the HR Innovation team at Diageo and temporary project sprint teams at Arup and other organizations. What's common across all these case studies is that a product-led strategy can only be achieved through teams working as a multidisciplinary collective.

So, how do you develop the skill profiles and capabilities necessary to build a multidisciplinary, problem-solving collective? The answer is T-shaped people in T-shaped teams.

What is a T-shaped professional?

A T-shaped professional is a person with a breadth of general skills, as represented by the horizontal part of the T, combined with one or a few deep specialisms, as represented by the vertical part of the T (see Figure 9.1).

First, let's consider the general skills – the horizontal part of the T. These are skills in which you have a general level of capability. You're not an expert, but you have a solid working knowledge of the topic and its application

FIGURE 9.1 T-shape career framework explained

Generalist   Specialist   T-shaped

within a business setting. It follows that the greater the breadth and diversity of these general capabilities, the better the ability to flex and adapt across various business scenarios and projects.

Now, let's consider the vertical part of the T, which represents your specialisms. These are the specific skills where you have deep expertise and can offer advice and direction. On these topics, you contribute to projects and product design as a subject matter expert or leader in your field.

How does the T-shape benefit you? Well, it links back to the need to move beyond traditional job titles and the outdated concept of being either a generalist or specialist within the people profession. Instead, you need to be both in today's complex business environment. The T-shaped approach helps you achieve this by strategically developing general business and commercial capabilities supplemented with deep specialisms in specific L&D and people topics (or other business areas). By combining both breadth and depth, you're able to build a skills profile that essentially makes you more capable and employable, you're better able to adapt and respond to change, as well as transfer your skills across different business scenarios as and when required.

Additionally, the T-shape framework allows you to focus on developing or strengthening skills deemed vital for your current organizational context, such as the increasing need for L&D professionals to be comfortable working with data analytics or genAI. You don't need to become an expert or change job titles in such examples. Instead, by thinking T-shaped, you focus on building a general level of capability through activities like digital learning, talking with experts and testing a few things out in projects.

The ease with which L&D and people professionals have started to use the T-shape framework across the many teams I've been fortunate to coach has amazed me. This demonstrates how immediately applicable it is and offers a practical, modern approach to developing careers that celebrates and builds on different career backgrounds rather than interpreting every new job as a complete career switch. Gone are the days of pre-defined career pathways linked to job groupings and functional-based hierarchies. Instead, the modern career is about flexibility and adaptability, where people move up, down and sideways as new work opportunities and experiences arise.

It's also helpful to note that the T-shape framework is not just for L&D and people professionals. Many organizations use the framework to guide capability development within other business teams, such as marketing and tech or, for some, the whole company.

Example T-shape

Every person has a different T-shape that reflects their personal experiences, career journey and, of course, motivations and preferences (see Figure 9.2).

For example, a person might have a general level of capability in skills like data analytics, change management or Agile ways of working, coupled with deep specialisms in design thinking or L&D. By contrast, someone else might only have a general level of capability in L&D but a deep level of expertise in data analytics and DEI. It's also important to note that any one

FIGURE 9.2 Example T-shape for a person solving L&D and OD problems

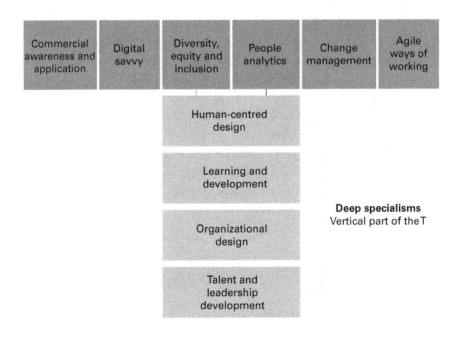

skill is not intrinsically general or specialist but that a person's T-shape reflects the level of capability they hold in that skill.

The overall aim is to acquire a good range of general capabilities and, based on your career preferences and the capability requirements of your organization, also pursue specific specialisms. This means your T-shape continuously evolves and is shaped through different career opportunities, targeted development and the skills demanded by the business context in which you operate.

Where does the term T-shaped professional come from?

There is debate about whether the T-shape phrase was coined by McKinsey & Company in the 1980s or by Tim Brown, CEO of IDEO Design Consultancy, in the 1990s (Bodell, 2020). Either way, it's become synonymous with Agile teams and organizational design. This is because, contrary to common belief, the majority of our daily work tasks don't require specialist skills, meaning a T-shaped team can complete most tasks required day to day (Yipp, 2018). Also, because a T-shaped professional is not limited to a single niche, they're more flexible across the organization. A T-shaped team collaborating in a multidisciplinary way also encourages cross-training, which means leaders can do more with the same number of people.

It's also good to note at this point that a few different interpretations of the T-shape career framework exist within business literature. Some practitioners limit the T to one job function, for example it would solely represent all the skills necessary to excel in L&D or recruitment. It's also common to see the vertical of the T interpreted as only representing one specialism rather than several (see Figure 9.3), as shown earlier (see Figure 9.2).

In contrast, the T-shape framework in this book represents your whole career. It aims to move beyond pre-set job roles or singular specialisms regarding career development and workforce planning. For example, someone in L&D might have a marketing specialism gained from a previous job. This should be celebrated and recognized in their T-shape because it gives them an edge in any learning-related projects requiring communications, branding or product design.

Alternative shapes

Other extensions of the T-shape exist, known as the M-shape (or pi) and X-shape. The M-shape or pi-shape is an alternative way of visualizing more

FIGURE 9.3 Alternative interpretation of T-shape

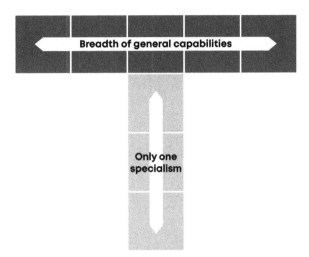

than one specialism (on the vertical) connected to the horizontal representation of general skills (see Figures 9.4 and 9.5). In contrast, the T-shape framework presented in this book adds multiple specialisms to the same vertical.

The X-shape (see Figure 9.6) extends the T-shape from being multidisciplinary to transdisciplinary, but a few interpretations exist. The concept of an X-shaped learner by Heather McGowan (2019) explores the interplay of humans and technology as we move into the fourth industrial revolution. In future careers, McGowan predicts that people will move between 15 jobs or more, and we need to transcend the outdated concept of skills linked to specific identities (degree, job title, company brand) and instead apply knowledge and skills at a moment in time. 'This is a shift from storing stocks of knowledge to working in flows of emerging knowledge with a trans-disciplinary mindset of human and technology collaboration' (McGowan, 2019).

Another interpretation views the X as an intersection of empathy and design thinking. David Clifford (2019) argues that this represents an advanced ability to notice and reflect on our own thinking and biases. In this example, the X-shaped person is more human-centred and inclusive. The final interpretation of the X-shape is of a leader who holds deep expertise in specific skills on one axis and leadership skills on the other axis. An X-shaped

FIGURE 9.4 Alternative M-shape

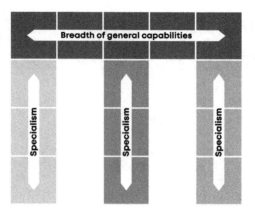

FIGURE 9.5 Alternative pi-shape

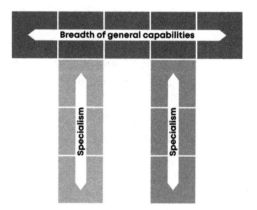

FIGURE 9.6 Alternative X-shape

person can therefore lead diverse teams and stretch into new domains (Designlab, 2016).

Danny Seals (2023), founder of Knot, an employee experience design and innovation consultancy, and Vice President, Employee Innovation, Listening and Effectiveness at RAKBANK, interprets the X-shaped person as an M-shaper who can apply their knowledge and skills more meaningfully through interdisciplinary thinking. What's significant for Seals is that you want people demonstrating the M-shape and X-shape learning curiosity when building an HR innovation team because they're better able to blend and collaborate across multiple disciplines. Seals calls this the 'antifragile team' able to ride the waves of uncertainty and take advantage of adverse conditions. An antifragile mindset underpins experimentation and the ability to navigate complexity and change (Taleb, 2012).

What's common across these alternative interpretations of the T-shape framework is a recognition that the modern career is interdisciplinary, multidisciplinary and fluid. It was this recognition that prompted people leaders interviewed for this book to question the traditional HR functional structure and its numerous topic silos. As Arne-Christian van der Tang (2023) from TomTom highlights, within a large HR function, up to twenty-five different disciplines might exist, such as L&D, talent, total reward, international mobility, employee brand, internal comms, organizational design, and the list goes on. For Van der Tang and others, it was increasingly recognized that a more multidisciplinary approach within HR was the answer. 'We needed a way to bring all our domain expertise together and make it easy to build impactful products that make sense for the company and our customers will love.'

T-shaped teams

As already explored through earlier chapters, business agility demands a more fluid movement of people, better reflecting customer needs and capability requirements. The idea is to group people together based on what's needed, the problem to solve or the product to deliver, as opposed to what function or job people are in. The T-shaped career framework offers an excellent foundation for building this skills-based approach in how organizations hire, deploy and develop capability. Rather than looking at a pre-set list of tasks required to fill a job, workforce planners can instead use the T-shape to seek out specific skills or skill clusters and group them together as and when needed.

What does a T-shaped L&D or people team look like?

A T-shaped team comprises people with a range of similar general skills combined with a variety of specialisms unique to everyone (see Figure 9.7).

Along the horizontal (representing general capabilities), most people in the team would have a solid knowledge of similar skills such as commercial awareness and application, change management or applying Agile ways of working. Some or ideally all team members would also have deep knowledge in at least one topic, such as human-centred design or diversity, equity and inclusion (DEI).

Such a breadth of skills coupled with deep specialisms means this type of T-shaped team can take on a wide range of people-related business problems. This team also perfectly illustrates the Agile goal of having all the required skills in the team to get the whole job done. Such T-shaped teams can be further strengthened by including people from other parts of the business, especially when seeking specific specialist skills for particular projects or product design. By having all the skills required from the start, dependencies and handovers are decreased or even eliminated, and the teams are in an excellent position to respond rapidly to changing customer needs.

FIGURE 9.7 Example T-shaped L&D or people team

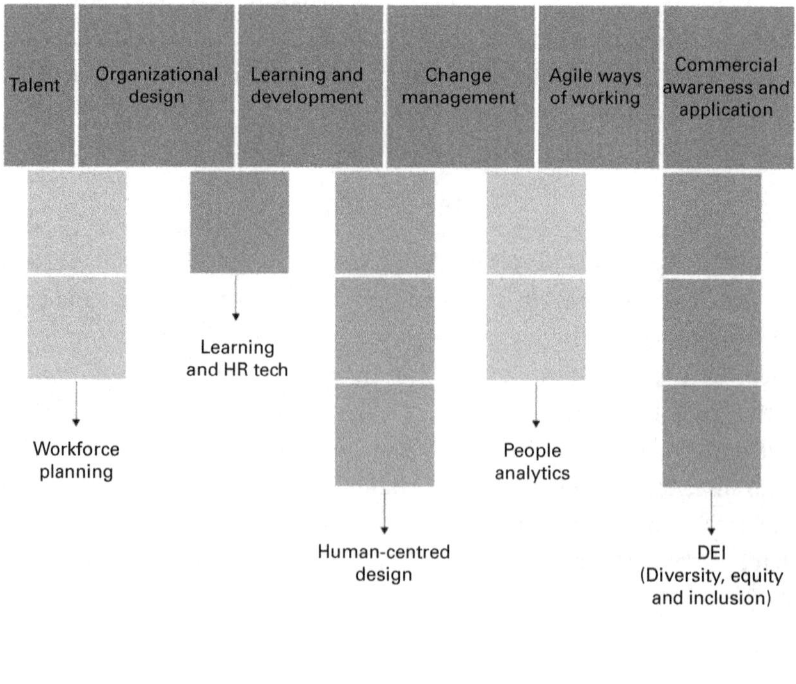

Case study: TomTom's T-shaped people team

TomTom is an excellent example of a people function needing to reinvent itself to be in the best position to support the broader reinvention of the business. The company is a market-leading specialist in independent location, navigation and map technology. While many companies talk about the impact of rapid technological change, market disruption or losing industry position to a competitor, TomTom has faced all three over the last decade and can now share a successful tale of business evolution. A big part of this story has been the people function's ability to build an award-winning employee experience and attract highly skilled engineering, tech and scientific talent in a competitive skills market.

To do this, it became necessary to transform every component of the operating model – starting with developing T-shaped capabilities and then moving on to ways of working and ending up with a completely new team structure and organizational chart. Let's explore this excellent case study, which I also contributed to as a coach and consultant.

Delivering the value that matters most

For Arne-Christian van der Tang (2023), Chief HR Officer at TomTom, HR agility is the ability to deliver value to your people and organization quickly, but also crucially, *'where it matters and when it matters'*. To do this, you first need to know who your customer is and what matters to them and the broader organization. You almost need to predict what's going to be important based on strategy, trends and people data because it's about delivering value for the things that matter now rather than delivering solutions in a few months or a year's time. Furthermore, delivering quickly implies an ability to stop or pause other things to focus on what matters the most now. If you don't, it will be too late once you finally have the spare capacity to get started. Finally, you need to ensure the value gets into the hands of your customer. This is a goal that requires deep customer knowledge and building products that are fit for purpose and, at times, very targeted.

As far back as 2019, the people function of approximately one hundred professionals set themselves the challenge of delivering the value that matters most to TomTom employees. Like most HR functions, they started by experimenting with Agile tools and design thinking to get closer to the customer and co-create value. Van der Tang reflects that while this led to some great initial products and employee feedback, they still lacked sufficient evidence to confidently say that each process and project was the most critical for the business and was driving the right strategic result.

Then, about two and half years ago, Van der Tang personally led a dedicated transformation team that saw the necessity to break this complex business challenge down into three main problems to solve:

1 How might we design our processes and ways of working to deliver value at pace?

2 How might we organize the team structure and operating model to deliver the value that matters most?

3 How might we ensure we have the right people with the right skills and the right mindset to realize our vision?

As stated by Van der Tang, 'In the earlier years, we talked about becoming Agile and applying Agile ways of working, but without specifically thinking, okay, what does that mean? What does that entail? And what do we need to do in order to get there?' Breaking the problem down into three separate areas made it easier to prioritize where to start. Acknowledging that structure was a standalone topic allowed the team to accelerate progress in the other two areas, knowing they could return to the structure question once they felt better equipped.

It also became apparent that any structural change was highly sensitive, potentially impacting people's careers and desire to work at TomTom. It was important to clarify that while there would inevitably be a few bumps along the way, the change wasn't about downsizing, reducing headcount or an opaque, one-way, top-down, magic cure solution. The only way it would work was if everyone was in it together, open to change and willing to speak up as soon as something didn't work or felt too difficult.

From 2021, the people function focused on building a common way of working across all teams. This was interlinked with strengthening Agile capability plus related skills like data literacy, stakeholder management and analytical thinking. The goal was for every person to actively contribute to an ongoing monthly cycle of *plan, do, review, adapt*, and for all work to be visualized through a people portfolio. Powering this rhythm was a set of design principles that focused on knowing your customer, working through comprehensive feedback loops, applying data-backed prioritization, scaling products and, crucially, collaborating through a T-shaped approach. Indeed, while the T-shape framework was initially introduced to help people identify which skills and behaviours to develop next, it quickly became a favoured method for discussing career development and how teams formed around specific projects and deliveries.

Despite a few stumbling blocks and a surprising length of time to unearth all the work across the different HR topic domains, the people team began to gain momentum as a product-led function. What this served to highlight, however, was that the existing model, based on functional domains, kept slowing them down. It simply took too long to form T-shaped project teams around specific problems to solve. So then, in April 2023, the people function changed its structure. 'So even though we split the transformation up into process, structure and skills, for us, we consider day zero as the day we finally changed our team structure', states Van der Tang.

New people team model

The new operating model (see Figure 9.8) consisted of four interconnected core teams revolving around their customers, who are considered new joiners, candidates, leaders, business units, the board, learners and leavers.

- **People strategy and business partners** – steer the people portfolio and act as a type of intelligence bureau. The team comprises strategic business partners, organizational development expertise, a small data insights team, portfolio management, finance and people directors leading each part of the broader function.

- **People essentials** – with a primary focus on platforms, policy and processes, this team of experts is like a streamlined modern-day COE and oversees all vendor spending. Their collective T-shape represents deep expertise in employee tax, reward, L&D, DEI and CSR (corporate social responsibility), while their generalist skills ensure consistent delivery and optimization of the entire employee lifecycle.

- **People services** – first customer entry point for candidates and all employees. Made up of talent acquisition, service desk, employee relations plus mobility and tax, this team supports, guides and advises customers in each phase of their employee journey.

- **People products** – an entirely new team of multidisciplinary problem solvers. A team of equals, working in autonomous sub-teams, each tackling different problems as prioritized by the people portfolio and often reflecting the company's wider OKRs. Made up of people with backgrounds in L&D, OD, business partnering, HR tech, analytics, reward and communications, the team has undertaken extensive exercises to understand both individual T-shapes as well as the collective team T-shape.

FIGURE 9.8 TomTom people team model

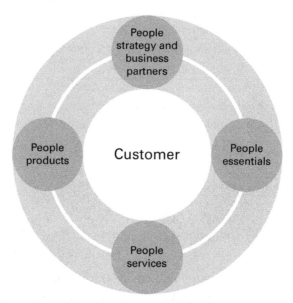

It's helpful to note that the people communications team sit alongside these four teams, working closely with each to ensure an aligned roadmap. They also provide an internal communications agency for the broader business.

Rapid value delivery

TomTom is an excellent example of transforming a people function using an Agile mindset and achieving outcomes incrementally and iteratively, rather than big-bang, one-size-fits-all. Everyone felt included by embracing an ethos of learning from each other and viewing the change as an opportunity for personal and professional development. When speaking with several people from across the function, it's clear that everyone feels part of the journey. Also, even if, in hindsight, Van der Tang would have preferred to arrive at their current state a little quicker, this transparent, feedback-driven approach harnessed true co-creation and job crafting.

But has it worked? A key proof point has been the ability to swarm on urgent real-time issues. When a meaningful problem surfaced at the company executive board level, it became a perfect test case to see if one of the dedicated product sub-teams could pause existing work and rapidly develop a solution. Within 5.5 days, a full report with detailed analysis and recommendations was sitting back with the board. Also, the team's T-shape meant they easily ran with the issue despite the required mix of employee relations, reward and employee brand skills. Interestingly, the final decision was the polar opposite of the initial opinions expressed by the board when the issue was first raised, due to that data-driven approach.

Van der Tang now views this ability to swarm and rapidly reprioritize to deliver value quickly as the most significant differentiator from a year ago. It was almost like the people function were solving problems as a side gig to the main day-to-day focus. So, every time they felt they had failed to deliver value quickly, it wasn't because of capability, it was because the environment hadn't been created for teams to laser focus on one business challenge at a time.

T-shaped team formations

There are various ways to form a T-shaped team. Here are some other examples from the interviews I held with different people or from my work with L&D and people teams.

Sarah Ford (2023), Head of HR Innovation at the global drinks manufacturer and industry giant Diageo, has used the T-shape framework to build the HR Innovation team, a first for the company. Initially, Ford thought hiring for mindset was the right approach but discovered this was quite challenging. She then created a T-shape map to identify the capabilities needed to succeed in the team at general and specialist level. For example, skill in Agile ways of working or experience as a Scrum Master. As Ford highlights, it doesn't imply people need all the skills: 'It just means that you have to be able to contribute in some way.' Now, Ford tracks capabilities using the T-shape, with green indicating skills covered and amber for skill areas they still need to develop.

Setting up temporary T-shape sprint teams is also a common approach mentioned by the leaders interviewed for the book. This recognizes that you're not ready to change the structure permanently or there is a need to gather a particular skillset from across the business for specific projects. For example, Kate Walker (2023) runs hackathon-style sprints of a few days to accelerate L&D and people projects at Arup. Another illustration is from the Agile HR coach Nicki Somal (2023), who recently ran an eight-day sprint with a T-shaped group of seven sprinters sourced from the L&D team, tech systems, and people partnering. Over the eight days, the team worked between 10am and 3pm, allowing each person to catch up on activities such as email replies. The sprint was structured around the design thinking sequence. This saw the team create six personas, use empathy mapping to identify pain points, and formulate a selection of problem statements based on the prototypes. By the end of the eight days, the team had tested and validated a series of enhancements for the performance management system and associated processes across the organization. At Macmillan Cancer Support they have created T-shaped Agile teams with people sourced from across the organization who work together certain days of the week to tackle critical business challenges.

At the housing trust Incommunities, Sara Sheard (2023), Executive Director of Business Operations, has structured her team to reflect the T-shaped approach, similar to the earlier TomTom example. The model aims to solve a common problem repeatedly highlighted among L&D and OD teams where people feel overwhelmed with BAU work and unable to complete important project work. The model comprises a people support team, where most of the BAU work sits alongside a few process improvement projects. Next is the People Experience team, a multidisciplinary team comprising general capabilities and specialist skills such as L&D and DEI, plus a small data insights group. This team covers the bulk of the people projects and associated product design. Sheard also formed a change team that acts as a type of Agile delivery lead function for the whole organization and coordinates projects across the people function as well as IT, communications and other parts of the business.

Finally, Laura Keith (2023), CEO of Hive Learning, embraces a T-shape model to run six-week product innovation sprints. This approach has also led to people strengthening their personal T-shape within the company and developing careers in new ways. For example, a copywriter who was an expert in content now obsesses over learning design and is a product owner who happily engages with customers. Another example is an ex data engineer now working as a product owner and overseeing the learning experience design for the platform.

These examples highlight the need to free up capacity within your existing structure to give people the space and bandwidth to problem-solve. Designing great learning and organizational development solutions isn't just a side gig. Building a T-shaped and collective approach ensures people can focus on one juicy problem at a time.

Essential Agile roles for L&D and people teams

Working T-shaped helps L&D and people teams develop the depth and breadth required to operate as a multidisciplinary collective, solving complex business problems. We've also seen that the structure and formation of the T-shaped team can vary across organizations depending on size, context and customer needs. However, no matter the team structure, several key roles are becoming increasingly essential when applying agility within L&D and people teams. While the roles are essential, they don't always need to be permanent, and it's common for people to move across these for specific projects or cycles of work. Let's look now at each role and an example of how it can be utilized within L&D and people T-shaped teams.

PO (product owner) or Product Manager

The PO or Product Manager takes the lead in translating the project or product vision into a prioritized backlog and is ultimately responsible for realizing the value of what's being delivered. The role is commercially focused and oversees the roadmap and release plan. It's helpful to note that some organizations use the titles of Product Manager or Product Lead rather than PO because they don't use the Scrum framework. While these titles differ, the responsibilities and remit are often very similar, and the different wording reflects organizational context and title preferences.

A good PO or Product Manager engages customers and stakeholders continuously to refine the vision, manage delivery expectations and offers an outside-in perspective. If the broader people function manages a People Portfolio (see Chapter 5 for more information), they take the lead in syncing their specific project or product deliveries with the higher-level portfolio roadmap.

It's often said within Agile that the team owns *how* the project or product will be delivered, while the PO or Product Manager owns *what* to deliver. At the end of a work cycle or sprint, the role acts as a type of sign-off by approving what value can be released and whether it meets quality and customer expectations.

PO OR PRODUCT MANAGER EXAMPLES

The autonomous people product sub-teams at TomTom self-select a person from within the group to take on the role, which they call a Product Lead, for each specific project and then rotate for the next project. At Diageo, the

PO is sourced directly from the HR Innovation team and leads a project group of people identified as subject matter experts or working closer to the customer from the broader business or people function. Another example comes from Citizens Advice, where the Head of L&D and Executive Director of People acted as joint POs for a large competency framework project. In this example, the PO signs off value released each cycle, and an Agile Delivery Lead (see the role description in a later section) undertakes duties like backlog management and roadmap planning. At Macmillan Cancer Support and a few other organizations, the PO is the L&D Director or team manager. One thing to note is that the PO or Product Manager should have time to own and manage the backlog and, as such, this role generally does not suit a Head or senior manager.

People Portfolio Manager

This is a type of chief PO overseeing the prioritization and visualization of all the products and services making up the people portfolio, usually at a functional level (see Chapter 5 for more information on Portfolio). The role is similar to a project programme manager or 'office' (often known as a PMO) but with a much stronger Agile feel. The Portfolio Manager plays a vital coordination role and often helps steer projects by introducing standard tools and procedures, such as the business challenge canvas or project scope canvas (see Chapter 7).

PEOPLE PORTFOLIO MANAGER EXAMPLES

At TomTom, this role sits within the Strategy team and helps the function prioritize and coordinate deliveries in line with company OKRs and other business goals. As another example, at Incommunities, this role is provided by the Change Team, which coordinates projects across the whole organization, not just L&D and HR.

Agile Delivery Lead

Working across a large team, an entire people function or sometimes the wider business to coordinate projects, sync roadmaps, and remove impediments, an Agile Delivery Lead also tracks metrics and analyses data to assess the value and impact of different L&D and people initiatives. Many who undertake this role also talk about the need to coach others to help lift the general level of Agile capability within teams, especially within management teams.

AGILE DELIVERY LEAD EXAMPLES

At Citizens Advice, this role coordinates and upskills an L&D team of twenty people and takes the lead in broader organizational-wide projects. An Agile Delivery Lead also sat within a people leadership team for a function of about 35 people at a tech company. In this example, the person helped the leadership team prioritize the strategy and people portfolio while helping different project teams within the function build and prioritize backlogs, plan roadmaps and sync deliveries.

Agile Coach

The Agile Coach helps a whole function or organization enhance agility and generally has a broader mandate than a Scrum Master, who typically only focuses on a single team. The aim is to optimize Agile working methods, tools and capability development and strengthen Agile maturity over time. Such roles are commonly sourced as temporary contractors or consultants, often advising on organizational structure and capability.

AGILE COACH EXAMPLES

Nicki Somal (2023) is an experienced Agile HR coach and regularly works with L&D and people teams. For example, Somal currently coaches across an entire people function for one organization and mentors the Agile Champions who operate at the team level. Somal comments that this coaching group operates as a collective, ensuring a consistent approach across all the teams, and is an effective way to unearth impediments, which Somal raises at a functional level if unsolved at the team level.

Scrum Master or similar team-level coach

With its roots in the Scrum framework, a Scrum Master is considered the guardian of the Agile cycle. An alternative title is often used for teams that don't use Scrum, such as Agile Champion or Agile Expert. Working at a team level, the role aims to improve performance and delivery through continuous coaching and facilitation. This means they generally facilitate events such as team retrospectives and often wear multiple hats of coach, mentor, trainer and protector of the team. Within Agile, a Scrum Master is considered a servant leader to the team. To do this, they constantly unearth and remove impediments or blockers slowing the team down. They may also need to collaborate with the PO and multiple stakeholders to help the team move forward. A Scrum Master also aims to protect the team from outside disturbances, such as senior stakeholders asking for urgent requests or support with other projects.

SCRUM MASTER EXAMPLES

At TomTom, the teams prefer the term Agile Expert because they use a mixture of Agile tools and don't always follow the Scrum framework. In the Product Team, the Agile expert is again self-selected and generally sourced from a different sub-team to ensure objectivity and neutrality when facilitating rituals like a team retrospective. Another typical example within L&D and people teams is a temporary Scrum Master nominated from within the team to facilitate specific project sprints. It's worth noting that the Scrum framework argues that a Scrum Master shouldn't do any other project work. However, in nearly all the L&D and people team examples explored for this book, the Scrum Master role is a percentage of someone's time.

User experience (UX) researcher

A common role in other business teams, like product design, tech, customer experience and marketing, is an L&D or people UX researcher. They seek to understand the human experience of work and how people interact with the products and services that make up the employee lifecycle. They use a range of research tools such as interviews, usability testing, user journey mapping, personas, observation and focus groups. By observing and listening to users and collating data on user behaviour, needs and motivations, the UX researcher feeds crucial data into the design and personalization of the employee experience.

UX RESEARCHER EXAMPLES

Jodie Pritchard (2023), experienced Agile practitioner within L&D and former Head of Learning at Citizens Advice and now at Barnardo's children charity, argues that being user-led and human-centred is critical to any Agile delivery. Within a team of twenty, Citizens Advice has two UX researchers who lead all discovery work for any significant business challenge. However, in many other teams, a UX researcher is not a permanent role; people add this capability to their T-shape. Others will source skills temporarily.

Conclusion – five takeaways for L&D and people professionals

- T-shaped people in T-shaped teams represent an end to the siloed legacy existing within the L&D and people profession and help you deliver product-led impact.

- A T-shaped professional is a person with a breadth of general skills, as represented by the horizontal part of the T, combined with one or a few deep specialisms, as represented by the vertical part of the T.

- The T-shaped career framework offers an excellent foundation for building a skills-based approach to how organizations hire, deploy and develop capability.

- A T-shaped team is better equipped to tackle complex problems than a functional silo and operates as a multidisciplinary collective.

- New roles within these T-shaped teams include Product Owners or Product Managers, Agile Delivery Leads, People Portfolio Managers, Agile Coaches and UX researchers.

References

Bersin, Josh (2023) Redesigning HR: An operating system, not a model, https://joshbersin.com/2023/03/redesigning-hr-an-operating-system-not-an-operating-model/ (archived at https://perma.cc/F8VL-47TZ)

Bodell, Lisa (2020) Why T-shaped teams are the future of work, Forbes, 28 August, www.forbes.com/sites/lisabodell/2020/08/28/futurethink-forecasts-T-shaped-teams-are-the-future-of-work/ (archived at https://perma.cc/8T55-PE8Y)

Clifford, David (2019) Forget about T-shaped people. We need X-shaped people, TEDxChristchurch, TEDx Talks, 24 September, https://youtu.be/EezmRPE3fpQ (archived at https://perma.cc/F9LP-KPWM)

Designlab (2016) How to get hired: Understand if you're an I, T, or X-shaped person, Medium, 10 January, https://trydesignlab.medium.com/how-to-get-hired-understand-if-you-re-an-i-t-or-x-shaped-person-58f440f9a29 (archived at https://perma.cc/4JH8-J3SX)

Ford, Sarah (2023) Interview with Natal Dank, recorded 14 July

Gartner (2023) HR Operating model: Revolutionize HR and adapt to change, https://www.gartner.com/en/human-resources/topics/what-is-an-hr-operating-model (archived at https://perma.cc/8EYA-MVXC)

Keith, Laura (2023) Interview with Natal Dank, recorded 21 July

McGowan, Heather (2019) What if the future of work starts with high school?, Forbes, 3 April, www.forbes.com/sites/heathermcgowan/2019/04/03/what-if-the-future-of-work-starts-with-high-school/#2a52fb2c5964 (archived at https://perma.cc/KB8S-6QFS)

Perri, Melissa (2018) *Escaping the Build Trap: How effective product management creates real value*, O'Reilly Media Inc, Sebastopol, CA

Poppendieck, M. and Poppendieck,T. (2006) *Implementing Lean Software Development: From concept to cash*, Addison-Wesley, Boston, MA

Pritchard, Jodie (2023) Interview with Natal Dank, recorded 20 July

Seals, Danny (2023) Interview with Natal Dank, recorded 26 June

Sheard, Sara (2023) Interview with Natal Dank, recorded 4 August

Somal, Nicki (2023) Interview with Natal Dank, recorded 19 July

Taleb, Nassim Nicholas (2012) *Antifragile: Things that gain from disorder*, Penguin Books, London

Van der Tang, Arne-Christian (2023) Interview with Natal Dank, recorded 14 July

Walker, Kate (2023) Interview with Natal Dank, recorded 6 July

Yipp, Jason (2018) Why T-shaped people?, Medium, 24 March, https://jchyip.medium.com/why-T-shaped-people-e8706198e437 (archived at https://perma.cc/U5HF-69C6)

10

Principle 4: Experimentation

What's the difference between an experiment and a pilot? The answer is based on whether you can fail or not.

The concept of failing fast to learn quickly underpins Agile experimentation. However, for many L&D and people professionals, just mentioning the word *failure* seems to invoke panic. This fear of failure is not uncommon in the business world, where there is a preference for things to be predictable and controlled. With this comes a reluctance to experiment unless people can be certain of the result, which by definition means it's not an experiment. Too often, I come across L&D and people teams embarking on an experiment to prove their hypothesis is right, rather than readying themselves to simply observe and learn from the results. When experimenting, it's often the data you don't expect or the people who choose not to use the product or participate in the programme that you learn the most from.

As humans, we experiment constantly throughout life. As children, we learn to walk through trial and error. As a young adult, I enrolled in university, hypothesizing that I would be a good economist, only to discover a preference for people over numbers and instead finding myself a career in human resources. In a complex adaptive system, the only option is to experiment (Heffernan, 2020). When faced with myriad possibilities and constantly changing circumstances, the only way to move forward is through an emergent test-and-learn process. By experimenting, you gather data, which gives you the confidence to take the next step. Even if the experiment results in the exact opposite of what you first assumed, you've still learnt something and at least now understand not to continue in that direction. As expressed by Tracey Waters (2023), well known HR Agilist featured in this chapter, experimentation is asking yourself, '*What is the lowest cost, lowest effort, first step I can make that gives me confidence I'm going in the right direction?*'

Some might argue that the social and organizational experimentation required in L&D and OD topics is more challenging when compared with testing something like a digital app or a new range of ice cream. However, it is because of this very complexity that it's just as vital to experiment in the workplace as it is with commercial products. This is because it's only through experimentation that you can rise above opinion and hearsay and confidently recommend organizational change.

Experimentation versus pilots

The fear of failure probably goes some way to explain why many L&D and people teams have favoured pilots over experimentation in the past. Perhaps there is a misunderstanding that experimentation is the riskier approach. The problem is that if the pilot is the first time a customer experiences the product, it will fail nearly every time. This is because pilots usually involve trialling something fully formed, like a new learning programme or a piece of workplace tech. In these examples, the pilot is launched into the business for, say, three to six months and then assessed. Generally, to get to this point, a substantial amount of money, time and energy, not to mention much influencing of senior stakeholders, has already been invested. So much so that it's now costly and, let's be honest, embarrassing if it fails. So, you don't let it. It becomes important to save face or make the most of the investment. To rescue the situation perhaps the learning programme is tweaked and rebranded, or a communication campaign is launched to sell the benefits of the workplace tech. At times, desperation to make the new product work can even lead to some L&D and people teams to embark on a culture change initiative aimed at evolving people's learning mindset, rather than admit defeat.

Pilots are not inherently wrong, and can be hugely successful, but they should only ever follow a period of rapid prototyping and experimentation. So, while a pilot aims to demonstrate and validate an MVP (minimal viable product; see Chapter 4 for more detail) in the real world, an experiment is how you develop the MVP in the first place. As such, a pilot tends to be longer in duration and more static, and will require more resources when compared with an experiment.

FIGURE 10.1 Prototype and test stages of design thinking sequence

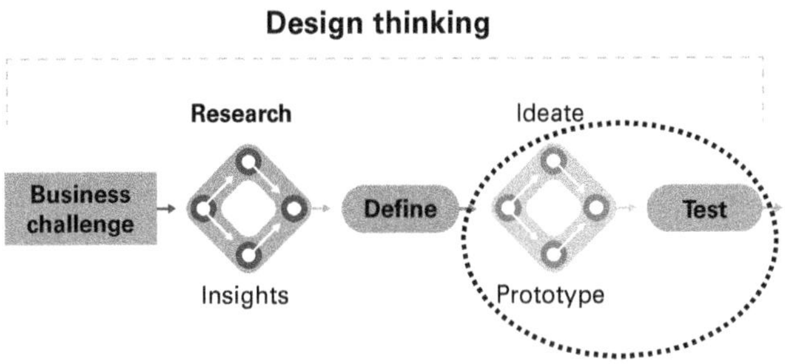

Experimentation combines the prototype and test stages of design thinking (see Figure 10.1) and can be over in a couple of minutes or last for several months. The aim is to quickly and cheaply test whether your hunch proves correct. It's essentially a low-risk form of learning where you test a proof of concept and a hypothesis. Experimentation can be as simple as sketching a few ideas on a blank piece of paper and asking five people what they think or as elaborate as setting up a UX lab to observe users engaging with a product simulation. Either way, you should be able to fail quickly without it costing too much or feeling too embarrassed.

When interviewing Tracey Waters (2023) for this book, she likened a workplace experiment to what we used to do in Year 10 science. So, let's put on our lab coats and explore how to build, run and evaluate an Agile L&D or OD experiment.

How to build an L&D or OD experiment

It's best to keep an experiment simple and not overcomplicate it with too many variables. The main thing is being clear on what you're actually testing. This might sound obvious, but it's a common area where L&D and people teams get confused. It's easy to fall into the trap of thinking your experiment is testing the whole solution you have in mind. Instead, what you're doing at the experiment stage is testing the hypothesis and assumptions on which your solution rests. The testing of the actual solution comes later. Let's explore an example to understand this further.

Let's say you've been researching a business challenge linked to career development. Following a series of interviews, people data analysis and external research, you've discovered that a key problem to solve is making internal career moves easier to apply for and more visible. You've also discovered that increasing internal hires directly impacts the business bottom line. Internal candidates are hired at a faster rate, perform better in the role and are more likely to stay. This leads to some ideation exercises (see Chapter 8 for more detail) and prototyping, where several possible solutions are explored by sketching out ideas on paper and asking people facing the problem for feedback. From this exercise, a central idea forms around creating an internal job marketplace website, which invites people to connect their LinkedIn profiles and have internal career moves recommended to them. You've even found a possible vendor. The whole thing sounds great, but how can you quickly test it without needing to buy the website or embark on a long procurement process first? Let's take a look.

An experiment is made up of the following elements:

a   **Aim** – the overall purpose of the experiment.

b   **Assumption** – the supposition you're exploring through the experiment.

c   **Hypothesis** – what are you testing and what do you think will happen as a result? For example, if you do X, then Y per cent of users will do Z.

d   **Method** – step by step outline of the experiment, including duration, resources, variables and people involved.

e   **Measurement** – what data needs to be collected and assessed in the experiment to determine the result?

f   **Post-experiment recommendations** – what are the recommended next steps based on the outcome, the data collected and insights learnt?

Now, let's return to our career development example from earlier (see Figure 10.2).

In this example, the experiment first needs to test whether people want to use an internal job marketplace website. It's not the website itself that we're testing at this stage. It's whether the potential functionality of the website is appealing and helps people solve the problem identified. At this point, we're not testing the hypothesis that the website makes finding and applying for internal jobs easier and therefore increases the rate of internal hires. Instead, we're simply testing whether people want to use the website. If they don't or are hesitant to use some of the functionality, such as connecting their LinkedIn profile, then the idea won't be worth pursuing any further.

FIGURE 10.2 Experiment canvas

Experiment name Give your experiment concept a name	
Hypothesis What are you testing and what do you think will happen as a result? For example, if you do X, then 10% of users will do Y.	
Design your experiment Outline your low-risk, low-cost experiment to test your assumption and measure the behaviour of real users. No surveys!	
Success metric What data needs to be collected and assessed in the experiment to determine the result?	

To do this, the team decide to run an experiment using cardboard cutouts of fake website landing pages. They've named the experiment 'Career Compass' (see Figure 10.3). The steps were as follows:

a **Aim** – test whether a selection of users find the prospect of an internal job marketplace website appealing and valuable.

b **Assumption** – based on the assumption that an internal job marketplace website will facilitate internal career moves and improve career development perceptions.

c **Hypothesis** – the team formulated three hypotheses to test:

  o People want to link their LinkedIn profile to an internal job marketplace website.

  o People will be delighted by personalized job recommendations from the internal job marketplace website.

  o People will click on a recommended role.

FIGURE 10.3 Experiment canvas with example

Experiment name Give your experiment concept a name	Career Compass
Hypothesis What are you testing and what do you think will happen as a result? For example, if you do X, then 10% of users will do Y.	1. People will want to link their LinkedIn profile to an internal company website 2. People will be delighted by personalized job recommendations provided by the internal company website 3. People will click on a recommended role
Design your experiment Outline your low-risk, low-cost experiment to test your assumption and measure the behaviour of real users. No surveys!	How? By asking employees to experience a mockup ON CARDBOARD of the website, which is made up of a landing page plus five 'click through' pages 1. Sit with test employee 2. Send them a 'sign up email' 3. If they click, show mock landing page 4. If they click on 'create a profile', show next mockup with LinkedIn link 5. If they click on 'link your profile', show next mockup with recommendations 6. If they click on 'recommended for you', show next mockup 7. If they click on one of the recommendations, STOP.
Success metric What data needs to be collected and assessed in the experiment to determine the result?	1. Observed user behaviour of test employees (number of clicks) 2. Quotes and words said by test employees during experiment 3. 'Intent to use' rating (1–10)

d Method:

   o Twenty-five employees are invited to experience a mockup of the website on cardboard, comprising a landing page plus five click-through pages.

   o The employees represent a target group selected from parts of the business where the career development issue is most pronounced or falls within the tenure of one to three years, which is when most people leave.

   o The group also aims to test for some diversity and include females, people with disabilities, different ethnic backgrounds and sexual identities (note, with such experiments, you might need to target specific groups, for example what the experience is like for neurodiverse people).

- o The experiment steps are:
    - i.   Sit with the test employee
    - ii. Send them a fake 'sign up email'
    - iii. If they click, show the mock landing page (on cardboard)
    - iv. If they click on 'create a profile', show the next mockup page with the link to connect their LinkedIn profile
    - v.   If they click on 'link your profile', show the next mockup page of the profile and a link to recommended jobs
    - vi. If they click on 'recommended for you', show the next mockup page of a series of recommended jobs
    - vii. If they click on one of the recommendations, STOP.

e   Measurement:

- o Observed user behaviour of test employees (how many fake clicks)
- o 'Talking out loud' behaviour
- o Intent to use rating (1 to 10)

f   Post-experiment recommendations:

- o Recommended to move to the next phase of product development and testing based on an overall intent to use rating of 8 (out of 10) plus 80 per cent of test employees choosing to connect their LinkedIn profile and select a recommended role (note, we've assumed a favourable outcome here for illustration purposes).
- o The next phase is to negotiate a thousand licences to test the job marketplace website for a period of three months, again for a specific target audience.
- o During this time, you'll evaluate user behaviour but also whether people applied and succeeded in an internal career move.
- o Also, remember, you're just as interested in the people that don't apply or succeed in a new role as the ones that do.

How to write a hypothesis

A dictionary definition of a hypothesis is: '*An idea or explanation of something that is based on a few known facts but that has not yet been proved to be true or correct.*' (Oxford Learner's Dictionaries, 2023.)

A hypothesis is your hunch or best 'educated' guess based on anecdotal evidence that has been made specific and can be tested. For example, you often hear statements like, '*Hybrid working isn't productive – everyone needs to come back into the office five days a week.*' However, without any meaningful data, a statement like this is only ever an opinion that, in this case, has also dangerously assumed the solution. So, what if we wanted to test this assumption and perhaps even challenge the statement?

Let's start with the assumption:

Assumption: Hybrid working isn't productive.

Now we need to translate this into a testable hypothesis. To help, it's useful to write several different versions and gather feedback on whether your hypothesis accurately describes what you want to test. Doing some initial research also helps. You can then write the hypothesis as a prediction or a question. For example:

Hypothesis example A: Performance indicators X will decrease for a hybrid working team over Y period compared with a full-time office working team.

Hypothesis example B: What is the impact on performance indicators X when a team works hybrid over Y period?

It's good to understand variables when writing a hypothesis. An independent variable is what you change or vary in the experiment, whereas the dependent variable is what you observe or measure. In the hypothesis here, the independent variable is the hybrid working team. You'll compare a hybrid working team (as defined by your organization, for example two days in the office and three days working from home) to full-time office working teams. The dependent variables are the performance indicators. We expect these to go down, up or remain stable. Of course, in this example, you'll need to select appropriate performance indicators, which will either reflect the type of work the teams do or data already being recorded. These might include service delivery times, performance ratings, customer net promoter scores (NPS), absenteeism, sales, logged hours, or self-rated productivity scores. You'll also need to establish a baseline reflecting the standard performance expected for office-based teams.

There must also be control elements that are not directly related to the study and remain constant in order to accurately assess the variables being tested. In this example, it's important to compare two teams over the same length of time (Y). Other controls include the type of work the teams do, the location and the team size.

Now, let's consider how we can test this hypothesis. First, once you have a hypothesis, it becomes much easier to conduct research. For example, you could compare any existing performance data collected for known hybrid working teams with data for teams fully office-based. You might also be able to access external studies, which provide incredibly helpful examples and data to reference.

Next, you can set up an experiment by inviting a team or department to use hybrid working methods for a specific period and compare the outcomes with those of a control group who continued to work in the office unchanged.

CASE STUDY
Executive leadership development experiment

Tracey Waters (2023) is a world-leading HR and L&D Agilist. Former People Experience Director at Sky UK, Waters now heads up Leadership and Talent at a large Australian bank. One of the first initiatives she was asked to focus on when starting in her recent role was the strategic development of senior leaders. Immediately, Waters saw a dilemma. If they followed the traditional design for senior leadership programmes, they would end up with a three-day offsite hosted by a prestigious business school, which would be costly and out of step with the organization's more modern, digital and global focus. Second, if approached from a topic perspective, it could end up too generic and focused only on strategy. Conversely, if made more specific, might only suit certain leaders from either the revenue-generating side of the business or corporate functions.

Wanting to approach the design from a different angle, Waters and her team started by prototyping various ideas on pen and paper. They then pitched these programme ideas to fifteen different leaders. What they extracted from this exercise was a core framework and, crucially, a set of design principles that would become the basis of their programme design and experiment. For example, they discovered that status and pride were important and that the leaders wanted to learn from internationally recognized experts. From these insights, Waters and the team landed on the *four Cs – Content, Coaching, Connection and Context*. These design principles then guided how they formulated their experiment and tracked results against five hypotheses.

Content – knowing that it wasn't feasible to fly people around the world to attend expert sessions, the team sought a more agile and flexible source of learning content. They also knew that if the experiment was successful, they wanted to scale the solution, so learning content couldn't be based on a twelve-month programme that only twenty people could attend in any one year. This led the team to some UX testing of two aggregated learning platforms that provided online learning experiences by partnering with the top business schools. Interestingly, they selected the platform that had the better user experience despite having less content. The programme then ran as a six-week learning sprint, with the team closely tracking user behaviour and comparing these results with expected completion rates. The hypothesis was that people will want to learn from experts they perceive as world leading.

Coaching and Connection – these design principles are a recognition that online learning is lonely. Waters reflects that this was her most significant learning from her early days testing out Agile, when everyone would say, 'Oh, let's just give everyone a licence, and they can choose their own adventure, and it's all on demand.' But by going digital first, they had forgotten the human element. 'People want to feel like they're part of a group; they're social. They want to feel like they're being stretched, but also that they know what they can improve.' So, this experiment tested if it was possible to design something that brought the best of both worlds but with a lower cost and lower resource requirement. The design included coaching circles to harness peer-to-peer networking and learning accountability to capture these elements. The hypothesis was that people value the ability to network and seek coaching to hold them accountable and develop through personal feedback.

Context – the team involved the Group Strategy Executive Director to meet the final design principle. This leader provided the upfront framing of why the programme mattered and how to approach it. They also assessed the results of each learner's strategic projects as part of the programme. As Waters states, this aspect gave the programme business credibility and legitimacy. There was also a danger that because it was based on a public online programme, other participants might not hold as senior a position as the bank's learners. As a result, Waters' team were particular with the provider to ensure their learners were partnered with leaders that operated at a similar senior level at other organizations. To give an element of authorship, participants selected from two programmes and selected the business challenge to solve. When it comes to context, the hypothesis to test was whether the project solves a real problem. Ultimately, the participants needed to feel that there was a direct return for the time invested. The second test was whether the Group Strategy Executive Director felts the quality of the project was aligned with the business strategy and that it added value.

On top of these design principles, the team also tested whether participants recommend the programme to others. The first experiment started with nine leaders, and the results were so promising that they immediately set up a second experiment to test that it wasn't just a one-off. Providing the results remained favourable, the team aimed to run at least three more experiments over a year, hosting ten leaders at a time. Waters points out that you need to be ready to scale up your experiments and overall solution by making the preparations in parallel. As such, the team are working through various checks linked to procurement, tech, finance, data, privacy and information security to ensure no delay in launching as soon as they are confident enough to run more programmes.

CASE STUDY
The F word – an experiment in workplace flexibility

Tombola is something of a local success story in the north of England town of Sunderland. Beginning with fourteen people in 2016, the business now has over 800 people and with offices in nine different countries. Many attribute the successful business model to Tombola's online emulation of the bingo hall community so many bingo players seek.

Amanda Bellwood (2023) joined Tombola as their People Director in September 2022, following over six years of leading one of the first Agile people teams in the UK at another popular tech-gaming company. Soon after joining, Bellwood and her team introduced an employee listening platform to track feedback data through regular pulse checks. From the start, the data highlighted workplace flexibility as a critical topic. Also, considering the company had a relatively fixed view of what constituted workplace flexibility, the team thought it was worth further investigation.

Reflecting its Sunderland legacy, Tombola was centred around a fun and innovative head office building where employees enjoyed free meals and regular social activities. All employees were expected to work the core hours of 10am to 4pm, but teams could decide on their own exact start and end times. Also, following the pandemic, the whole company embraced a fixed hybrid policy of three days in the office and two days working at home.

Over time, however, it became apparent that the company needed to consider sourcing talent from beyond the standard commuter journey to grow and scale further. Bellwood and her team also discovered that employee experiences were different and inconsistent despite the fixed hybrid policy. For example, customer service teams outside the UK worked fully remotely; for other teams, flexibility was often at managers' discretion. It was clear that they needed gain a better understanding of what flexibility meant to existing employees and if any future candidates might see a lack of workplace flexibility as a blocker to joining Tombola.

Bellwood shares that at the start of this project, she naively assumed that, providing that the team undertook a good amount of research and discovery work, they would come up with the perfect answer. Bellwood thought, 'We'll get our data, we'll then solve this problem, and we'll fix it, and this is what that fix looks like.' So, after announcing to the company a focus on flexibility, the team talked to over eighty people through a series of focus groups, alongside further pulse surveys and an outside-in perspective on their EVP (employee value proposition) from external talent. Yet, like many complex workplace topics, this research failed to unearth any clear fix or one-size-fits-all solution. 'So, it made us then really think, what the hell now? We've got all this insight, and we've not found the answer. How are we going to solve for it?'

The team discovered that workplace flexibility is personal and linked to choices people have about where and when they work. Trust was another strong theme. People wanted to be trusted to manage their own time and be valued on output, not hours worked. Fairness was also important. This meant that a blanket policy for the whole organization wasn't always fair because of the different types of work people did. For example, granting more flexibility to office-based teams didn't help people already working fully remotely, and some teams, like Facilities, didn't have a choice but to work in the office.

Off the back of these findings, the team was fully transparent and shared with the whole organization about both the outcomes of the research and the fact that there was no single definite fix. The team then launched the *F word* (flexibility) campaign with the aim of experimenting at the local team level to see if it was possible to create solutions that were relevant to specific locations or functions.

The first experiment was with Tombola's Spanish office, where people followed the three days in the office rule in line with the Sunderland headquarters. However, for the Spanish location, the average commute was lengthy, and the cost of travel was relatively expensive. Also, because people could decide which three days they worked in the office, sometimes people would travel in to find only a few other people there. This led to a hypothesis that people would be more satisfied if the choice of which days they came into the office was removed, but could spend fewer days in the office overall. So, as a collective team, the Spanish office agreed that they would all come into the office on Tuesdays and Wednesdays, with the option to work at home on the other days. A baseline measurement using pulse survey data was taken, and the experiment ran for three months. The outcome was a significant improvement on all the targeted flexibility survey questions and an endorsement across the Spanish office to make the new policy a permanent change.

The success of this approach has led to other locations and functions wanting to run their own experiments. To help, Bellwood and her team have set up a toolkit to guide local-level discussions. Then if a group wants to experiment, the people team helps to manage the overall approach, work out what hypothesis to test and specify how the data will be tracked. Based on the outcome, a collective decision is made on which, if any, changes should become permanent.

A few things to watch out for

As mentioned earlier in this chapter, it's common for people teams to set out to prove a hypothesis correct rather than being open to a range of results, including it being wrong or inconclusive. Danny Seals (2023a), founder of Knot, an employee experience design and innovation consultancy, and Vice President, Employee Innovation, Listening and Effectiveness at RAKBANK, discusses the dangers of bias influencing your experiment outcomes. The most obvious is confirmation bias, where you filter out the data that challenges your assumption and proves you wrong. Other biases to watch out for include sampling bias, where we fail to test with a fair and diverse representational group, and performance bias, where people perform better during the experiment compared with normal because they feel special and singled out. When interviewing Seals for this book, he stressed the importance of measuring experiments beyond your own silo (Seals, 2023b). For this reason, he advocates the EXO measurements (employee experience data plus operational and business data) we'll look at in Chapter 11 when exploring how to deliver with impact. For every experiment, it's important to include both employee experience metrics, such as user behaviour and feedback, alongside operational metrics, like sales, retention or service delivery levels. Seals also suggests setting up a 'chain of custody' (2023c) when recording experiments. This acts as a central repository where all the experiments across the organization are tracked and monitored. While this can be as basic as an Excel spreadsheet or Kanban board, it ensures good governance and helps you keep track of the cost and value of each experiment.

Another danger to be wary of is confusing the difference between causation and correlation. Causation is based on cause and effect, and the two variables have a clear relationship. For example, an experiment where one sales team is given an online coach and another team doing the exact same job continues to operate as usual results in higher sales for the team with the online coach. Correlation, however, describes a relationship between two variables and does not automatically imply that a change in one variable will cause a change in the other variable (Australia Bureau of Statistics,

2023). For example, you might launch a new learning management system and, simultaneously, see an improvement in job satisfaction feedback as recorded through a regular engagement survey. At this stage, this is simply a correlation, and other factors may have influenced the engagement result, such as it being summer, and people feel more relaxed and refreshed from having a holiday. In this example, you would need to run a controlled experiment to understand any direct cause and effect.

Finally, L&D and people teams often ask me how to influence and gain buy-in from other business teams or senior leaders to run workplace experiments. This point links back to the preference for certainty in the business world. The key is using a language of risk management and emphasizing the potential sunken cost if you undertake a project that fails and which wasn't first validated through data and other evidence. I've also found that just by using the term *experiment* and co-creating the hypothesis to test with business leaders, you get greater permission to play. You appear more credible and commercially aware when people see that you're serious about experimentation and ready to base decisions on the outcomes rather than just your opinion and recommendation.

Conclusion – five takeaways for L&D and people professionals

- An experiment is not a pilot; to quickly test a hypothesis, you must be able to cheaply and safely fail.
- A hypothesis is your hunch or best 'educated' guess based on anecdotal evidence that has been made specific and can be tested.
- A workplace experiment is similar to what you did in Year 10 science and is relatively easy once you get the hang of it.
- Don't test for your whole solution immediately; instead, set up an experiment to test the hypothesis and assumptions on which your solution rests.
- Watch out for bias influencing your experiment outcomes.

References

Australia Bureau of Statistics (2023) Correlation and causation, www.abs.gov.au/statistics/understanding-statistics/statistical-terms-and-concepts/correlation-and-causation (archived at https://perma.cc/PTM7-XDEJ)

Bellwood, Amanda (2023) Interview with Natal Dank, recorded 24 July
Heffernan, Margaret (2020) *Uncharted: How uncertainty can power change*,
    Simon & Schuster, London
Oxford Learner's Dictionaries (2023), Oxford University Press,
    www.oxfordlearnersdictionaries.com (archived at https://perma.cc/7AJY-EMJE)
Seals, Danny (2023a) Let's Talk Experimentation 101, updated 3 July 2023,
    www.weareknot.co.uk/post/lets-talk-experimentation-101 (archived at https://
    perma.cc/J4NE-FCJB)
Seals, Danny (2023b) Interview with Natal Dank, recorded 26 June
Seals, Danny (2023c) Merchant of Death, 3 August, www.weareknot.co.uk/post/
    merchant-of-death (archived at https://perma.cc/V8AG-2SBW)
Waters, Tracey (2023) Interview with Natal Dank, recorded 26 July

11

Principle 5: Deliver with impact

'We can't be all things to all people all of the time,' states Nebel Crowhurst (2023), Chief People Officer at Reward Gateway, former People and Culture Director at Roche and Head of People Experience at River Island. 'There's only so much time, resources and budget. What you want to do is deliver the things that are going to have the biggest impact on the most people and make the most difference to the organizational performance and to individuals in the business.' These are wise words from Crowhurst, a long-time Agile HR collaborator and interviewee for the book. 'Then what you need to consider is how you continuously monitor that, when you're delivering a product or an initiative or a solution, that you've got the mechanism in place to have the continuous feedback loop to know that what you're delivering still has impact' (Crowhurst, 2023).

When I asked Jodie Pritchard, former Head of Learning at the large UK charity Citizens Advice and now Director of L&D at the children's charity Barnardo's, to define Agile, she replied, 'in a nutshell, delivering with impact' (2023). Pritchard adds that several factors drive this outcome, but ultimately, it's how you combine them to deliver impact across the organization. Of particular importance for Pritchard is the Agile pursuit of continuous improvement, a way of working that keeps you current, or even ahead of the curve and ensures your products don't just sit on the shelf gathering dust (Pritchard, 2023).

Laura Keith, CEO of Hive Learning, a genAI-powered skills and collaborative learning platform, describes Agile as a quest for 'marginal gains' (2023). 'Not trying to solve something upfront but putting something out into play that's 60 per cent, 70 per cent done, and then looking at increasing marginal gains to make it better as you go.' Hive aims to build product value gradually and sustainably for customers through an evidence-based test and learn cycle. For Keith, this continuous pursuit for marginal gains is how an

Agile business successfully rides the S curve. Instead of stalling at the predicted plateau, momentum and growth are maintained through a willingness to keep innovating, testing and learning as a business (Keith, 2023). The ability to deliver with impact operates on multiple levels – a mindset, a product-led model, a team effectiveness framework, and a way of running a business.

Delivering with impact is the fifth principle in the Agile L&D playbook. It's also the final principle because it requires a combination of all the practices and tools explored in this book. You can't deliver with impact only by designing and launching new products. Instead, the impact is understood by tracking over time whether the product is fixing the problem you've set out to solve. You also won't deliver with impact if you're only measuring results at the end of an L&D programme or OD project. Rather, measurement needs to be a continuous feedback loop of data reflecting the same cadence as the Agile cycle. Therefore, to deliver with impact is to become data-obsessed in the ongoing pursuit of marginal gains. Moreover, if successful, you should achieve an effective, sustainable and continuous flow of value throughout the organization.

To help you put it all together and deliver with impact, this chapter starts with prioritization and how value guides your L&D or people strategy. We'll then look at different ways to measure and track the impact your strategy and its various initiatives have on business performance. As mentioned in Chapter 7, a lot of traditional L&D and people strategy focuses on output rather than outcomes. Such strategy is often just a wish list of topics such as talent management and leadership development that are measured through things like content, programmes, processes and surveys. But these lists only capture activity and deliveries planned. What you want to know is what happened as a result. What has been the impact on business performance? Did you solve the problem? And, because of this, what value was created? Only by understanding the outcome do we know if the activity and output were worth the effort.

How value guides L&D and people strategy

Too often, strategy is made out to be an elusive, highly specialized activity reserved only for top senior leaders. As a result, it's generally based around a glorified strategy offsite or a significant piece of documentation that stops everyone else from moving forward until it's agreed. Yet, as expressed by Felix Oberholzer-Gee (author of *Better, Simpler Strategy*), it's nonsense that strategy is a mysterious, complicated thing that only really senior people can do. 'Strategy is simple. It's a plan to create value' (Harvard Business Review, 2022a).

I often coach teams who despair that they don't have a strategy yet and are just treading water while they await the direction of play. It is an all-too-common scenario when strategy is misunderstood as an annual activity only reserved for an exclusive few. This type of approach also means strategy falls prey to a build-and-forget mentality. In these situations, a huge amount of time is dedicated to crafting a beautiful strategy one-pager, only for the objectives to be forgotten as the day job takes over. Unfortunately, this dilemma even leads to some teams feeling too busy just getting stuff done to even set a strategy in the first place.

Strategy also doesn't start with profit or financials. These are the end points, the consequences and outcomes of your strategy. As explained by Oberholzer-Gee, strategy looks forward and begins with a sense of how much value you create and how to build more (Harvard Business Review, 2022a). The same is true with L&D and people strategy. It doesn't start with listing employee engagement scores. Instead, it begins with understanding why the engagement scores are the way they are and how to make people's working lives easier to positively impact the employee engagement scores.

In this sense, value can be measured by what an organization can offer a person versus what they are looking for in a job, plus the total reward they are happy to receive (Harvard Business Review, 2022a). Yes, organizations can always pay more to attract great talent, but this doesn't mean people will stay if a higher salary is offered elsewhere. Increasing pay also eats into an organization's profit margin, ultimately decreasing the overall value realized by the business. Additionally, just increasing pay is easy for your competition to replicate. Rather, value is created when you can attract great talent with a delightful employee experience without the need to pay more. Now, at this point, it's good to note that I'm not advocating a low-pay framework. Salary and benefits should always be competitive and ideally in the higher percentiles where possible. Instead, it articulates how value forms the basis of L&D and people strategy and why it's also a vital component of any overriding business strategy.

It's also important to differentiate strategy from planning. As explained by Roger Martin, former dean of the Rotman School of Management at the

University of Toronto: 'there is no such thing as strategic planning' (Harvard Business Review, 2022b). A plan is a list of things you intend to do, whereas strategy has a theory. It's a theory that explains why you've made a set of integrated choices and how you will win on a playing field of your choice. Interestingly, as highlighted by Martin, with strategy comes vulnerability and angst (Harvard Business Review, 2022b). When planning and listing intended deliveries, you feel in control and comfortable. But with strategy, there is no guarantee that it will work. Strategy can't be perfect. All you can do is set out your theory and then iterate and evolve the strategy as you go.

Perhaps this sense of vulnerability leads many L&D and people teams to confuse strategy with a list of things they intend to deliver. See Figure 11.1 as an example of a familiar people strategy one-pager shaped as a house and a list of solutions to be provided. Strategy presented as a list of topics or solutions doesn't set out your theory of why you should deliver these things, how you will do it and what the impact on business performance will be. However, it is not just L&D and people professionals who fall into this trap. When you ask executive leaders like the CEO what the business issues are, they often say something like 'talent management'. Yet, talent management isn't an

FIGURE 11.1 Traditional L&D and people strategy

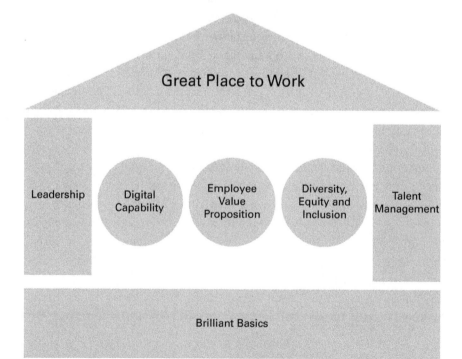

organizational issue; it's a solution. To build a strategy, you need to under-stand the problem with talent management. What do you need to solve exactly?

The other common trap is creating an overly ambitious strategy that tries to cover far too much. While you might start with an extensive wish list, you need to break this wish list down into manageable chunks based on the most critical problems to solve. You're aiming for a ruthlessly prioritized road-map of value creation: a roadmap that is easily linked to the overarching business strategy and the most pressing organizational issues.

Some readers might wrongly assume this section isn't for them. However, no matter your position or role, understanding how to craft and contribute to strategy execution is a vital capability. As an L&D consultant, you'll need to identify critical issues to solve either within an organization or for the business unit you represent. As an OD or HR business partner, you'll need to prioritize and agree on a strategy with your business stakeholders. As an L&D adviser or designer, you'll need to align your contribution to a team or functional strategy. While, as an L&D or people leader, you'll need to build a collective team vision around a motivating strategy. Ultimately, strategy is only as good as your ability to make it happen, and this execution of strat-egy is a team job. So, the steps and tools we'll explore in the next section apply to all readers.

L&D and people strategy

See Figure 11.2.

STEP 1: IDENTIFY

This step represents a regular diagnostic that seeks to understand the follow-ing four areas (see Figure 11.3):

1 **Business priorities and burning issues** – gained through ongoing conversations with other business leaders and teams, the overriding business strategy, financials and business performance metrics such as sales revenue, customer net promoter score and customer retention rates. Notably, this diagnostic includes regular conversations with other support functions like risk, legal and compliance.

   'I host a monthly drop-in for managers across the business to just chat to me. I find that very useful because it gives me a temperature check of what's going on. And I also use that as a forum to ask them questions, to gauge things and for them to ask me things. I just call it What's Brewing.' (Nebel Crowhurst, 2023, Chief People Officer at Reward Gateway)

FIGURE 11.2 How value guides L&D and people strategy

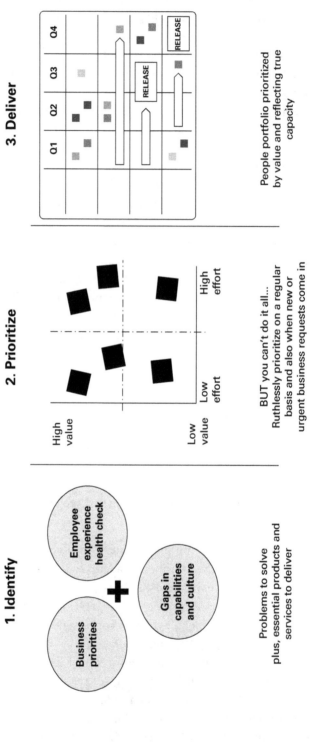

1. Identify

Business priorities

+

Employee experience health check

Gaps in capabilities and culture

Problems to solve plus, essential products and services to deliver

2. Prioritize

High value

Low value

Low effort   High effort

BUT you can't do it all...
Ruthlessly prioritize on a regular basis and also when new or urgent business requests come in

3. Deliver

	Q1	Q2	Q3	Q4

RELEASE

RELEASE

People portfolio prioritized by value and reflecting true capacity

2 **Employee experience health check** – assessed by tracking people data, ideally linked to an employee experience dashboard or journey map. The aim is to continuously monitor essential moments and key touchpoints throughout the employee experience cycle. Metrics might include pulse survey results, internal hires and retention. The objective is to gather insight on what's performing well versus what's bubbling up and becoming a pain point.

'Your engagement survey gives you a bit of an idea of what's going on, but that's only valuable if you are genuinely using the principles of pulse and constantly delving in. You should be utilizing the information that you're getting from your stakeholders. You should be using business analytics and business information. How is the business performing, and what does that tell you about what you need to adapt?' (Nebel Crowhurst, 2023, Chief People Officer at Reward Gateway)

3 **Gaps in culture and capability** – once you've reviewed business priorities and employee experience data, assess the organizational culture and capability required to respond.

'We describe ourselves as the pioneers of the HR function. So, taking inputs from HR, employees, or even other functions, like IT, marketing, etc, and then also potentially things externally. So, look at key trends, whether technology or social trends and use that outside-in mindset.' (Sarah Ford, 2023, Head of HR Innovation at Diageo)

4 **Problems to solve and products and services to deliver** – based on the first three steps, list the significant problems to solve alongside any employee experience processes or products you might need to innovate or change. You also need to list existing products and services that will continue. Assessing what needs to be maintained versus killed off or innovated is a crucial discussion that influences effort and capacity. The aim is to clarify how much of your expected strategy is already covered by existing deliveries versus how much of the strategy requires new stuff and, therefore, additional effort. At this stage, make this one big wish list. Prioritization comes next.

'This is where we should be utilizing data and insights from a variety of angles. That comes from employee voice, that comes from stakeholder viewpoints, that comes from our own expertise as HR people. It also comes from external perspectives and the latest trends. You need a variety of insights and perspectives to inform how you prioritize what you're going to deliver.' (Nebel Crowhurst, 2023, Chief People Officer at Reward Gateway)

FIGURE 11.3 Step 1: Identify

Business priorities and burning issues	Employee experience health check	Gaps in culture and capability		Problems to solve and essential products and services

FIGURE 11.4 People identification example strategy

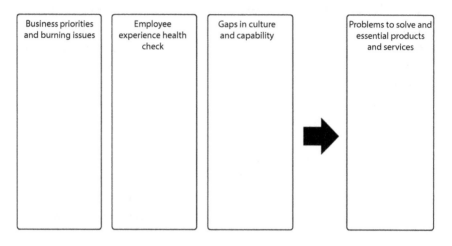

Business priorities and burning issues	**Employee experience health check**	**Gaps in culture and capability**		**Problems to solve and essential products and services**
Business challenge: Five critical roles have been vacant in technology for three months. Unable to source candidates with the right digital capability. Metric: Critical role unfilled >30 days.	Business challenge: A significantly high proportion of people are leaving within the first two years. Metric: Nearly 80% of new hires are external, with 55% leaving within the first two years.	Not seen as a tech company but need digital capability. Perceived lack of career development within organization.		Problem (Project): How might we develop and source new digital capability, starting with skills in genAI? Problem (Project): How might we improve career development opportunities to retain more people? Essential service (BAU): Track feedback through pulse engagement survey.

A good approach is to undertake this identification step every quarter and iterate the strategy if needed (see Figure 11.4). Next, align your quarterly iterations with monthly check-ins to capture any new burning issues demanding a more immediate response. Of course, at times, something might be so urgent that you'll need to assess it within a matter of hours or days, but generally, these are exceptions (and won't necessarily require a whole team or cross-functional response). While strategy should continuously evolve and respond, most elements will remain stable from month to month. As such, strategy is more about regularly tweaking different aspects rather than reinventing the whole document each time.

STEP 2: PRIORITIZE

You can't do it all in today's complex and ever-changing world, nor should you try. Prioritization is one of the most important skills an L&D and people professional can develop. A lot of self-discipline is required to successfully prioritize your wish list and remain committed to your choices in the face of ongoing business demands. What makes prioritization extra tricky is that it's a team action. While it's relatively easy to prioritize your own wish list, once it involves collective effort, dependencies and trade-offs within a team or function, the task becomes much more complicated.

I focus a lot of coaching time towards helping L&D and people teams build an effective prioritization method linked to an ongoing Agile cycle of *plan, do, review, adapt*. One of the biggest challenges is helping teams visualize and, thus, prioritize all work. Most teams happily spend time prioritizing new projects, often termed strategic work. But this is only half the story. It's crucial to understand your spare capacity after you've delivered existing BAU processes. Only by combining the two can you hope to achieve prioritization nirvana and successfully agree on a realistic, sustainable rhythm of work.

Value versus effort   The value versus effort grid (see Figure 11.5) is one of the most effective ways to prioritize and agree on strategic commitments. However, you first need to define your value drivers to use the grid (see following points). Ensure the whole team agrees on how each value driver will be assessed before you start the prioritization exercise. Then, assess each new project against the list of value drivers by rating it high, medium or low. You can then assess the total value of each project. For example, a project might be deemed a high business priority, but if it's low in time criticality, impact level and potential risk, it might be possible to postpone, thus allowing you to focus on something rated higher across each value driver.

Value drivers

- Strategic business priority – this might link to company OKRs or specific goals in product innovation, market expansion or mergers and acquisitions.
- Time-critical business issue – is it a crisis, and you must act now? Is it deadline-driven?

FIGURE 11.5 Value versus effort grid

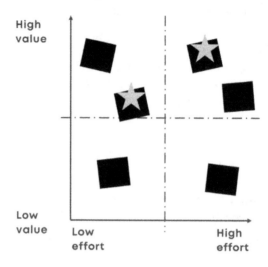

- Impact level – organizational reach or for a business-critical area.
- Risk – reputation, financial or legal. Most teams refer to criteria agreed upon by the risk management team or representative within the business.
- Employee experience – does the initiative link to an identified pain point or shared problem to solve in the employee lifecycle?

Effort criteria

- Dependent on other business functions.
- Time to complete (relative).
- Capabilities required and whether you have them in the team.
- Level of complexity.
- Constraints – tools available, budget required or any compliance restrictions.

TIP: VALUE AND EFFORT

Assess value first, then discuss the effort. It's important not to blur the two. Next, step back and explore where different projects have landed once you've placed several projects on the grid. Now, return to the effort discussion. Can you approach effort differently if you need to commit to several projects? For example, can you break the project into smaller chunks and focus on a few elements to begin with, thus requiring less initial effort? Or is it possible to run a highly focused time-boxed sprint to get a specific project done quickly before you move on to other projects that require longer time commitments? Remember, task switching slows people down. Aim for hyperfocus and explore how to get valuable things done by embracing novel working methods. And remember – you can't do it all. Be ruthless in your prioritization.

STEP 3: DELIVER

Now, it's all about delivery. Visualize your work and commit to an effective Agile cadence to help achieve this.

Visualize   Visualizing the work across a team or function at two levels is essential. The first is a portfolio view, which visualizes the big chunks of work or key deliveries across the team or function (see Figure 11.6). The second is more detailed backlogs for each big chunk of work or key deliveries, some of which may sit with different sub-teams who own the specific project or process (Figure 11.7). Many tools are available on the market today to help you – for example Product Board, Trello, Jira, Monday, Basecamp and so on. See Chapter 5 for more detail on visualization.

Cadence   I recommend that L&D and people teams or whole functions agree on a cadence that tracks the strategy and related portfolio rather than individual projects. What do I mean by this? Well, most L&D and people teams and nearly all functions cover multiple projects and BAU processes simultaneously. Each project and process usually has its own agreed cycle. For example, a career development project might have a two-week *plan, do, review, adapt* cycle. However, it's critical to help everyone in the team or function to appreciate the strategic big picture and coordination needs across the team or function. The goal is to monitor when and how different projects and BAU processes are being released across the organization. The best way to do this is to commit to a monthly cycle of *plan, do, review, adapt*. Now, depending upon the size of your team or function, it might be best to appoint specific roles to coordinate different stages of the cycle so you don't burden groups with too many meetings. For example, you might appoint an Agile delivery lead or portfolio manager to oversee much of the coordination (see Chapter 9, T-shaped people in T-shaped teams, for more detail). However, as much as possible, you want to ensure alignment and

FIGURE 11.6 Portfolio

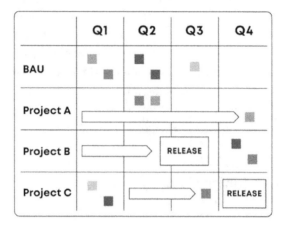

FIGURE 11.7 Team backlog

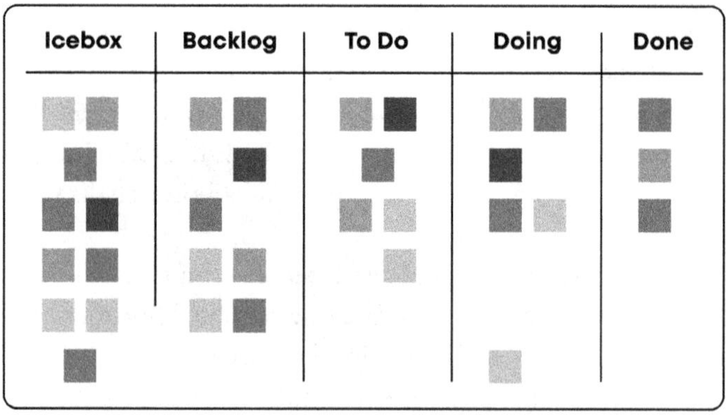

syncing across the multiple deliveries, and the best way to achieve this is through whole team or function check-ins.

A good illustration is a function of 100 people that committed to a monthly cycle made up of:

- Adapt and plan – a type of virtual obeya room (a term that originates from the Toyota production cycle. and means large room in Japanese) that kick-started each monthly cycle, where team leads project leads and roles like HR business partners agreed key priorities and delivery goals in line with the strategy and portfolio.

- Weekly check-ins – an open virtual call that anyone from the function could join to share updates on progress and, crucially, discuss blockers, challenges and any new urgent priorities.

- Product demos – different teams or project groups nominated themselves to showcase a specific delivery or product release to the wider function. The aim here was to demo and test unfinished work and collect invaluable feedback rather than review a finished product.

- Team retros – retrospectives took place at the team level, including the leadership team, with key messages and learning shared across the function.

Strategy one-pager

It's crucial to articulate your strategy on one page that anyone in the business can read and understand. Keep it simple and aim to share key messages succinctly and effectively. See Figure 11.8 for a strategy one-pager template and Figure 11.9 for an example of this.

FIGURE 11.8 Strategy one-pager template

Vision		
Mission (Why we do it)		
What (Initiatives / Problems to solve)		
Deliverables		
Measures of success		

FIGURE 11.9 Strategy one-pager example

Vision	A place where people can be the best version of themselves	
Mission (Why we do it)	Make it easy for people to connect, grow, lead and have impact	
What (Initiatives / Problems to solve)	Enhance career development and retain a higher percentage of people beyond 2 years	Target and accelerate genAI skills development
Deliverables	Discovery and design sprint Prototype to test by X date	Discovery and design sprint Prototype to test by X date
Measures of success	Increase internal hires by X% within X period	genAI skills identified and utilized in X% of teams

As a separate activity, undertake a co-creation exercise with your team to formulate your vision and mission. This helps people understand the bigger picture of what they're working on and why. Generally, the vision and mission are longer term and usually only tweaked year to year rather than entirely reworded. Details on how to set a powerful vision are given in Chapter 5.

Measuring impact

The great thing is that once you know the problem to solve, it's relatively easy to track results. Many L&D and people teams have found measuring impact difficult in the past because most focus on the content or activity as the solution. This will always be difficult to measure because what's meant to happen is unclear. Skills development or training alone won't shift business performance. There will always be other factors, such as confidence, the opportunity to practise, incentive, motivation and support, that contribute to whether the person can do something with the skills learnt.

A good example is the continued obsession within the workplace with changing behaviours, which Thomas F. Gilbert, founder of performance technology and author of the 1978 book *Human Competence: Engineering Worthy Performance* (2007), calls 'the cult of behaviour'. Gilbert realized that formal learning programmes generally only brought about a change in knowledge, not a behaviour change. Other factors, such as the opportunity to enact the behaviour, must be in place to ensure this behavioural change happens. Guy Wallace (2021), an influential thought leader in L&D instructional design and performance analysis, defines performance competence as the ability to perform tasks that contribute to business, organizational and societal results. For Wallace, it's not about learning; it's about performance. The critical test is whether people can produce more value because of the learning programme, and this value needs to be a thing, an outcome. For example, this might be a better relationship, a more detailed report, a quicker decision or a balanced budget.

Carl Binder (360Learning, 2022), CEO of the Performance Thinking Network and founder of the plain English Performance Thinking Network, calls these *accomplishments*. These things can be identified as work outputs and are products of applying behaviour or skill. Binder is particular that these need to be countable nouns, such as a report or a relationship. A good illustration is a learning programme designed to develop communication effectiveness. When described only as a competency, communication effectiveness is too vague. Instead, it needs to detail what will happen because of learning content. For example, the learner will respond to a series of questions in a tough negotiation. By describing the learning objective as an accomplishment rather than just a vague competency, it becomes targeted and measurable. Now, by focusing on accomplishments rather than competencies, you can assess a person's fluency in doing the accomplishment. Determining the wider organizational factors required to support this person in producing the accomplishment is also easier.

Another common trap is confusing the launch of a new product with impact. A good example is EVP, which Nebel Crowhurst (2023) commented on when interviewed for this book – a story many readers probably recognize. 'I've seen so many HR leaders and businesses say, we've got to design our EVP.' This leads to a whole project based on designing the EVP, often involving a vast array of activities such as listening groups and redesigning values. 'Then they launch their EVP, which is normally a beautiful artistic document that's wonderfully, gloriously articulated and got beautiful colours on it. And HR goes tick, "We've delivered EVP," and then nothing happens.' What they don't realize, emphasizes Crowhurst, is that the work has only just begun.

EXO metrics

Many L&D and people professionals ask me what's the best metric to track. My advice is to always start with the data you already have. Nearly every team I know wants to build its people analytics capability and collect more data. These are worthy aims to have. But while you build this out, start by selecting one or two metrics your organization already tracks for each problem you need to solve. Take a baseline measurement and then follow what happens as the project progresses. Aim to use EXO metrics which are employee experience data (such as engagement scores or retention) combined with operational and business data (such as customer NPS or lead-to-customer conversion ratios). Also, when tracking data, be mindful of which indicators are immediate, for example, open-click rates on an email, versus which indicators lag, such as retention rates or engagement scores.

'Ultimately, when we're talking about measurement, we need to stop thinking about measurement in a silo,' states Danny Seals (2023), founder of Knot, and Vice President, Employee Innovation, Listening and Effectiveness at RAKBANK Seals suggests using a measurement map or engine, as he calls it, that looks at O, X, I and P data:

- O is operational data – for example, your people data dashboard, which will include numbers like turnover, vacant roles and new hires.

- X is experience data – for example, feedback from exit interviews, recommendations on external websites, ratings and feedback from new joiners. Aim for a mix of qualitative and quantitative data as much as possible.

- I is innovation data – for example, cost per experiment and average testing results.

- P is your products, practices and processes data – for example, measuring the lifetime value of your employees, similar to the ratio of customer lifetime value (LTV) to customer acquisition cost (CAC) that most organizations use to track the lifetime value of a customer versus the cost of acquiring that customer.

EXAMPLES OF MEASUREMENTS TO TRACK

Here are some of my favourite measurements to track for L&D and people products.

People data

- Time to productivity – especially when linked to onboarding a new hire or a person moving into a new role or skill requirement
- Time to upskill
- Employee retention – especially when linked to specific groups, for example people who participated in a particular learning programme
- Internal hires – movements and promotions
- Recruitment and onboarding costs
- Time to hire
- Internal referrals
- Voluntary and involuntary turnover
- Absenteeism
- Ratings on external websites like Glassdoor
- Employee net promoter score
- Volunteering or charity days taken
- Exit (before they leave) and stay (why they are still with your organization) interviews
- Feedback surveys – engagement, wellness, post-programme and so on
- Annual leave days taken
- Average length of employment
- New hire retention
- Retention of people in critical roles
- Number of people accessing employee assistance helpline or employee assistance programme (EAP) services

Product and business data

- Conversion rates – downloads, click rate, email opening rates, click-through rates, website traffic and search rate
- Logged-in time or viewing time

- Customer and employee net promoter score
- Sales quota achievement or time to first deal
- Customer retention rates
- Time-to-deploy
- Rate of errors or accidents
- Project completion rates
- Lead generation, client follow-up or client proposal output
- Overtime rate
- Number of bugs or defects
- Number of errors
- Number of customer complaints
- Number of units produced
- Customer service calls, digital contact handling time or first-contact resolution rates or time
- Customer service contact quality rates
- Revenue or profit per employee
- New ideas generated or patents filed
- Number of successful cross-functional projects
- Sales revenue
- Net profit margin
- Monthly recurring revenue

Scalability

Scalability is another crucial component of delivering with impact. As suggested by David James (2023), Chief Learning Officer at 360Learning, the aim is to scale what works. James comments that scaling should not be confused with launching a new LMS (learning management system) which would give you instant reach and push out a huge amount of content. Instead, scalability is about speeding up and automating the testing and design of your employee experience products. For this reason, James encourages L&D and people teams to use various digital tools to speed up iteration and automate product features like nudging, peer-to-peer chat and coaching bots. By embracing smart tech, much of the data tracking and analysis can be automated, saving you considerable time.

L&D Director Jodie Pritchard (2023) suggests making scalability a design principle or part of your definition of done from the start. For example, the team approached scaling in three phases for a recent apprenticeship project at Citizens Advice. This was particularly important because it was the organization's first foray into working with an external provider on apprenticeships and using apprenticeships to support community advice. In the first phase, they got an MVP up and running to test every aspect of the solution, including the application process, provider relationship and communications. This was based on forty people set up on apprenticeships. The second phase is scaling the solution across the organization and recruiting people into ongoing apprenticeship posts. The third phase is commercializing the solution and providing the product to a broader network of organizations and volunteer groups that work with Citizens Advice. For Pritchard, launching a product across an organization should be easy if you design and test for scale from the beginning. If it's built on solid foundations and validated through prototyping and testing, it shouldn't matter if it's for 10 or 10,000 people.

A good example was when Citizens Advice evolved its competency framework for a federated organizational model of 250 individual charities. First, a core working group of 16 specialists agreed on the specific competency for each one-month sprint and designed a prototype. This was shared with a second user testing group (over 100 people from various roles and demographics across the charity network) for feedback via an online portal for two weeks. Once the feedback window closed, the prototype was returned to the core working group for iteration. A final draft was signed off by Pritchard, who acted as the joint PO (Product Owner) alongside the Executive Director of People, followed by release into the organization. While the test group gave feedback on one prototype, the core group could design the next prototype in the same two-week window. As Pritchard highlights, 'The dilemma with these products, like competency frameworks, is that they need to be a living thing, and they never are. But this process allows it to be so, it's really amazing.'

Conclusion – five takeaways for L&D and people professionals

- Measurement needs to be a continuous data feedback loop reflecting the same cadence as the Agile cycle.
- The ability to deliver with impact operates on multiple levels – as a mindset, a product-led model, a team effectiveness framework and a way of running a business.
- Your L&D and people strategy needs to set out your theory of how you will deliver value to the organization – and value is achieved by solving customer problems.
- When measuring impact, always aim for EXO metrics – a combination of employee experience data, such as engagement scores or retention, with operational and business data, such as customer net promoter score or lead-to-customer conversion ratios.
- Test the scalability of your product from the start.

References

360Learning (2022) Pivot to Performance episode 2, with Carl Binder, 360Learning Live Event with Carl Binder, David James and Guy Wallace, 19 October, https://app.livestorm.co/360learning/pivot-to-performance-episode-2-with-carl-binder (archived at https://perma.cc/CRK7-8X2H)

Barlow, Buckley (2023) The S curve of business: The key levers to sustaining momentum for your brand, Rocket Source, www.rocketsource.com/blog/s-curve-of-business (archived at https://perma.cc/7N8N-LGKJ)

Crowhurst, Nebel (2023) Interview with Natal Dank, recorded 17 August

Ford, Sarah (2023) Interview with Natal Dank, recorded 14 July

Gilbert, Thomas F. (2007) *Human Competence: Engineering worthy performance*, Tribute Edition (International Society for Performance Improvement), Pfeiffer (Wiley), San Francisco

Harvard Business Review (2022a) What is strategy? It's a lot simpler than you think, Harvard Business Review YouTube, 23 February, https://youtu.be/o7Ik1OB4TaE?si=YbWj4QGN5cP94E9Q (archived at https://perma.cc/5SYH-F7XE)

Harvard Business Review (2022b) A plan is not a strategy, Harvard Business Review YouTube, 29 June, https://youtu.be/iuYlGRnC7J8?si=0fC8x37kqr34QutG (archived at https://perma.cc/U7HD-PU6R)

James, David (2023) Interview with Natal Dank, recorded 2 August

Keith, Laura (2023) Interview with Natal Dank, recorded 21 July

Pritchard, Jodie (2023) Interview with Natal Dank, recorded 20 July

Seals, Danny (2023) Interview with Natal Dank, recorded 26 June

Wallace, Guy (2021) Beware Gilbert's cult of behavior by any name, EPPIC – Pursuing Performance, 6 August, https://eppic.biz/2021/08/06/beware-gilberts-cult-of-behavior-by-any-name/ (archived at https://perma.cc/55YV-3APG)

12

Wins, lessons learnt, pitfalls and where it can go wrong

When interviewing L&D and people leaders for this book, it was fascinating that many found it easier to describe what Agile isn't rather than detail exactly what it is. From these discussions, I also discovered that by conducting a type of strategic retrospective on their experiences leading Agile transformation, we could gather a lot of useful data to share as lessons learnt. So, in this chapter, we'll explore all the excellent insights and real-world examples gained from the interviews. This is a collection of stories based on what went well, what didn't go to plan and what the leaders would do differently if they could do it all again. Use this chapter as a checklist to help you and your team get started, continue to build momentum, lead functional and organizational-wide Agile transformation and, perhaps most importantly, navigate your personal change journey.

> I think that it is really quite important that if we're not willing to change our own mindset then it's a very difficult transition to go through with the team. If I could give myself advice three years ago, I would say that as a leader, you need to commit to this change… it cannot be window dressing. And it cannot be look at us; we're going to create solutions with our business stakeholders, we're going to do all these cool things and use all the buzzwords and show that HR is a value-creating team. Yes, all that's possible – but you have to truly understand how by doing it yourself.
> (Arne-Christian van der Tang, Chief HR Officer at TomTom, 2023)

Define why and explain the purpose for embracing Agile

Many readers will now appreciate that Agile is, first and foremost, a response to complexity. However, you can't just go Agile. You need to set out why, and the specific problems you aim to solve by introducing Agile working methods.

As explained by Eoin Cannon (2023), a business agility coach and experienced Agile L&D consultant, it's critical to anchor all your Agile work to business outcomes. Be deliberate and concrete when connecting the work to the business mission. This is crucial to manage the common problem of Agile being 'a sexy new thing', rather than a practical and business-led method of working:

> Yes, Agile is a new way of working, but you don't just change working methods without a clearly defined reason. Agile doesn't make sense to people if they don't know why they should work that way, how it will benefit them, what work you want to deliver using Agile and what you're trying to solve by changing in this way. (Cannon, 2023)

'I think the biggest challenge is helping people understand the why,' states Adam Hepton (2023), former software developer and tech people manager who moved into HR and OD at Sky Betting and Gaming and then Tombola. You need to help people understand why they should even entertain the thought of doing things differently or as an alternative to what they've experienced in other organizations. To champion the cause, Hepton continually shares with the team evidence of progression and how they are working better because of Agile, for example tracking results from team health checks over time to show that they deliver more, and team engagement has increased. Hepton also points out that such resistance to change is not confined to L&D and people teams; he also experienced this in software development.

To help, Hepton suggests setting out your stall and being clear on your purpose and goal from the start. 'In the true spirit of Agile, you don't need to get everything right straight away, but you do need to think about what it is you're trying to achieve... If you have a problem and have the chance to put a reset on it, it's a gift. So, treat it as such.' For example, when Hepton moved into the people team at Sky Betting and Gaming, he helped them work through a series of problems to solve by applying Agile. First, they wanted to share work as a collaborative team and no longer operate as a group of individual HR business partners. In response, they surfaced and visualized all their current work and then prioritized the most important projects and deliveries for the whole team to commit to, not just individuals. Next, the team asked: 'How do we decide who works on what if we all know different things? Well, let's make sure we're telling each other about what's going on.' Hepton adds:

> I came in blind to that HR team, right? I'd never done an HR role in my life. So, there were a lot of technical things that I didn't know within that realm that I needed skilling up on. That was really valuable in itself having somebody who didn't know that specific technical skill because by necessity, you have to bring people along, you have to pull people up to gain that knowledge.

Conversely, Hepton found that his previous experience leading successful and mature Agile tech teams created a virtuous win-win cycle. This saw Hepton coach the team in Agile practices while others taught him the fundamentals of OD and HR. As a result, the team delivered a series of significant projects in career development, reward, performance and organizational design that wouldn't have been achieved at such a high level of quality and pace if they had continued to work as a collection of individual HR business partners.

Cassie Soady (2023), former Head of Culture and People Transformation at Woolies X and Chief People Officer for Digital Data, Analytics, Technology and Enterprise Operations at National Australia Bank, warns that you can't just 'go Agile for the sake of it'. One of the biggest dangers is teams and organizations jumping straight to a new Agile delivery operating model without 'knowing what problem you're trying to solve'. Soady comments that this situation is quite common, not because people are disingenuous but because they feel the pressure to attract great talent in the market. As a result, they announce they're going Agile because they think it will strengthen their EVP and brand position without truly comprehending what this implies.

Greg McCaw (2023), Chief People Officer at BKL and former Director of People Experience and DEI at Flutter, states 'I think the first thing that can go wrong is you, your behaviours. When trying to drive cultural change within an organization, it has to start with you and your framing of Agile, the benefits and payback it can bring'. McCaw points out that Agile transformation is like rewiring a team or company. 'And when you're rewiring organizations, it's almost like diffusing a bomb that has to be done really carefully because people can react to Agile, and there's a lot of common misconceptions with it.' For McCaw, some of these misconceptions include people incorrectly assuming that increased speed to market implies that the quality of the work is diminished and not completed to the same standard. Another common misunderstanding is confusing Agile with being fast and loose. 'I've worked with teams in the past that have gone, well, it's totally fine; we'll just move the deadline. We're Agile, we'll move it. And I'm like, well, no, that's not okay because you committed to your customer that you were going to deliver on that date. So, you can be transparent, but you need to reset your expectations with that customer.'

This leads McCaw to view Agile transformation as starting with yourself. 'The change needs to begin inward before it happens outwards.' This also means it's best to start small or begin by applying Agile within smaller teams. Essentially, you need to work with people who are willing to be pioneers or are perhaps already evangelists convinced of the benefits because they've seen Agile work elsewhere. If you're a large people function, McCaw suggests starting with the L&D team or people partnering. It's best to take a smaller team through the change first and then use the learning to understand how to evolve other parts of the function or the wider business.

> Because fundamentally, that's what Agile is about. And it's about how you work. It's about how you behave, act every day, the mindset you bring to work when you show up. (McCaw, 2023)

Jodie Pritchard (2023), former Head of Learning at the large UK charity Citizens Advice and now Director of L&D at the children's charity Barnardo's, agrees that you can underestimate the impact of the change as a leader. Pritchard warns that it can go 'very, very wrong' if you don't approach the transformation as a significant culture change for the team. This means it's critical to bring people along with you, clearly support them, answer all their worries and be conscious that they are going through the change curve. For this reason, Pritchard took an incremental approach and constantly worked on the team's engagement by clearly stating, 'This is what we're going to do, and these are the reasons why we're going to do it.' The aim is to build psychological safety within the team by letting them know it will sometimes feel 'clunky' and uncomfortable. Pritchard warns against going too fast or making any significant change without the full engagement of the team; instead, support and encourage people by saying, 'Let's just give it a go and let's just try it.'

Nicki Somal (2023), experienced Agile HR coach and consultant, highlights the importance of a sponsor or leader 'that gets it and gets the why and is really clear on the vision and has a hypothesis'. Somal confirms the need to clearly state your why when embracing Agile. 'Why is it that you want to do Agile? What's the problem you're trying to solve?'

For Sara Sheard (2023), Executive Director of Business Operations at Incommunities and former Deputy People Director at Mencap, the word *intentional* is how she describes this role of the Agile leader and sponsor. For example, you need to be intentional when defining Agile. Sheard has observed teams confuse agility with simply changing their minds whereas this could hardly be further from Agile methodology. Agile is highly disciplined and deliberate in construction, and there will be unforeseen ramifications if Agile working methods are not clearly understood. Once defined, be mindful of the team's readiness and have strategies to manage the pace of change. 'You can think it's the best thing in the world. But if you haven't got the hearts and minds of people', you will fail to take them with you.

Agile can't be 'side of desk'

Agile can't just be done on the side or in addition to a person's core day job. Too many organizations ask people to embrace Agile as an extra project on top of their existing responsibilities. This leads to several problems. The first is capacity and people feeling stretched. Consequently, people struggle to find the time to apply Agile and, because it's often more difficult when you first attempt new working methods, people will feel less and less inclined to keep trying. Secondly, motivation quickly disappears if Agile is not incentivized or included within existing performance measurements. Thirdly, building momentum and increasing a team's velocity is extremely difficult if they only work piecemeal or inbetween other projects and BAU work. It's critical to give the space for people to learn and explore together when applying Agile.

Ideally, role expectations are redefined so people can focus 100 per cent on the Agile project or be part of a team working fully Agile. Alternatively, carve out space each week for the team to come together and apply Agile. For example, as mentioned in earlier chapters, the team dedicates one or two days a week to the Agile project; on those days, everyone else knows not to request other work. On these dedicated days, the team undertakes important Agile ceremonies, such as planning or team retrospectives, but crucially gets actual project work done without needing to constantly switch tasks. The other popular approach is to carve out time for a time-boxed sprint, such as one week, and use this to progress an Agile project. Also, while each day is dedicated to the project and people effectively down tools on other work, sprinting between 10am and 3pm is often advisable to allow people to catch up on emails and other minor tasks.

As highlighted by Goeff Morey (2023), Head of Colleague L&D at Macmillan Cancer Support, just dipping your toe into Agile and doing it as a side gig doesn't work. Morey tried that and failed. Consequently, he created space so people could give up to 50 per cent of their time to an Agile project. This worked much better. Currently, he's testing what happens if it's 100 per cent. If you don't give people the capacity to apply Agile, Morey fears, teams do it half-heartedly, and it's doomed from the start.

With her experience of leading teams over the years, Tracey Waters (2023), former People Experience Director at Sky UK and now Group Leadership and Talent lead at a large Australian bank has found that capacity issues, resource constraints and the need to multitask are all common issues. Waters states

> Whereas I think the ideal is that you've got a team dedicated to solving a single problem or one part of a problem, what ends up happening is that you are juggling multiple plates, and you're trying to do it in a way that is more collaborative, more iterative, more data-informed, but it can feel a bit chaotic at times.

Jodie Pritchard (2023), agrees that commitment is key. 'You can't just do Agile off the side of the desk and just expect people to change overnight.' Pritchard suggests that you can do it in phases, and it's unnecessary to apply all the methods at once. 'You can pick the bits that are best suited for you and your organization without any doubt.' Pritchard would always start by applying a user-led approach to product design and introducing team retrospectives.

This highlights the importance of a leader who appreciates the need for Agile to be properly resourced and accounted for when capacity planning. Kate Walker (2023) is the People Programme and Projects Lead at the well-known sustainable development consultancy Arup. She stresses the importance of adequately resourcing Agile projects or taking time out of the day job to run an Agile hackathon or design thinking sprint. 'It's people having the confidence to know they won't have to return to that work in addition to the work they've just done in the two-day hack. I think there's confidence about knowing your work's covered.' In the projects Walker leads, most people cannot give 100 per cent of their time. So, it's a critical question to transparently discuss and resolve at the start of any project. Agile can't just be on the side.

Don't jump immediately into a new Agile operating model

There is no easy fix when it comes to upskilling people and teams in Agile. This is why it's important to embrace the values of Agile and take an iterative approach to gradually build up capability and confidence over time. You will eventually need to restructure the organizational design and operating model to allow teams to work more effectively and in multidisciplinary ways. Still, it's dangerous to rush into this structural change.

Cassie Soady (2023) believes too many teams and organizations try to jump straight to the structural change without first allowing time to evolve ways of working and, thus, harness an Agile mindset. 'You can't jump straight into a new delivery model without solving existing ways of working or introducing quarterly planning first.' Soady has worked with business areas that want to immediately set up an Agile delivery model made of squads, tribes and chapters without appreciating that Agile requires a complete overhaul of the day-to-day working rhythm.

Instead, Soady encourages people to start with an experiment, which we'll explore as a separate topic later in this chapter. For example, start with introducing team retrospectives or do a daily check-in. There are lots of different methods to test as a starting point. Soady suggests organizations focus on 'purpose, values, ways of working, quarterly planning. Get that flowing for at least a year. If you're a big organization, start with some trials. You know, solve a core chunk of your business before saying you've got to wrap everything into it.' Soady believes it takes at least four quarters of quarterly planning and cross-functional collaboration before you start seeing the full benefits. Soady also highlights the costly investment of implementing a whole organizational big-bang Agile restructure. This potential cost of failure is even more reason to do the changes iteratively and take your time. To illustrate, Soady meets leaders who don't want to invest in an Agile coach because they think they can do it themselves or can't afford it. Yet, the potential cost of the Agile transformation failing far outweighs such upfront investment.

Another interesting point that Soady raises is that Agile transformation is never really finished. In many ways, it's a continuous evolution, where you strive for mastery in collaborating as a team and innovating the product you deliver. Ultimately, any Agile transformation should replicate the Agile cycle itself. This cycle propels you forward by responding to an ever-changing business context and driving continuous improvement through the feed-back-driven loop of *plan, do, review, adapt*.

Be prepared to change the team or organizational structure

Despite the need to approach Agile transformation incrementally, Sara Sheard (2023), from Incommunities, thinks it is important to consider the future design and structure of your team or organization early on. In Sheard's experience, the traditional operating model of L&D and people teams quickly becomes prohibitive and creates a blocker to Agile transformation. To pre-empt this, Sheard encourages leaders to be brave and get ready to restructure at some point. Sheard suggests still doing this preparation even if you only feel 80 per cent certain of the future organizational design. While Sheard tested possible structures with key stakeholders and based the design on research and validated customer needs, in the end, people require certainty. So, following an initial experiment, Sheard was able to transition into the new operating model to enable Agile to succeed and give everyone involved a sense of security.

Sheard highlights the need to be mindful that the legacy of HR functional remits and competing topic owners will most likely act as a continual blocker to any Agile transformation within L&D and people teams. Adam Hepton (2023), who brings an outside-in perspective by starting his career in software development, notes that HR contains more specialisms than he has probably seen anywhere else in the business. 'There are a lot of, what do we call it, I-shapes, aren't there?' he says, referring to the need for more T-shaped teams within the L&D and people profession and that many remain in their vertical skill silo (see Chapter 9 for more information on the T-shape). Hepton points out that even when these I-shapes are brought together, it often results in multiple vertical work streams rather than the team sharing and collaborating across all the work as a collective unit. Hepton says:

> Fundamentally, that is one of the biggest, most common issues with
> implementing any sort of trial. Trial is always a dirty word. Experiment is
> always seen as a difficult word. Transparency is another one.

These experiences lead Hepton to conclude that you will often need to shift team members away from these traditional HR operating models and related habits. This means it's always new, even if some team members have previously worked in an Agile way. 'And that is fundamentally the reason behind the challenge. The kind of challenges that we see are trying to do things differently or trying to understand why you should do things in a different way to what everyone else (in HR) is doing'.

Treat Agile transformation as an experiment

As mentioned earlier in the chapter, many L&D and people leaders interviewed for this book suggest viewing your transformation as an Agile experiment. Interestingly, even just using this description helps remove the pressure and allows people to feel that it's okay not to know everything and not be skilled from day one. Be clear, however, that if the experiment fails, you're ready to listen to feedback and return to the old ways of working if necessary. I personally have yet to come across a team that went back.

This is why Nicki Somal (2023), Agile HR coach earlier, advises teams to start small and view transformation as an experiment. Somal shares:

> My experiment here is that we will do this for three months, and my hypothesis is this. If the problem in the team, for example, is siloed teams, then the hypothesis is that by applying Agile, we're going to break down the silos. Or it might be the problem is that our learning isn't meeting our customer needs and we're not delivering at pace as an example. And the hypothesis is then by working in an Agile way and pulling in design sprints where you're delivering and designing a manager programme, for example, in a shorter space of time, you can see that value.

By setting out the experiment with a clear hypothesis to test, you can better measure results and understand what elements to continue with or eliminate post-experiment.

Another reason to experiment is that people initially experience few setbacks or get things wrong. These hiccups are more accepted, sometimes even laughed at, if it's an experiment where everyone learns together. However, breaking down old habits and supporting the necessary behavioural change is harder if you go too big, too early. As Somal comments, 'I think where people go wrong is they think that they're just going to *do* Agile and not *become* Agile.' Unfortunately, this can lead to *WAgile*, which happens when people overlay Agile with a traditional Waterfall mindset. 'What you find is people are doing *WAgile* and [get] focused more on the tools and to-do lists versus backlogs and delivering value. I think it comes from going big too soon. I think that's where it goes wrong.' In these situations, people continue to work as individual contributors, sharing to-do lists in daily check-ins instead of collaborating as a team on how a backlog item will deliver value. 'We're not jointly scoping work; there's no collaboration or co-creation with our stakeholders or product. We're not connecting with the PO (product owner).' Somal finds coaching a *WAgile* team one of the most challenging situations to deal with.

> It's probably easier to work with a team with no experience and no exposure to Agile than it is to transition a *WAgile* team into Agile. I've worked with two *WAgile* teams now, and it just took so much longer. (Somal, 2023)

Greg McCaw (2023) also stresses the importance of not thinking that Agile is achieved only by introducing a few new tools. For example, a team starting to use a Kanban board to visualize their work doesn't instantly mean they're now Agile. 'Because then you'll go to the Kanban board, and you go, you do know that there are a hundred and fifteen tasks on this board, and they all have a priority of medium. And they're all due next week.' To counter this, McCaw encourages people to view Agile first and foremost as an outcome of mindset and behaviour. The tools, such as a Kanban board, are the enablers of the expected actions: 'tools that help bring Agile to life and activate it'.

When coaching teams in these situations, McCaw asks questions to encourage reflection and learning on how best to work with tools like a Kanban board. As an illustration, McCaw will ask the team to explain the definition of done for a ticket on the Kanban board or explore how a certain ticket connects to the problem the team wants to solve. 'I really just want to know what problem we will try to solve when we put that on the board. And why is it a high priority?' When approached this way, McCaw feels it's less threatening because it's positioned more as him just being curious.

For these reasons, Sara Sheard (2023) from Incommunities recommends keeping the experiment incredibly simple. For example, select a few key projects and develop methods over time into something more sustainable. You've got to be ready to play the long game. At Incommunities, Sheard and the change team have set out their ambitions. However, they understand that shifting the wider organization from Agile awareness into application will take time.

Kate Walker (2023) at Arup suggests starting with practices and tools that resonate with people and suit your business context. 'Think less about it being, so, we're going Agile and more about let's just try and test some tools that we think could add value, then let's assess if they add value. And then let's share those stories.' A good illustration was using the strong affiliation within Arup with process improvement to help people appreciate the value of a team retrospective. 'Just changing the name from "lessons learned" to "retros" and using the retrospective language, people were really comfortable with that because it's got quite an L&D feel to it.' Walker then discovered that talking about how the team were delivering the work and collaborating, rather than just assessing the quality of the work produced, was a 'real game changer'. 'It's thinking about a high-performing team environment, thinking about how we can work closer or better together.' Another good example was empathy mapping. Within Arup, HR people are passionate about applying a human-centred approach and want to design people-friendly solutions. This meant Walker found it relatively easy to introduce empathy mapping as a practical technique to document different perspectives and ensure all voices are heard in the design process.

Creating an experiment where people can experience *aha* moments that help shift their mindset is critical when supporting team transformation. Returning to Sara Sheard (2023):

> People really need to experience Agile to get it. So, you can read a textbook on it and think it sounds great. But the best way of getting people on board, I think, is living and breathing and doing it or showcasing it.

For example, at Sheard's previous organization, they showcased a great case study of a user-led self-service system design that allowed people to make changes directly to their employee data. The success story was so well received that it got people interested in Agile and willing to give it a try, even without first experiencing it directly themselves.

However, a final word of caution with the experiment approach. As business agility coach Eoin Cannon (2023) highlights – don't let the experiment become a fun novelty. Cannon witnessed this happening after running a series of successful, high-energy design thinking sprints at a large drinks manufacturer. While this time-boxed hackathon approach was great at delivering results, it failed to embed Agile within the organization because everyone returned to their day job at the end of the one or two-week design sprint. Instead, Cannon advocates learning in the flow of work and applying Agile tools and techniques to a 'project that is live and matters to you and the people you're working with regularly'. Cannon suggests it will take several months from that point to get the new working methods to stick.

Get comfortable with some basic Agile terminology

When exploring the definition of Agile with Danny Seals (2023), founder of Knot, and Vice President, Employee Innovation, Listening and Effectiveness at RAKBANK, he made a point of 'humanizing and simplifying the language'. Seals felt this was necessary because many people get too caught up in the related Agile terminology. Geoff Morey (2023) from Macmillan Cancer Support agrees. 'For me, people get really hung up on the tools and the jargon associated with Agile rather than embracing the Agile mindset.'

Consequently, Morey comments on an interesting dilemma that results from people misunderstanding Agile terminology. On the one hand, people fear Agile as last minute, unplanned and chaotic. This is a view amplified within the charity sector because of a tendency to be risk-averse and bureaucratic in nature. Unfortunately, this leads some to incorrectly interpret Agile as the riskier option. However, as Morey points out, when Agile is done well, it successfully manages risk because you take smaller iterative steps and validate decisions as you go with data.

On the other hand, Morey observes people feeling overwhelmed and a bit anxious when first introduced to Agile terminology. For example, terms like burndown chart, Kanban or Scrum Master, can feel quite alien to people. 'And, what we found is just remove some of that language and rather than say daily stand-up, we say check-in. And then people go, okay, I get that.' As highlighted by Morey, it's essential to make Agile terminology accessible and help people get comfortable with the language and associated tools as enablers of the overall mindset.

Returning to Jodie Pritchard (2023) from Barnardo's, she also feels people get too absorbed in or focused on the jargon rather than what you're trying to achieve when embracing Agile. 'We hardly use jargon in my team. And we've done that mindfully. Because I think sometimes the language and the jargon, not just Agile, of new things, can just disengage people.'

To manage this challenge, Kate Walker (2023) from Arup is conscious of gradually developing understanding and comprehension across the different teams she works with. What's interesting is that Walker now feels the wider HR function is much more comfortable with the language and the value of applying Agile techniques a few years on. 'I think now people are saying we're ready for that language. We're ready for the step change. We want to do things differently.' Walker views this more of a pull from the teams wanting to embrace Agile rather than feeling like she needs to push the benefits of Agile. However, Walker argues this traction resulted from being cautious when introducing Agile and mindful of which words to use and what tools to introduce.

Sarah Ford (2023), Head of HR Innovation at Diageo, also warns there is a danger of people not speaking up if they don't understand the new ways of working and concepts. Ford recommends remaining grounded in the business context and related problems you're trying to solve so as not to scare people. Sara Sheard at Incomunities feels this is particularly important when engaging the wider business. 'We love it and might want to discuss design thinking and Agile. People in the business don't care. It will become a buzzword.' For this reason, Sheard introduced a 'ways of working toolkit' in her previous organization, which contained Agile tools alongside other useful OD, project management and change management techniques. Sheard likens this to 'unbranding' Agile to make it more accessible. For example, a section of her toolkit was simply called 'killer questions'. Based primarily on design thinking, the toolkit guided the user in how best to research business challenges in a language that resonated with their organizational culture.

These examples highlight a significant dilemma to resolve when introducing Agile and is a problem I face regularly when working with new teams. The dilemma is that you need to give Agile a go and start using some tools and related terminology to create an environment where people have *aha* moments and evolve *their* mindset. As noted earlier, the Agile mindset can't be taught in isolation or only from reading a book. Therefore, keep it simple and introduce a collection of core practices deemed the most useful for solving the specific problem. *Go slow, don't rush people and allow them to gradually build up confidence in using Agile terminology.*

Take your senior executive leaders on the journey with you

Amanda Bellwood (2023), People Director at Tombola, reflects that her previous experience leading Agile transformation at another organization before moving into her existing role was fortuitous. 'I think, on reflection, it's because I've been there and done it and seen it work, that I've had so much confidence in being able to showcase how this can work in the People space.' However, unlike previous organizations where most of the business already worked in an Agile way, her whole team was new to Agile along with many of her senior executives. For these reasons and because there are no other reference points within the organization, Bellwood operates openly and transparently, constantly showcasing the people team's journey. Bellwood also updates the executive on the next steps and shares any team development activities. The goal is to help other business leaders 'see it and feel it' so they too begin to evolve their thinking.

It's good to note at this point that it's always advisable to utilize any other examples of Agile teams operating within your organization as a reference point when embracing your own transformation. Aim to learn from others by spending time with these teams or asking to observe some of their Agile ceremonies, such as a planning session or product review. The concept originates from the Toyota production system and is often termed a *Gemba walk* within Agile circles. A Gemba walk is commonly referenced in connection with Lean, the process improvement methodology and the project management framework, Six Sigma (Six Sigma Daily, 2018).

Arne-Christian van der Tang (2023), Chief HR Officer at TomTom, also keeps his fellow senior executives updated with the change journey the people team are experiencing. However, Van der Tang adds that he is mindful not to make a big show of it because the best way to gain peer support is to demonstrate the change over time through the value delivered. To illustrate, when it came to day zero for the new people team operating model, Van der Tang sent an update to his colleagues on the executive board and advised them to share the information openly with others. The email provided a brief explanation and visual of what the model looked like. Van der Tang deliberately took this low-key approach because he wanted a chance for the people function to settle in and feel comfortable before they launched any high-profile, organizational-wide communication campaign. 'Because if the team is not there yet, then they're not going to be able to answer any questions.' Then, relatively soon after the restructuring, Van der Tang was able to showcase a great proof point of how the new model delivered more value to the organization. The insight here is a need for balance. While providing enough information to ensure your fellow senior leaders feel informed and comfortable with your actions is important, protecting the team's development journey is also critical.

Van der Tang also learnt a lot from other senior executives. For example, the chief product officer provided inspiration and guidance when the TomTom people team formulated their design principles. Van der Tang highlights the crossovers between the product-led vision within the people team, how other parts of the business operate, and the company's overriding 'go-to-market' strategy. 'So, it's also close to their hearts. So, we learn a lot from them. As much as we also learn from our go-to-market organization, it's not just about the product; it's also about getting it into the hands of our users.' This is a great story that demonstrates it is possible to get other business leaders excited about the people team applying the same Agile tools and skills used or originating from their domain.

Eoin Cannon (2023), business agility coach, believes it's not enough for the executive board to only say they support Agile; they need to do it themselves. 'Culture eats strategy for breakfast, and I also think culture eats HR processes for lunch. I think you've got to understand culture and power and use it as a tailwind. That means you've got to say, okay, where is the power in this organization as it stands, and how can I use that to leverage Agile behaviours, to embed them?' Cannon argues this is critical if you need to manage situations where the people at the top of the organization openly support Agile, but the next layer down doesn't appear convinced. Cannon hypothesizes that the lack of role models at the board level means the next layer down is unwilling or reluctant to change themselves. This thinking is based on Cannon's observations when working in different organizations where the leadership team declares support for Agile and adds it to the business strategy but fails to shift the needle. Further emphasizing an earlier insight that people need to experience Agile to get it.

Another danger highlighted by Cannon is if people don't truly understand Agile, especially at the executive, they try to implement it in a way that isn't conducive to Agile, such as a top-down, Waterfall style, big-bang approach. This makes Cannon reluctant to use the term transformation. 'It's an overpromise in itself.' As highlighted earlier in this chapter, Agile transformation is more like an ongoing evolution than a single desired end point.

Geoff Morey (2023) at Macmillan Cancer Support has also learnt 'the power of the end result'. At the start, yes, 'there's a bit of bravery and a bit of risk', with the need to build trust. But then momentum and support of other business teams quickly follow if you can showcase a few proof points and success stories across the wider organization. Morey, however, also mentions the potential tension that Agile introduces for leaders of an organization. This tension results from many leaders wanting to be seen as the expert and decision maker. However, within Agile, the team takes on most of this decision-making by self-organizing around the product vision. This calls on the leader to help people connect with the vision and strategy, essential to the *what,* but be comfortable to coach and support the team to decide on the *how*. Morey talks about the need to help leaders make this transition and appreciates that delivering value through others is a sign of great leadership.

I'll also comment here that this same tension can arise within L&D and people teams. Suppose you have a group that previously operated as individual contributors and owned different functional remits or business relationships. In that case, you'll need to help them appreciate the value of working as a collective, T-shaped team. To begin with, some may question whether they'll gain the same sense of self-achievement. However, I've found that by celebrating the more significant impact that an Agile team approach delivers, people start to value the new ways of working and the opportunity to achieve more together over time.

Build a supportive network

Many leaders interviewed for this book discussed the importance of learning from other leaders outside their immediate organization and accessing coaching. Indeed, several people I interviewed had worked together over the years or acted as a mentor and sounding board for each other. This outside-in perspective and 'voice of experience', as described by Agile HR coach Nicki Somal (2023), is a vital support mechanism to help you personally along the change journey.

Having had that support when starting out with Agile, Somal now provides the same coaching support to others. Somal coaches teams at the start of their Agile transformation and throughout their ongoing adventure to help keep the mindset alive: 'That voice of experience is almost like the drumbeat, the heartbeat that keeps it going, keeps Agile living and breathing.' Additionally, because the coach has experienced the ups and downs before, they act as a useful guiding hand, helping to accelerate the application of skills.

Somal points out that the servant leadership of an external Agile coach or internal Scrum Master is critical: 'The coach is able to encourage innovation, creative thinking, and also challenge from a neutral place and not get the death stare for it.'

Somal comments that people respond differently to a neutral, non-directive coaching voice, which is essential when developing psychological safety within a team. It's also why the leader will struggle with any attempt to provide a Scrum Master or coach role while also acting as a sponsor. It is simply too much to take on, and you'll find it hard to remain objective in your coaching style. Interestingly, Somal also advises against the Head or team leader providing the product owner (PO) role unless they can directly own and manage the backlog. Otherwise, they are better off working as sponsors, aiming to remove impediments and blockers at the higher enterprise level.

When Jodie Pritchard (2023) led the Citizens Advice L&D team of twenty people, she hired an Agile delivery lead, which proved essential in driving team engagement and bringing everyone along the change journey. Based on this experience, Pritchard recommends having a role that acts as a coach and a coordinator at the team level. 'They're the ones that are in it. They're doing it every day and then working with the leader to go, okay, so what's next?'

Finally, many L&D and people professionals are asked to lead or contribute to an organizational-wide Agile transformation. So, it's useful to share tips from the interview with Cassie Soady (2023), who has led multiple culture and structural Agile transformations. Soady's main advice is to combine the OD and L&D expertise of people professionals with the experience and background of an Agile coach. 'I still wouldn't embark on something like that without a great Agile coach with me.' While Soady brings many years of organizational design and change management, she values partnering with a person with deep Agile expertise. Soady also advocates a T-shaped approach to any Agile transformation, in the same way that this book encourages an L&D or people team to operate when solving a business challenge. For example, she recommends having a collection of skills that cover strategy, finance, operations, product management and customer experience, as well as L&D, OD and other core HR skills. This T-shaped transformation team then uses human-centred design to ensure a great change and team experience for people going through the transformation, just like we would when designing the customer experience in connection with a product.

Conclusion – five takeaways for L&D and people professionals

- Define why and explain the purpose for embracing Agile and the problems you need to solve by working in an Agile way.

- Treat your Agile transformation as an experiment and set out to test your hypothesis. For example, 'By working Agile, we will remove silos and deliver higher quality work at pace.'
- Agile can't just be added to a person's core day job as a 'side of the desk' activity.
- Don't be afraid to access the support of a coach and seek an outside-in perspective and a voice of experience by connecting with others who have done it before.
- Be ready to change yourself.

References

Bellwood, Amanda (2023) Interview with Natal Dank, recorded 24 July
Cannon, Eoin (2023) Interview with Natal Dank, recorded 12 July
Ford, Sarah (2023) Interview with Natal Dank, recorded 14 July
Hepton, Adam (2023) Interview with Natal Dank, recorded 21 July
McCaw, Greg (2023) Interview with Natal Dank, recorded 23 June
Morey, Geoff (2023) Interview with Natal Dank, recorded 23 June
Pritchard, Jodie (2023) Interview with Natal Dank, recorded 20 July
Seals, Danny (2023) Interview with Natal Dank, recorded 26 June
Sheard, Sara (2023) Interview with Natal Dank, recorded 4 August
Six Sigma Daily (2018) What is a gemba walk and why is it important?, 17 January, www.sixsigmadaily.com/what-is-a-gemba-walk (archived at https://perma.cc/6CWG-VQ94)
Soady, Cassie (2023) Interview with Natal Dank, recorded 30 June
Somal, Nicki (2023) Interview with Natal Dank, recorded 19 July
Van der Tang, Arne-Christian (2023) Interview with Natal Dank, recorded 14 July
Walker, Kate (2023) Interview with Natal Dank, recorded 6 July
Waters, Tracey (2023) Interview with Natal Dank, recorded 26 July

13

Conclusion: Designing for the *now* of work

Considering how much of this book emphasizes the need for the people profession to work in a more T-shaped and multidisciplinary way, some readers might wonder why I still felt Agile L&D as a topic warranted its own book. Several reasons are important to explore as we move into the book's conclusion.

L&D suits Agile

Despite advocating an end to the traditional HR and people operating model, most L&D and OD professionals currently work within a discrete L&D or talent team. Some readers may also operate as solo L&D representatives within an organization. As a specialism, L&D is ripe for Agile disruption. The type of work that sits within L&D naturally suits Agile working methods. The majority of work is project-based and requires some type of product design. Moreover, the intended outcomes are generally linked to an experience, whether this is learning or behavioural change. It's also a discipline that is digitizing at pace and, thus, lends itself nicely to iterative product design and experimentation. It naturally follows that the five design principles fit the L&D and OD remit perfectly. Interestingly, most leaders interviewed for this book also commented that, out of all the functional areas that sit within the people profession, L&D needs to *go Agile* the most.

L&D as the role model

Perhaps because Agile suits the nature of L&D and OD work, it's common and often advisable for the L&D team to lead the way and be the first to *go Agile* within a broader people function. As mentioned in the previous chapter when first embracing Agile, it's best to start small and treat the transformation like an experiment. As such, the L&D team is often the starting point to test and evolve an approach before inviting other teams within the people function to join in. It's also generally assumed that L&D and OD professionals are well suited to coach others in Agile and potentially become Scrum Masters or Agile coaches both within the people function and the broader organization. Furthermore, considering many L&D teams are then tasked with leading an organizational-wide transformation, it is critical that this team should upskill and be ready to role-model the Agile mindset.

L&D doesn't always identify as HR

L&D doesn't always sit within HR. For example, when I started my L&D career twenty years ago, I worked as an onsite coach and trainer, reporting directly to a business unit and operating independently of the HR function. A few years later, when I took up a role as an L&D specialist within a more traditional HR structure, I was surprised when first asked questions about topics like payroll and employee relations because up until then I had never associated myself with the HR profession. I've since learnt that this experience is not uncommon.

The L&D and OD profession also represents a significant industry in and of itself. Within this industry is another valued group of readers – independent consultants, instructional designers or business leaders providing L&D products and services. Indeed, some of the leaders interviewed for this book currently work for a digital learning platform or in a specialist coaching and facilitation consultancy. In such environments, because of the nature of their product offering, many people are already familiar with Agile and design thinking tools, and this book will help consolidate and progress these practices.

L&D and people strategy

L&D and OD represent salient components of any organization's people strategy. While the amount varies, leaders across all industries appreciate the importance of allocating a learning budget. Not only is career growth perceived as a vital employee benefit, but the development and strengthening of skills underpin people and organizational performance. For example, led by Google's 20 per cent rule, many companies now allocate a certain percentage of time within people's job roles for learning new skills and pursuing innovative ideas (Clark, 2021). This is because skills development and career growth are seen as significant parts of the employment deal: a two-way contract where an employee offers their skills, energy and time in return for compensation and a sense of career progression. As highlighted in Chapter 11, Deliver with impact, value is realized if the employee experience product strengthens a person's desire to stay without a corresponding increase in compensation.

Many readers are also probably all too familiar with managers attempting to hold on to people they deem key talent by offering them career development opportunities, such as an MBA or a leadership role. Also, until relatively recently, it was common practice to treat people perceived or assessed as top talent as an elite cohort requiring exclusive career development. So, while some readers may highlight that it's often the L&D budget that gets cut when a company hits hard times, this tends to reflect short-termism rather than L&D not being perceived as an essential part of the people strategy. As we'll discuss later in this chapter, skills gaps and talent shortages now represent significant business risks for most organizations. This is a situation that demands L&D- and OD-themed solutions.

Solving for the *now* of work

The final reason why Agile L&D warranted its own book is that many organizational challenges faced by businesses today either sit directly within the L&D and OD domain or require these types of skills when solving the problem. Each challenge is immensely complex and reflects long-term megatrends reshaping the world of work. Also, while Agile does not answer each challenge, the mindset and related collection of tools and techniques help you discover possible solutions. In this way, Agile equips you to start solving for the *now* of work so we can build a better future together. Let's explore three of the most significant challenges as we conclude this Agile L&D playbook.

Climate emergency

The need to reduce emissions and limit global warming now constitutes the most pressing and perhaps the most formidable socio-economic challenge ever faced by humanity. As a result, organizations across the globe are pledging net-zero targets with significant implications for L&D and people strategy. Increasingly, this shift towards a net-zero business model reflects changing government policies and a potential competitive advantage for organizations able and willing to lead the emerging green economy. Recent studies based on the FTSE Russell's Green Revenue dataset indicate the green economy, made up of companies working in clean energy, energy efficiency, water, waste and pollution services, is growing rapidly. Today, with a market capitalization of over US$7 trillion and a weight of 7.1 per cent of global equity markets, would in itself constitute the fifth largest industry and comparable in size with the fossil fuel sector (FTSE Russell, 2022).

Additionally, ESG (environmental, social and governance) criteria are beginning to influence investor decisions and shape a company's access to equity in most countries. Larry Fink, CEO of Blackrock and the world's largest asset manager, declared climate risk an investment risk (Blackrock, 2022). Any business not planning a carbon-free future will likely be left behind. Advancements in technology and science let you switch to more sustainable solutions, such as powering your office or warehouse with renewable energy, which is more cost-effective and cheaper over the longer term.

Yet, despite the potential financial upside of going green, it's customers and employees who are having to force businesses to adapt. Ultimately, people are voting with their feet and are increasingly likely to base consumer and employment decisions on the sustainability actions of companies. This impacts L&D and people strategy in two significant areas.

The first is the need to develop green skills, defined by LinkedIn Learning (2022) as skills that enable the environmental sustainability of economic activities. A good illustration is how the company Tesla disrupted the car industry by going fully electric and, by doing so, created new roles linked to self-driving technology and electric car batteries. Another example is a large European bank upskilling employees to seek out cross-selling opportunities linked to home mortgages, such as the installation of solar panels.

The scale of transformation required within companies over the coming decade means all sectors will need to develop, acquire and harness green skills in some way. For example, the prominent British public transport provider First Bus is undertaking an organizational-wide culture change and spending £100 million a year for the next decade to replace its entire diesel fleet with electric and hydrogen vehicles to reach its carbon-neutral target by 2035. To achieve these goals, First Bus is upskilling drivers and engineers and supporting employees to influence the broader community that catching the bus is better for the planet (Whitehouse, 2022). This growing demand for sustainable skills even saw LinkedIn Learning launch a suite of green skills development programmes in 2022, a strong indicator that the recruitment market now views green skills as a significant differentiator.

The second area where the climate emergency impacts L&D and people strategy is an opportunity to attract and retain great talent by aligning your EVP with a purpose-driven mission linked to net-zero. For example, an IBM Institute for Business Value survey reported that Covid-19 influenced the sustainability views of 93 per cent of global consumers and 71 per cent of all employees (IBM, 2021). As a result, a large proportion of candidates now find environmentally sustainable companies more attractive. Studies also show that younger generations have a higher level of eco-anxiety and are more likely to seek employment with a brand committed to sustainable business practices (Ro, 2022).

Tackling the net-zero challenge to gain a competitive advantage is a highly complex problem requiring changing attitudes, beliefs and working methods. Agile capabilities will be essential if L&D and people teams are to help organizations achieve a decarbonized future.

Digitalization and AI

The race to digitalize both the customer and employee experiences to boost profit and achieve productivity gains means that, in 2022, organizations invested $1.85 trillion in digital transformation, a figure that is projected to nearly double by 2026 (IDC, 2022). This scenario is unsurprising given a Gallup (2022) survey that found companies across 19 countries with high utilization of digital skills achieved annual revenue that was approximately 168 per cent higher than businesses not using digital skills after adjusting for size, country and sector. This means at the time of writing this book, most L&D and people teams are currently supporting or have recently supported digital transformation within their organization. When combined with the increased prevalence of video calling and online collaboration in connection with hybrid working patterns, understanding how to design workplace solutions for a digital context is now an essential skill.

As a result, an acute demand for digital skills exists within most businesses. In the UK alone, only one in ten workers possesses digital skills. At the start of 2023, 72 per cent of businesses had vacancies for roles requiring digital skills, and over two-thirds found it difficult to hire digital skills (Gallup, 2022). This is a major challenge that stems from the relentless advancement of technology within our society and, thus, the rapid obsolescence of digital skills in the workplace.

A perfect illustration is the recent rise of AI (artificial intelligence), particularly genAI (generative AI). Since the launch of ChatGPT in November 2022, AI has entered the everyday discourse. It even resulted in a long-running strike by screenwriters and actors in Hollywood over the threat AI poses to workers in the creative industry. Intriguingly, this strike also led to one of the first workplace agreements introducing new guardrails for how AI interacts with human workers and is used in creative projects (Anguiano and Beckett, 2023). Many readers will also be familiar with the associated debate and media coverage on whether ongoing AI development requires new government legislation to ensure positive intent. It's predicted that over the coming eighteen months, some AI companies are planning to train models with one hundred times more computation than exists today and that no one, not even to workers building these systems, understands how powerful they will be (Milmo and Helmore, 2023).

'It's going to be a friend and a foe. If we don't embrace it, then those that are going to use it in the bad ways are going to get ahead,' states Laura Keith (2023), CEO at Hive Learning, a company leading the way in the AI transformation of the L&D industry. For Keith, AI represents a shift for L&D and people professionals from creator to editor. For example, by powering their coaching bot with AI, Hive has personalized users' learning experience. AI also helps internal L&D teams extract crucial data on how a person utilizes skills learnt, where skills gaps persist and what other factors are necessary to accelerate workplace performance. Such an approach could revolutionize an L&D team's ability to identify problems to solve and target personalized learning solutions in the flow of work.

Hive is a good illustration of how AI can significantly enhance the workplace learning experience, but it also demonstrates the importance of L&D and people professionals leaning in and quickly upskilling in AI and digital skills to contribute to ongoing development positively. In this example, it's clear that AI does not replace the L&D professional and instead boosts productivity and the pace of design. However, it is also clear that an L&D professional must understand how AI and internal data are used and interpreted. Most HR and people platforms have started introducing AI, including leading brands like Workday, Microsoft and LinkedIn. For example, Hive follows the AHAH principle – AI-assisted, human-led,

AI-resourced, human-checked – and is conscious of applying a diversity and inclusion lens to all their work. Such an approach is crucial to limit and detect potential biases often built into a machine learning algorithm.

As David James (2023), Chief Learning Officer at 360Learning, suggested, 'AI is simply the co-pilot. We're still the captain. And I think that's important to acknowledge. We need to act as the captain.' For James, digital learning solutions can positively transform the L&D profession and learning outcomes within organizations but only if digital learning moves beyond just pushing out content and instead crafts solutions targeting moments that matter. For this reason, James argues that it's important not to position digital learning as an either-or option:

> We've got an opportunity at this time using Agile approaches, smart integrated tools and AI to do what humans haven't been able to do since they were sitting next to a person and handing over a really predictable and manual job.

As business complexity increases, delivering learning at the point of need and solving workplace problems in real time is becoming more challenging. Learning in the flow of work is still a type of nirvana within L&D circles, and James views digital adoption platforms as one of the most essential mechanisms in helping the profession achieve this outcome. All learning, whether digital or face to face, needs to be curated and represent 'the simplest, easiest, fastest route to competence in any given task'.

Learning in the flow of work is about the ability to solve real-time workplace problems by aiding and supporting a worker at the point of need. To achieve such an outcome, you need to embrace each of the five design principles we have outlined in the Agile L&D playbook. First, research, define and prioritize which problems to solve. Next, experiment and test possible solutions. Then, track and measure ongoing value. As highlighted throughout the interviews for this book, the proactive nature of the Agile mindset helps you stay at the forefront of workplace digitalization and product design.

From jobs to skills

Throughout this book, a central theme linked to business agility is the redesign of internal organizational structures away from rigid hierarchy towards more fluid role-based networks. As outlined in Chapter 9, the concept of T-shaped people in T-shaped teams can enable greater flexibility and responsiveness in organizational design. The aim is to group people together based on the skills needed (as opposed to job functions and titles) to solve business problems or innovate products. This promise of organizational flexibility has led to skills being viewed as a new type of currency for workforce transformation. However, to understand what a skills-based approach to talent and workforce planning entails, it is important first to appreciate how traditional jobs can be broken down into roles and skills.

Roles represent the things that must be done, what people contribute and clear deliverables for the task at hand. The implication being that a person could potentially fill multiple roles at the same time or move across roles as needed by the business or personal career aspirations. It also follows that one specific role may be filled by different people depending on skills, capacity and business requirements.

The next layer is composed of the skills required to perform effectively in a role. Skills are the expertise or talent needed to contribute to a role or complete a task, for example, coding, analytical thinking or problem-solving. When a person participates in a role, it can be viewed as a collection of skills.

Taking a skills-based approach helps enormously with sourcing and the internal mobility of people. Instead of looking at a pre-set package of skills to fill a job, you can seek out specific skills or skill clusters and group them together as needed. For example, most job descriptions still detail a complete skillset, so skills A, B, C, *and* D must be utilized together, as well as specifying levels of experience, qualifications or previous job titles. Instead, by looking at skills individually and exploring the possibilities of transferable skills that don't require a certain number of years to acquire, you're able to source what is required from a more diverse mix of people. Similarly, a skills-based approach facilitates a more creative redeployment of people within organizations. To illustrate, as specific tasks or job functions become automated and digitized, you're able to move people internally based on adjacent skills, or, as described in Chapter 9, into roles that take advantage of other skills contained within their T-shape.

All of this leads to a re-evaluation of career development within organizations. A recent Gartner (2023) survey found that 89 per cent of HR leaders believe career paths are unclear for most employees and that 66 per cent thought existing career paths were not compelling to many employees. Much of this reflects that, until now, most career development guided people along defined pathways structured around the now-defunct models of job groupings and function-based chains of command. As explained by Lynda Gratton and Andrew J. Scott in their book, *The 100-Year Life: Living and working in an age of longevity*, these traditional career pathways also reflect a legacy within society of viewing life in three stages – education, work and retirement. Now, as generations live longer and the world of work continually evolves, people will need to acquire and recreate intangible assets to transition through multiple stages in life and, thus, alternative career experiences. As a result, corporate career practices and processes need to be reframed to fit our increasingly complex and ever-changing business environment.

In the traditional organizational model, employees rose in salary and importance according to the number of managerial levels a company had. However, today, an individual contributor can potentially have a far more significant impact on the business bottom line than all the managers put together. As discussed in Chapter 9, the T-shape offers a modern-day framework that helps people move beyond just climbing the ladder to gain a sense of career progression. Instead, through the T-shape framework, career development means accessing different projects, roles and experiences to acquire and master an array of different skills. It's time for L&D and people teams to design for people moving up, down and in and out of multiple roles and companies to strengthen the T-shape and employability.

Such a skills-based approach to career development and workforce planning has the potential to transform our organizations into flexible, fluid networks. Indeed, many view this as the holy grail of modern and Agile organizational design. However, this complex business challenge won't be solved by buying an off-the-shelf skills inventory or embarking on a large Waterfall-style project to identify and record every skill in the organization. Instead, like the earlier challenges discussed, it's about focusing on how to solve talent problems *today*, as opposed to building succession plans for the future. For example, by focusing on a crucial capability or strategic need within the business, you can experiment and test applying a skills-based and T-shaped approach to solve it. This smaller working example can then be further iterated and potentially scaled if successful.

Agility as a modern-day business skill

Over the years, I've come to appreciate Agile as a modern business skill. Part of the reason I wanted to write this Agile L&D playbook is that I meet too many people professionals feeling overwhelmed and burnt out as the world of work becomes increasingly complex and more demanding to navigate. It's clear something has to give, and our existing working methods must change.

To solve today's complex business problems, L&D and people teams require a new Agile and multidisciplinary operating system: a collective, strategic and ruthlessly prioritized approach that moves beyond traditional job titles and the functional silos of L&D, OD, talent and HR business partnering. This represents an evolution within the L&D and people profession that demands new skills, roles and working methods underpinned by a product and experimental mindset. I hope this Agile L&D playbook and the five design principles provide a valuable guidebook to help steer your transformation. Agile can't just be a side hustle on top of your day job; it needs to be an ongoing experiment aimed at continually improving working methods and delivering value for the *now* of work. Because, in the end, the health of the L&D and people profession reflects the health of our organizations. If they are thriving, we are, too.

References

Anguiano, Dani and Beckett, Lois (2023) How Hollywood writers triumphed over AI – and why it matters, *The Guardian*, 1 October, www.theguardian.com/culture/2023/oct/01/hollywood-writers-strike-artificial-intelligence (archived at https://perma.cc/P8C4-4H2B)

Blackrock (2022) Larry Fink's 2022 letter to CEOs: The power of capitalism, www.blackrock.com/corporate/investor-relations/larry-fink-ceo-letter (archived at https://perma.cc/2AX5-3JEC)

Clark, Dorie (2021) Google's '20% rule' shows exactly how much time you should spend learning new skills – and why it works, CNBC, published 16 December 2021 and updated 7 January 2022, www.cnbc.com/2021/12/16/google-20-percent-rule-shows-exactly-how-much-time-you-should-spend-learning-new-skills.html (archived at https://perma.cc/E62Q-RHMW)

FTSE Russell (2022) Investing in the green economy 2022: Tracking growth and performance in green equities, ftserussell.com, Index Insights, May, content.ftserussell.com/sites/default/files/investing_in_the_green_economy_2022_final_8.pdf (archived at https://perma.cc/V6AZ-73ZZ)

Gallup (2022) AWS Global Digital Skills Study: The economic benefits of a tech-savvy workforce, February, https://assets.aboutamazon.com/dd/e4/12d668964f58a1f83efb7ead4794/aws-gallup-global-digital-skills-study-report.pdf (archived at https://perma.cc/F4EN-V87S)

Gartner (2023) Top 5 priorities for HR leaders in 2024: Actionable insights to tackle challenges and plan for success, *Gartner 2024 HR Priorities Survey*, emt.gartnerweb.com/ngw/globalassets/en/human-resources/documents/trends/top-priorities-for-hr-leaders-2024-ebook.pdf (archived at https://perma.cc/HTX5-4XL5)

Gratton, Lynda and Scott, Andrew J. (2020) *The 100-Year Life: Living and working in an age of longevity*, Bloomsbury, London and Dublin

IBM (2021) Sustainability at a turning point: Consumers are pushing companies to pivot, The IBM Institute for Business Value, April, www.ibm.com/downloads/cas/WLJ7LVP4 (archived at https://perma.cc/8FLE-EMTD)

IDC (2022) IDC spending guide sees worldwide digital transformation investments reaching $3.4 trillion in 2026, 26 October, www.idc.com/getdoc.jsp?containerId=prUS49797222 (archived at https://perma.cc/6KES-PYRT)

James, David (2023) Interview with Natal Dank, recorded 2 August

Keith, Laura (2023) Interview with Natal Dank, recorded 21 July

LinkedIn Learning (2022) Closing the green skills gap to power a greener economy and drive sustainability, course released 2 February

Milmo, Dan and Helmore, Edward (2023) Humanity at risk from AI 'race to the bottom', says tech expert, *The Guardian*, 26 October, www.theguardian.com/technology/2023/oct/26/ai-artificial-intelligence-investment-boom (archived at https://perma.cc/R3T2-25ZN)

Ro, Christine (2022) How climate change is re-shaping the way Gen Z works, BBC, 1 March, www.bbc.com/worklife/article/20220225-how-climate-change-is-re-shaping-the-way-gen-z-works (archived at https://perma.cc/Z7FT-V85B)

Whitehouse, Eleanor (2022) Kevin Green: 'HR can't just sit at the side and create nice messages', *People Management*, CIPD, 27 January, www.peoplemanagement.co.uk/article/1746383/kevin-green-hr-cant-sit-side-create-nice-messages (archived at https://perma.cc/7X3U-62GR)

INDEX

Note: Page numbers in *italics* refer to tables or figures.

Looking for another book?

Explore our award-winning
books from global business
experts in Human Resources,
Learning and Development

Scan the code to browse

www.koganpage.com/hr-learning-
development

More from Kogan Page

AGILE HR

Deliver Value in a Changing World of Work

Natal Dank and Riina Hellström

ISBN: 9781789665857

Printed in the USA
CPSIA information can be obtained
at www.ICGtesting.com
JSHW062046220324
59757JS00004B/18